Southern Families at War

SOUTHERN FAMILIES AT WAR

Loyalty and Conflict
in the Civil War South

Edited by Catherine Clinton

OXFORD
UNIVERSITY PRESS

2000

OXFORD

UNIVERSITY PRESS

Oxford   New York

Athens   Auckland   Bangkok   Bogotá   Buenos Aires   Calcutta
Cape Town   Chennai   Dar es Salaam   Delhi   Florence   Hong Kong   Istanbul
Karachi   Kuala Lumpur   Madrid   Melbourne   Mexico City   Mumbai
Nairobi   Paris   São Paulo   Singapore   Taipei   Toyko   Toronto   Warsaw

and associated companies in
Berlin   Ibadan

Copyright © 2000 by Catherine Clinton

Published by Oxford University Press, Inc.
198 Madison Avenue, New York, New York 10016

Oxford is a registered trademark of Oxford University Press

Library of Congress Cataloging-in-Publication Data
Southern families at war : loyalty and conflict in the Civil War South /
edited by Catherine Clinton.
p.   cm.
ISBN 0-19-513683-7; ISBN 0-19-513684-5 (pbk.)
1. Confederate States of America—Social conditions.
2. United States—History—Civil War, 1861–1865—Social aspects.
3. Family—Southern States—History—19th century.   I.
Clinton, Catherine, 1952
E487 .S74   2000
973.7′1—dc21   99-052634

1 3 5 7 9 8 6 4 2

Printed in the United States of America
on acid-free paper

Dedicated to
Mary Tyler Cheek McClenahan
and to the
memory of Bobbie Simms

CONTENTS

CONTRIBUTORS

ANNE J. BAILEY is the author and editor of five books on the Civil War (most recently *The Chessboard of War: Sherman and Hood in the Autumn Campaigns of 1864*), numerous book chapters, and more than 140 articles and book reviews. She is the general editor of *Great Campaigns of the Civil War* and *The Civil War in the West,* and editor of the Society of Civil War Historians Newsletter. She teaches at Georgia College & State University and is currently working on a study of the March to the Sea.

E. SUSAN BARBER teaches in the Department of History at the College of Notre Dame of Maryland. She is the author of "Anxious Care and Constant Struggle" in *Before the New Deal: Social Welfare in the South, 1830–1930* (1999) and "Cartridge Makers and Myrmidon Viragos: White Working-Class Women in Confederate Richmond" in *Dealing With the Powers That Be* (forthcoming). She is currently working on a study of prostitutes in nineteenth-century Richmond, Virginia.

CATHERINE CLINTON is the author and editor of over a dozen books, most recently *Civil War Stories* (1998), the *Scholastic Encyclopedia of the Civil War* (1999), and *Fanny Kemble's Civil Wars* (2000).

JENNIFER LYNN GROSS is a Ph.D. candidate at the University of Georgia in Athens. She is currently completing her dissertation on the experience of Confederate widowhood and its societal significance in the postbellum period.

JUDITH LEE HUNT is a Ph.D. candidate at the University of Florida. She is currently writing a dissertation on nineteenth-century rice planters in Low Country South Carolina. She has taught at the Université de Versailles-St. Quentin and at the University of Florida.

MICHAEL P. JOHNSON, professor of history at Johns Hopkins University, has recently edited *Abraham Lincoln, Slavery, and the Civil War: Selected Writings and Speeches* (2000) and is the author of *Civil War Exodus: Slaves' Migration North during the 1860s* (forthcoming).

MICHELLE A. KROWL received her Ph.D. in history from the University of California, Berkeley. She is the author of "'Her Just Dues': Civil War Pensions of African American Women in Virginia" in *Dealing With the Powers That Be* (forthcoming) and is revising her dissertation, "Dixie's Other Daughters: African American Women in Virginia, 1861–1868," for publication.

AMY E. MURRELL is a doctoral candidate in history at the University of Virginia. She is completing a dissertation on families divided by the politics of the Civil War and is the interim associate director of the Virginia Center for Digital History.

TED OWNBY teaches history and southern studies at the University of Mississippi. He is the author of *American Dreams in Mississippi: Consumers, Poverty, and Culture, 1830–1998* (1999) and *Subduing Satan: Recreation, Religion, and Manhood in the Rural South, 1865–1920* and the editor of *Black and White: Cultural Interaction in the Antebellum South* (1993).

DONALD R. SHAFFER received his Ph.D. from the University of Maryland, College Park. He has taught at San Diego State University, SUNY-Plattsburgh, and the University of Wyoming before joining the department of history at the University of Northern Colorado. He is currently revising for publication his dissertation on African American veterans of the Civil War.

DANIEL W. STOWELL is director and editor of the Lincoln Legal Papers in Springfield, Illinois, and teaches at the University of Illinois,

Springfield. He is the author of *Rebuilding Zion: The Religious Reconstruction of the South, 1863–1877* (1998) and the editor of *Balancing Evils Judiciously: The Proslavery Writings of Zephaniah Kingsley* (2000) and *In Tender Consideration: Women, Families, and the Law in Abraham Lincoln's Illinois* (2001).

HENRY WALKER has a Ph.D. in history from the University of Alabama. He has taught at the University of Alabama, Mississippi State University, Mississippi University for Women, and, most recently, the University of West Alabama. He is currently working on a study of secession as a grassroots movement and the role of women within this movement.

LAUREN F. WINNER is Richard Hofstadter Fellow in the Department of History at Columbia University. She is coauthor, with Randall Balmer, of a study of contemporary American evangelicalism (forthcoming), and author of numerous articles, including investigations of male devotees of Martha Stewart and white women's defenses of Jim Crow after *Brown v. Board of Education* (1954).

Southern Families at War

✹

SOUTHERN FAMILIES AT WAR

Loyalty and Conflict during the Civil War

Family metaphors abound in Civil War literature. The captivating image of a house divided against itself was meant not to conjure architectural disaster but, instead, to evoke biblical images of Cain and Abel. The heartrending tales of mothers with sons fighting on opposite sides of the conflict and women with husbands in one army and fathers in another create a powerful pull on our emotions. Family ties shattered by the onslaught of combat, blood against blood, together turning Antietam Creek red one September afternoon, prod us out of our complacency and thrust us into the very sinews of this historic struggle. With our national family grappling for survival, we recall the intensity of these life-and-death decisions—wrenching dilemmas that defy tidy outcomes.

Plotting untidy outcomes can enthrall. One person's treachery can be another's noble act—even within the same family. Sacrifice to one cause can be betrayal of another within the tangle of internecine warfare. And with war's resolution, the bitterness of the defeated can create currents of tension and despair long after armies have retired from the field. Following the Civil War, one of the greatest conflicts within white Southern families was the "loyalty oath" required by the federal government. To move on, to reclaim property, heads of household needed to reaffirm their allegiance to the re-United States, which seemed a direct slap of dishonor in the face of those who sacrificed so much in hopes of the Confederacy.

Exploring the history of the Civil War remains a process of peeling away the endless layers of interesting tales, remembrances, and revisions. More and more we are interested in learning not just statistics and official records but also stories that move us beyond the battlefields. How and why hundreds upon thousands died is outranked only by data on who they were and where they perished.

The human face of Civil War studies has shifted to the everyday and extraordinary people who participated in this titanic clash. Millions bore witness, and thousands left us records chronicling their impressions. The gigantic outpouring of letters and memoirs, journals, and oral histories—compelling accounts of lives forever marked by war—continues to slake the interest of scholars and readers.

Throughout the past century and a half, with so much academic and popular interest in the Civil War, we might imagine that writers and researchers would have exhausted every topic imaginable. However, each rising generation not only puts new historical methods and technologies into practice but often recovers some untouched body of evidence—perhaps dust-covered treasures from the attic or tales long ago buried and only recently unearthed. Many members of each new generation offer an updated set of sensibilities, which in turn offer a blueprint for revisionist analysis. This at times can lead to bitter infighting, and, in some fashion, a refighting of the war.

The Civil War as America's anthem and epic, more powerful and stirring than what had come before and certainly what has come after, has been deftly captured in a passage from Ian Frazier's remarkable volume, aptly entitled *Family*. In the passage that follows, Frazier meditates on the legendary death of Stonewall Jackson in May 1863:

> "Let us cross over the river, and rest under the shade of the trees." In this sentence, perhaps the most famous dying utterance in American history, Jackson concentrated a lifetime of prayer and struggle and aspiration—his, and that of the young country he had fought to divide. So many crossed water to get here, so many wanted to rest under the shade. . . . In his last words, Jackson created America's best known imaginary landscape. "Let us cross over the river, and rest under the shade of the trees." In the staccato rhythm of words I can see each step of the action. The sentence ascends in terraces to rest and peace, it undoes knots inside me, it exhales like a sigh. . . . Before the Civil War, America didn't know if it was a country or a lot of different Promised

Lands. People invented the America they wanted to live in and then struggled to live there. Across the river and under the trees combined all these invented countries into one. Across the river and under the trees descended like a beneficence in the last moments of a fierce man's life and crystallized his fierceness to purity. Across the river and under the trees carried no demurring subclauses or riders. It included us all—people Jackson considered infidels, men he would have shot unblinking in life. Across the river and under the trees was poetry to equal the nation-making poetry of Lincoln, and the only line of public poetry to come from the South in the war.[1]

Jackson may well have been the only Southerner to provide us with this kind of transcendent poetic imagery. But after the war a generation of white Southerners, bent on Redemption, full of poetry and pathos, tantalized the American imagination with their romanticized plantation epics and their compelling memoirs of loss, sacrifice, and honor.

Within American popular culture, literary elegy and epic films have burnished the image of the postwar South. In a sort of politico-cultural alchemy, white Southerners traded on their defeat, wallowing in their martyrdom, spinning straw into literary gold. Warriors put down their swords and took up their pens, enlisting women's help to translate fiction into fact, to write the literature of "the Lost Cause," exalting defeated Confederates.

Their children may have been robbed of their destiny, but Lost Cause celebrants wanted to make sure their descendants would be enraptured by their heritage. William Faulkner's description of Gettysburg in *Intruder in the Dust* symbolizes this literary conquest: "For every Southern boy fourteen years old not once but whenever he wants it, there is the instant when it's still not yet two o'clock on that July afternoon in 1863 . . . it's all in the balance, it hasn't happened yet it hasn't even begun yet but there is still time for it not to begin."[2]

This volume emerges from a very different set of historical issues, moving well beyond a Faulknerian timeline. *Southern Families at War* does not concern itself primarily with tackling truths trapped behind the myths. Rather, this collection of lively and thoughtful essays locates itself in a parallel universe. The contributors to this volume are well aware of the wider questions of slavery's impact on African American families, cognizant of the controversies surrounding questions of Confederate loyalty and disloyalty, and especially knowledgeable about the historical roles of white Southern women and black Southern men and women within this tangled web of allegiances.

Many contributors have participated in public debates over honoring the Confederate dead, raising the Confederate flag, and interpreting the cultural meanings of Confederate memorabilia. This volume was conceived to encourage other kinds of dialogue, to search the past for different questions as well as new answers.

We feel our work stems from the seismic changes in the field of Civil War history over the past two decades. Once, Civil War history might have been viewed as a fortress, the gates open only to students of military history and militants. Now the field seems to have been invaded by bands of renegades, beckoning comrades onward. Writers investigating the Civil War reflect a variety of backgrounds, a diversity of disciplines, pursuing multiple and competing agendas with zeal and abandon. Their most original and revisionist works seem literally unfathomable to earlier generations of Civil War scribes.

For several generations, Americans have characterized the Civil War as a "brother's war," both to underscore the universality of this bloody strife and to diminish other views of the conflict. If we reduce the Civil War to a kind of family squabble within our past—rather than the "Second American Revolution," or perhaps a "war for black liberation," or a time when the future of the entire continent and even the destiny of the hemisphere would hang in the balance—this casts the conflict into a completely different light.

We might even continue to characterize the Civil War as a "brother's war" if we recognize that on occasion the white soldier in gray faced his black half-brother in blue, for over 180,000 African American soldiers served in Union forces. These family connections were not always rhetorical or metaphorical, but sometimes the result of blood ties between black and white, slave and free, often unacknowledged outside the family.[3] Placing the African American soldier at the center of this discussion of the Civil War—its causes, conduct, and results—remains a relatively new development both within the academy and among Civil War buffs.[4]

These collected essays are an attempt to plant new ideas in ground that has been previously plowed. We are all well aware of the important work that has come before, but we hope to build new bridges to twenty-first-century Civil War scholarship. We hope that individuals and families may become as fascinating a subject for Civil War buffs as regiments and artillery. We know that the impact of the war on families was diverse and complex, and perhaps the reverberations are still rippling into the present. We intend this volume to contribute to the ongoing investigation of the Civil War's continuing fascination for millions of Americans.

These essays emerge from a conference held at the University of Richmond with funds from the Douglas Southall Freeman Professorship, a visiting chair held by the editor of this volume in 1997–98. In April 1998 over forty invited scholars from around the country and abroad, and another hundred participants, came together to exchange ideas about the issues of loyalty and conflict, family and conscience, race and rhetoric, fealty and betrayal within the Civil War South.

The original essays that follow address the important theme of how families coped with the impact of armed conflict, with the strife of division in the wartime South. Because we can no longer be content with projecting a monolithic interpretation of the South, white or black, before, during, or after the Civil War, these essays necessarily cover a wide range of topics and broad geographic, economic, ethnic, and racial spectra. Both white families and African American families were riven with internal conflicts, suffering from countless fissures that threatened to split wide open once the stresses of wartime exerted pressure. The great strength of this volume is that contributors have chosen such a wide array of source materials, subjects, and approaches to provide an enthralling exploration of war's most intimate ravages.

TO EMPHASIZE THE NATURE OF ITS DIVERSITY, THE VOLUME opens with three essays examining African American families, partly during but mainly in the aftermath of war. First, Michael P. Johnson examines the strategies of black couples, parents, and children in their quest for reunion at war's end. By looking at literally hundreds of notices placed in Christian journals and other periodicals, Johnson deftly sketches the meaning and impact of family ties for African Americans caught in war's terrible turmoil. His skillful interpretation of these elliptical snapshots of one of slavery's cruelest by-products—the involuntary separation of family members, perhaps permanent absences from loved ones—provides a powerful insight into wartime dislocations and the hope peace fostered for some.

Michelle A. Krowl offers us in-depth analysis of the way former slave men and women struggled to piece together their family lives within the thicket of issues confronting them in wartime Virginia. She describes the mass weddings of slave couples once their unions could be legalized and highlights the proud ex-slave husband announcing to his wife his intentions "to take you to freedom with me." She also illuminates the grief and famine that plagued slave families left behind when black men went off to war. Krowl demonstrates the ways in which "the federal government in Virginia created opportunities for women to negotiate their relationships with husbands" and "to make choices for children," concluding that the government sought to strengthen the traditional roles of husband and wife for African American freedpeople. Krowl portrays African Americans, especially black women, as active agents in the struggle to reconstitute black family life, which was a primary concern for liberated and liberating slaves during wartime.

Donald R. Shaffer mines the pension records of black Union veterans and other sources to delineate emerging attitudes toward marriage among former slaves. He discovers the ways African Americans struggled to reconcile their informal system of slave marriages with the formal legal options available after emancipation and the ways freedpeople adapted laws to their own advantage. He underscores the adaptability and flexibility of ex-slaves, who faced enormous obstacles on their road to achieving stable family life. Finally, Shaffer suggests that for many emancipated African Americans the persistence of folk customs was an essential by-product of cultural survival, perhaps even integral to the identities forged by this new generation of freedpeople.

Amy E. Murrell mines another important source of information about Southern families, looking at petitions to the Confederate government, the direct appeals for aid written by white Southerners to their newly constituted "state." She suggests that Confederates both on the battlefield and on the home front frequently made distinctions between their beloved "Cause" and the Confederate government. Citizens were willing to make inordinate sacrifices for Confederate patriotism while also railing at their state, particularly when it came into conflict with maintaining "healthy and stable families." Many women wrote to request exemptions for the good of their individual families, and a Georgia woman even requested that her brother be sent home for "the greater interest of the whole community," but they did not view their appeals as disloyal. Many white families, who supported Confederate independence while criticizing the crumbling "state" that was failing them, underscored the elasticity of white Southern loyalism.

For elite white planter families in the Confederate South, the crisis of war and its destructive elements were especially challenging to their "idealized conceptions" of their family "black and white." The overthrow of slavery and slaves' willing embrace of Union liberation were staggering blows to the slaveholders' reign. Judith Lee Hunt's examination of the Middleton family and its extended clan, which streched from South Carolina to Philadelphia, provides a powerful case study. As part of a "national elite," Williams and Susan Middleton of South Carolina found their kinship ties sorely tested by the nation's dividing in 1861. As these once proud Middletons were dragged into what Williams called a "vortex of disaster and ruin," they were forced to grasp the extended hand of Union kin offering assistance after the war reduced them to dependence. Hunt skillfully traces the way the war shifted priorities, alliances, and the allocation of resources for one grand clan during and after the conflict.

Elite white Southern women found themselves challenged by the accelerated pace of wartime. E. Susan Barber examines courtship and marriage patterns in the Confederate capital and finds that, contrary to conditions in the rural South, Richmond, "awash with soldiers," gave single white women a bounty of eligible mates. She finds neither the age of marriage declining nor the frequency of unions shifting significantly in this urban center. Yet some things did change. Naive young women might be drawn into ill-advised relationships, as was the hapless Emily Phillips, who was "strangled by her husband, a Richmond soldier she married after nursing him back to health," and as were the many young girls found dead from self-induced abortions in boardinghouses. And if they survived their husbands, the possibilities for young widows to find new mates, in Richmond and elsewhere, proved slim and dwindling.

Jennifer Lynn Gross's analysis of Confederate widows in Virginia details the way in which the sorrow of losing their husbands was compounded when they were forced to continue their struggles to survive within an increasingly harsh and challenging world. When men went off to war, women shouldered new burdens, and when men died, women were faced with few choices: autonomy was something most were saddled with, not something they sought. Gross argues that the legal disabilities women faced contributed to their search for new spouses. In one county she surveyed, only one of three women remarried, a statistic that starkly highlights what a limited option this was for the thousands of widows in the postwar South. Gross describes the impact of private charity and state assistance on poverty-stricken families of soldiers, asserting that state laws providing for widows' pensions reinforced the "ideological needs of patriarchy" and influenced gender roles in postwar Virginia, keeping women in their roles as "good angels."

Daniel W. Stowell offers a compelling analysis of the trials of one East Tennessee family within the Confederacy, and the Civil War's impact on the family's matriarch, Eliza Fain, a pious Presbyterian slaveholder's wife. When war is declared, her husband and three grown sons become soldiers, and Eliza is left behind with her remaining eight children and eight slaves. By 1863 her meadow is "swarming with blue coats" (enemy invaders), and by the summer of 1864 this plantation mistress confesses, "I have gotten so I do not have much confidence in Negro flesh." Her home is eventually occupied, then plundered; her slaves run away; her children go shoeless; and she finds the body of a mutilated kinsman in the woods. Throughout, she seeks solace in prayer and in her diary, which she keeps faithfully throughout the war. Stowell's adroit exploration of what this one woman endures brings us into the lone darkness of the Confederate heartland. Fain's stubborn and persistent faith is an important element of white Confederate family life, during and after the war.

Henry Walker examines the way wartime separations redefined gender roles in marriage, the way family crises intersected with wartime drama to transform a traditional, patriarchal union into a companionate marriage, in the case of Henry and Victoria Clayton of Alabama. Henry Clayton had been raised by a harsh and abusive father, but after the death of his older brother from a battle wound in 1863, a family conflagration erupted that was to propel Henry down a different path from that of his parents. During the war's early years, Victoria used sexual intimacy to expand her influence over her husband, and by 1863 the terrible toll of war's trauma allowed emotional intimacy between the couple, which peace rarely had fostered. The war created new demands on both Henry and Victoria Clayton, challenges each of them met. Victoria was anxious to take over the reins of plantation management, which Walker demonstrates she did with aplomb. This knack for independence was passed on to the next generation of Claytons, both daughters and sons. Henry and Victoria reshaped their family values, forever altered by the rigors of war.

Many families experienced severe bouts of gender conflict through prisms other than sexuality. Lauren F. Winner investigates neglected crises fostered by war with her engaging survey of Jews within the Confederacy. She suggests that the Civil War proved a boon to evangelical conversions of Southern Jews and describes the multiple meanings of shifts from Judaism to Christianity. Winner effectively chronicles the ways in which these conversions could and often did divide Jewish families, especially when one spouse refused to convert or resisted baptism or other rituals of Christian faith. Winner also describes how Jewish men and women warded off suspicions of disloyalty by channeling Hebrew aid societies and Jewish memorial associations into the Confederate cause, which proved patriotism while fostering ties with Hebrew traditions. Winner is even able to shed some light on those African Americans who followed in the faith of their owners, including one called "Paul the Jew" who strongly identified "with the Israelites' experience of being led out of Egyptian slavery." This fascinating look at how Confederate nationalism coerced many Jews into abandoning their faith, while strengthening others' resolves to maintain their religion, offers us innovative insights into the hidden scars of war, scars that remain invisible to us today.

Suspicions of disloyalty among the foreign-born remains a constant crisis of war, no different during the Civil War than any other. Although the Union army was full of first- and second-generation immigrants, less than 15 percent of America's foreign population lived within the Confederacy. The Irish were the largest immigrant group in the South, and over half of the second largest immigrant group, the Germans, were settled in Texas. Anne J. Bailey's striking portrait of the crisis for German Texans on the Confederate frontier—conflicts over conscription and banishment laws, raids and bushwhackers, the role of rumor and betrayal—offers a compelling backdrop. Bailey examines wartime conflict through the fortunes of one German immigrant family, the Coreths of Comal County, Texas. The three Coreth brothers enlisted in the Confederate army to preserve their property and fulfill their duties. They became steadily demoralized when their loyalties were constantly questioned. Bailey chronicles this steady decline. By the time two of the brothers had lost their lives, the family's loyalty to the Confederacy had dissolved. In 1865 the elder Coreth wrote about his strong feelings to his only remaining son and warned: "Burn this letter when you have read it. It could perhaps get into the wrong hands." The lone surviving Confederate Coreth eventually went into exile and died in Vienna.

What an afterlife would be like was surely something both men and women contemplated more seriously in the wartime South, and Ted Ownby speculates on ideas about Confederate heaven. He convincingly shows how images of God and family were blended by soldiers facing death, separated from loved ones, hundreds upon thousands dying alone on the battlefield. The notion of heaven as a family reunion was a comfort to many Confederates marching into combat. The way in which renewed appreciation of one's family translated into piety

around the campfires and in the trenches remained a wartime staple.
But Ownby also looks more closely at how gender and race relations
were reflected in these soldiers' visions of eternal life, commenting on
the absence of slaves in Confederate heaven and the way that patriarchal dictates were suspended in favor of a higher power.

The Civil War's cataclysmic impact on Southern families was
wrenching and profound. We can only begin to appreciate its vast and
diverse consequences in some of the scenes portrayed within the essays
that follow: from Friday evening seders in North Carolina to Baptist
family reunions in heaven, from burials in unmarked graves on the Texas
frontier to mass weddings of African Americans in wartime Virginia,
from a wife afraid to assert herself at family prayers in rural Tennessee to
a wife managing her husband's slaves solo on her Alabama plantation,
from the lonely garret of an abandoned pregnant woman in Richmond
to the splendors of Middleton mansions in the South Carolina Low
Country, from the pens of Confederate widows scribbling to ask
for government assistance to the voices of African American parents
negotiating for their children—and their children's children. The
many layers and dimensions of this tremendous transformation is still a
work in progress, as it will always be, and one in which we invite you to
share.

A MAJOR IMPETUS FOR THIS BOOK WAS THE GENEROSITY
demonstrated by the major donor to the Douglas Southall Freeman
Chair at the University of Richmond: Freeman's daughter, Mary Tyler
Cheek McClenahan. It is for this reason that she is acknowledged on
the dedication page. Her grace, wit, and commitment provide a shin-
ing beacon for those in Richmond—and her influence extends well
beyond her home community where she is so respected and beloved.

I first met Mrs. McClenahan in 1984 at the University of Richmond at a conference on the role of women in the South. When I returned to campus to accept an appointment as the Douglas Southall
Freeman Distinguished Visiting Professor of History for 1997–98, my
plans for a conference on the topic of Southern families during the
Civil War were warmly received.

During the more than eighteen months of planning, Professor
John Gordon, then chair of the department, was generous with his
time, his advice, and, above all, his supportive enthusiasm. Without
his guidance and hard work on behalf of the conference, this entire
project would have faltered. Other colleagues in the Department of

History at the University of Richmond, most especially Professor Robert Kenzer, were extremely helpful on several fronts. Mary Anne Wilbourne, Robyn Mundy, Matthew Corkern, Mary Pat Buckenmeyer, and David Arthur worked hard to make the event a success. Assistance provided by the Museum of the Confederacy, most especially by John Coski and Robin Reed, was warmly appreciated. Without the stellar efforts of Deborah Govoruhk, I would not have survived—I would have drowned in details.

Finally, the conference participants were part of an exciting group of senior and junior scholars whose talents are formidable. Their collective enthusiasm for a more comprehensive and eclectic Civil War history proved infectious. Both Carol Bleser and Carl Degler played a special role in shaping the collegial tone of the event. The twelve contributors whose essays have been included in this volume met several deadlines without complaint, cheerfully endured several rounds of editorial suggestions, and made the volume a pleasure to edit.

I have published over ten books with nearly as many different presses, but Oxford University Press remains a publisher with whom I am happy to work again and again. Much of the credit can be given to the wonderful editors with whom it has been my pleasure to collaborate. Most notably I wish to thank Thomas LeBien, who, on this and other projects, had been a trusted navigator through the shoals. Equally trusted, capable, and generous, Susan Ferber's input on this manuscript was invaluable. The contributors and editor remain in her debt. Enlightening reports from Bertram Wyatt-Brown (not unexpected, but always a pleasure) and an anonymous reader helped polish the book.

In the dedication to this volume, I have acknowledged my beloved aunt, Bobbie Simms, who was my most important link with Southern family. She was a support for me from my earliest years, and her generosity and spirit remain guiding forces in my life.

It may seem a cliché to thank one's family. But as my husband and two growing boys see me chained to the computer for yet another August, juggling publishing deadlines during yet another vacation season, the miracle of my family remains just that. It feels miraculous to have their love and support, and I remain unworthy of their many sacrifices. Thanks again to Daniel, Drew, and Ned Colbert.

Notes

1. Ian Frazier, *Family* (New York: Farrar, Straus & Giroux, 1994), 149–50.
2. William Faulkner, *Intruder in the Dust* (New York: Random House, 1948), 194.

ONE

LOOKING FOR LOST KIN

Efforts to Reunite Freed Families
after Emancipation

Michael P. Johnson

The Civil War gave Southern white families a small, relatively brief taste of the family separations, privations, hard work, and personal losses that slavery visited on Southern black families for more than two centuries. Separation of white men from their families was hardly unknown during the years before the war, but it *was* unknown for about 80 percent of white men of military age to be away from home in a four-year period. Southern white families had felt hardships before 1861, but seldom the shortages, hunger, and skimping caused by what Abraham Lincoln called "the mighty scourge of war." White Southerners had more than a passing familiarity with physical labor before the firing on Fort Sumter, but the rigors of war brought new, onerous, and mostly unwanted tasks for those behind the lines. The wartime deaths of more than a quarter million Southern white men in the prime of life left an unprecedented legacy of grief, blasted hopes, and unanswered prayers.

Despite these and other resemblances, the experiences of Southern white families during the war were far from slavery. Nobody bought and sold white family members. No white person suffered the legal proscriptions or racial degradations of slaves. Even the surface resem-

blances between slavery and the wartime trials of whites were miti-
gated by the countless legacies of freedom.

Consider the separation of soldiers from their families. For the
most part, Southern white men voluntarily left home to fight the Yankees, unlike slaves, whose families were routinely separated involuntarily and often without warning. Soldiers were more able to fend for
themselves than the majority of slaves—women and children—who
were sold away from kinfolk. Usually, soldiers went to war with neighbors; their families could communicate with them—imperfectly, to be
sure, but often with considerable frequency and facility, unlike slaves,
who normally had little chance to bridge the separation of kinfolk
with news. Wartime separations created anxieties registered on nearly
every page of white families' correspondence, including the letters
that said, "Nothing happening. I'm fine. I hope you are, too." Although
white writers and readers knew that such reassurances masked unset-
tling emotions, slaves seldom enjoyed more than rumors or guesses to
answer their nagging questions about those sold away: "Where are
they? How are they?" Southern white families could hope that, God
willing, their men in uniform would return home sooner or later, a
prospect in the realm of fantasy for most slaves separated by sale.
Overall, the war exposed one generation of white Southerners to four
years of a notably mild version of the family separations experienced
by ten generations of black Southerners for almost 250 years.

When the Civil War ended, surviving Confederate soldiers made
their way home for family reunions. Although the war and the Thirteenth Amendment ended slavery, freedom did not erase the blighting
legacy of bondage for slave families. Freed men and women seized
opportunities to try to reunite their families. No government agency
or volunteer organization stepped forward to offer them systematic assistance, such as that made available to displaced persons after World
War II by the Red Cross and the United Nations Relief and Reha-
bilitation Administration.[1] In general, freed families were on their
own. Some traveled from place to place searching for loved ones. Others solicited help from the Freedmen's Bureau or arranged for letters
of inquiry to be written by literate friends. Some hired agents to find
their missing relatives. And some tried to locate their lost kin by placing ads in the *Christian Recorder*, the weekly newspaper of the African
Methodist Episcopal Church.[2]

Tucked unobtrusively among political news and notices of baptisms,
marriages, and ministerial comings and goings, the *Christian Recorder*
ads displayed no typographical embellishment except the heading "In-

formation Wanted." In a few unadorned lines, freed men and women described lost family members and asked for help locating them. From 1861 through 1870, the *Recorder* carried a total of 268 such ads.[3] The ads represent only a tiny fraction of the hundreds of thousands of freed men and women who tried to reunite their families during these years, but they disclose some of the stubborn realities that plagued the family reconstitution efforts of most former slaves. The ads break the historical silence that, for the most part, shrouds the massive process of family reunion. Taken together, the ads form a miniature self-portrait of freedpeople expressing views of themselves, their kinfolk, and their community that other documents usually mute.

At first glance, the ads appear to be a strange combination of ambiguity and superfluous detail. They almost never answer the question that jumps immediately to a reader's mind: what did the missing person look like? The ads described the physical appearance of just 6 of the 754 people being sought. The only person identified by age (twenty-four), height (medium), complexion (light), hair (curly), eyes (gray), and build (stout) was Christopher Jones.[4] Nobody else was described so fully. The few physical features of the other five people could provide little help in identifying them. Charles Pembroke was "disfigured by a burn," but the ad said nothing about the appearance or location of the burn.[5] Frederick Collins was "slightly marked with smallpox," a fact that did not set him apart from thousands of others.[6] Perhaps most surprising of all, the ads described the skin color of only two people, Christopher Jones ("light") and Joseph Carter ("a bright mulatto").[7]

Initially, it seems puzzling that advertisers failed to provide physical descriptions of the people they were trying to find. Before emancipation, slave owners who advertised for runaway slaves carefully described the physical appearance of fugitives, often mentioning details about scars, clothing, speech, or mannerisms. None of the *Christian Recorder* ads said a word about clothing, speech, or mannerisms, and only three people were described as scarred (Charles Pembroke, Frederick Collins, and Noah Camper, a soldier who had lost a leg).[8]

Instead of describing the appearance of their lost kinfolk, advertisers provided other, seemingly unnecessary details. The four-sentence ad Martha Ann Good placed in April 1870 was fairly typical. She sought information about her sister, Sarah Williams, "who I left at Halifax Court House, Va., about 25 years ago." Back in 1845 or so, "at 12 o'clock at night, when quite small" Good was "taken way" from her master, a hotelkeeper at Halifax named Nathan Dexter, and "sold in Alabama." Her sister "belonged to a man whose name was William Early, who kept a dry-goods store." Like many others, Good concluded her ad with the request, "Ministers in the South, please read [this ad] in your churches."[9]

When Good's skeletal account is read for its assumptions about how her sister might be identified and located, the purpose of the details becomes clear. Twenty-five years had elapsed since Martha was the little girl who left her sister at midnight in Virginia, was sold in Alabama, probably grew up there, and by 1870 had come to live in Philadelphia. How could her sister be recognized now? Would her name still be Sarah Williams? When ministers read this ad to their congregations, how would listeners know whether they had information about this particular Sarah Williams?

Good answered these questions with the details in her ad. Her sister might have a different surname now, but she was probably still known as Sarah, specifically the Sarah owned by that dry-goods store keeper at Halifax Court House named William Early, the Sarah whose little sister Martha was owned by that hotel keeper Nathan Dexter and was taken away in the middle of the night to be sold down South. Each of these details was intended to spark a flash of recognition. Somebody might have heard something about Halifax Court House, William Early, Nathan Dexter, those two sisters Martha and Sarah, and that midnight departure twenty-five years ago. And what they knew might ultimately lead Martha to her sister.

Similar assumptions guided all the *Christian Recorder* advertisers. The fundamental reason their ads neglected physical appearance and instead offered details about names, family relationships, and places and times of separation was the audience advertisers hoped to reach. Slave owners' ads for runaway slaves appealed to the eyes of strangers, principally literate white people who—after reading the ad—might recognize an otherwise anonymous black person as a fugitive. Runaway ads described visible surfaces, features that could be noticed at a glance by any perceptive observer. The freed men and women who advertised in the *Christian Recorder* had a very different audience in mind. They conceived of their audience as a diaspora of keen-eared African American listeners who were not complete strangers, who either knew their lost kinfolk or had heard some scrap of information about them. Since most freedpeople could neither read nor write, the ads were intended to be read aloud and heard. They described missing persons by features that lay beneath the surface of appearance. To identify a missing person required memory of a known or rumored attribute of the person described in an ad.

As the mouthpiece of the advertisers, the *Christian Recorder* broadcast ads to African American readers throughout the nation.[10] Ministers amplified the ads by reading them to their congregations. According to the *Recorder*, AME membership doubled between 1861 and 1867, when it stood at 100,000, and more than doubled again by the spring of 1869. The *Recorder* estimated that four out of five members "were born in slavery" and were consequently "homeless and landless, moneyless, and many of them friendless . . . [and] ignorant, two-thirds of them cannot read."[11] But they could listen to their ministers. The number of AME ministers nearly kept pace with the growth in membership. More than 400 preachers were in the field early in 1867, and by 1870 there were just over 700, nearly three-fourths of them in the South.[12] The editor encouraged freed men and women to have the *Recorder* read to them by a minister of any denomination or, "if there be no minister in the city, town, village or county, let the steward, or class-leader, or some one who can read it properly, rise up and do so."[13]

The *Recorder* campaigned to be heard by freed men and women in order to spread its message of industry, responsibility, thrift, cleanliness, sobriety, piety, and education. Its advocacy did not extend to urging ministers to read "information wanted" ads to their congregations. Aside from printing the ads, the *Recorder* said nothing else about them.[14] Instead of arising from an orchestrated campaign to tell former slaves what was good for them, the ads grew out of quiet, unofficial, grassroots efforts of freedpeople to help themselves.

The people who placed ads in the *Recorder* differed from millions of other former slaves in several ways. First, unlike about 95 percent of other freedpeople, they had some connection to the AME Church. Second, they could spare the money to purchase an ad. The *Recorder* charged twelve and a half cents per line, cash in advance, for ads "of a private nature," and for $2.50 offered to run a ten-line ad for a month.[15] A person who earned cash wages could pay for an ad with several days of hard work, but most freed men and women did not earn wages, had little cash, and could not afford to spend what little they had for advertising.

A third way advertisers differed from most other former slaves was that they resided disproportionately in the North. Three out of four advertisers lived outside the former slave states; in the nation as a whole, only 7 percent of African Americans lived outside the South.[16]

A third of the advertisers lived in Pennsylvania, the home of the *Recorder*; almost half lived in the Northeast; and one-fifth lived in the Midwest.[17] The heavy majority of advertisers from the North probably reflected their greater distance from family members left behind in the South and, even more, their readier access to money from wages. It may also have expressed a desire not just to locate family members but to retrieve them from the South and bring them north. Rachel Ann Martienas advertised to find her three brothers because "I want them to come to Chicago, Ill.," where she lived with her husband.[18] Although no other northern advertisers said as much, many probably shared Martienas's aim.

After all, northern advertisers had formerly resided in the slave states. They differed from the advertisers who lived in the South at the time they placed their ads only by having migrated to the North, most of them during the Civil War or shortly afterward. In fact, a disproportionate number of advertisers—regardless of whether they lived in the North or the South when they placed their ads—had formerly resided in the most battle-scarred regions of the slave states, regions relatively close to the North. More advertisers (41 percent) had lived in Virginia when they were separated from their loved ones than in any other state.[19] The majority (56 percent) of advertisers had resided there or in the other mid-Atlantic slave states. In general, advertisers overrepresented the mid-Atlantic slave states more than threefold and the Ohio and Upper Mississippi Valley slave states by a third; they underrepresented the lower Atlantic Coast states twofold and the Gulf Coast states more than fourfold.[20]

More northern, more eastern, more prosperous, and more closely associated with the AME Church than the overwhelming majority of former slaves, the advertisers nonetheless had much in common with other freedmen and -women. Above all else, they shared the experiences of slavery, especially the disruption of families by sale.

Scores of advertisers hoped to reunite families ripped apart by sales. Ephraim Allen in Philadelphia sought his mother, who had been sold from Kentucky to Louisiana; his aunt, sold to Tennessee; and three cousins, sold to "Squire Black" and "Edd. Dickerson, negro trader."[21] Amanda Jane Bass, who now lived in Hamilton, Canada West, tried to locate her mother, who had been sold from Tennessee to Mississippi in 1856; her sister, who soon afterward was taken by her master to Kentucky; and another sister, who was sold to Texas.[22] George Henry Denna, a resident of Galva, Illinois, was looking for his mother and father, his three sisters, and three brothers; he had not heard from any of them since 1849, when they were sold from their home plantation in Faquier County, Virginia.[23] Phoebe Ann Jackson, who lived in Richmond and was one of three daughters and twelve sons in her family, knew that one brother and sister had been sold from Virginia to New Orleans, another brother to Georgia, and "Mother could only learn that Francis and Thomas were on the same boat."[24] Reverend Cyrus Boey, now in Oswego, New York, had been sold from Frederick County, Maryland, to South Carolina in 1837, along with his two brothers and six sisters, and he had "not seen them since."[25] Lucinda Johnson and her brother were sold away from her mother in Springfield, Missouri, "when I was eight years old, to the South."[26] William Thomas, now in Nashville, hoped to make contact with his mother, sister, and two brothers left behind when he was sold away from Washington "about forty years ago" when he "was very small."[27]

Advertisers did not always reveal why they had become separated from their families, but sales were by far the most common cause.[28] Slave sales were probably responsible for the lost kin of many other advertisers who did not explicitly say so. Silence about the cause of separation may reflect a widespread assumption among former slaves that family breakups were so integral to slavery that they need not be mentioned; they went without saying. Many advertisers, however, said outright that they were sold away. They accounted for 40 percent of ads that gave a reason for separation; they were trying to find half of all missing relatives.[29]

Other advertisers wrote that they "left" or were "taken" from their lost relatives.[30] They represented nearly a third of the ads and of the lost kin.[31] To our ears, the word "left" suggests volition; it hints that the advertiser absconded from the master, leaving kinfolk behind.[32] In the context of these ads, that meaning seems unlikely. Anna Jinkins, for example, hoped to find her six children: "They all left Tallader town, Alabama, about 20 years ago and came to Missouri." It is possible that John, Jesse, Susan, Juda, Caroline, and Emmeline Jinkins voluntarily picked up and collectively moved from Alabama to Missouri, leaving their mother behind. Far more likely, they were sold. For the most part, "left" and "taken" appear to be ambiguous synonyms for being sold. Although in some cases masters moved and literally "took" their slaves along, from a slave's viewpoint it made little difference whether sale or movement separated family members.[33]

In all, sales were responsible for four out of five of the advertisers' missing relatives.[34] But slaves were separated from family members for many other reasons. Abroad marriages (joining spouses who belonged to different masters) were common; some slaves moved seasonally from plantation to town or from one quarter to another; hiring often took both men and women from their kin, at least for a time; masters took their slaves from an old plantation to a new one; and above all, slave owners died, causing their chattel to be divided among heirs and creditors. Why did so many *Recorder* advertisers focus on separations caused by sale?

Part of the answer is that many separations of slave families were temporary. Even permanently separated kin were often a short distance away, close enough to hear news of each other from time to time, if not to visit. When an estate was settled and slaves were distributed to heirs, slaves often learned the identity of the new owners of their kinfolk and something about where those owners lived. Although separated from their kin, they were still embedded in the white family's network, which may have occasionally provided a welcome bit of news and more often the small comfort of knowing where their loved one was, with that master in that place. Slave sales, particularly long-distance sales, often made that knowledge very difficult to obtain. While the *Recorder* advertisers hoped to reunite with lost kin, their ads literally requested information that might provide the small comfort of knowing what happened to their loved ones after the separation.

Family members sold away often disappeared into a deafening silence. Somerset Cannon, for example, sought information about his brother and two sisters, "who were sold South" from Delaware 35 years earlier, "since which time I have heard nothing definite."[35] By mentioning that relatives were "sold South" or by imploring, "Ministers South please read [this ad] in church,"[36] advertisers expressed their lack of knowledge about where their lost kin might be. Advertisers who had been separated from kin by sale seldom failed to mention the state they were sold from.[37] But two-thirds of these same advertisers said—and presumably knew—nothing about the place their relatives were sold to.[38] From the viewpoint of relatives left behind, many slaves who were sold dropped off the face of the earth.

Most advertisers shared the dilemma of Richard Henry Croxen, who knew that his brother Madison Woods had been sold in Richmond but could only add that "he was there bought by a Southern planter" and that information would be welcome from "any one having any idea of his whereabouts."[39] With little idea about where to find their lost kin, advertisers supplied details that might somehow prove useful, such as the name of the former owner, the place of sale, and the name of the slave trader or new owner. Few advertisers could be as specific as John R. Scott, whose sister Mary Jane Page Scott was sold at Edgefield Court House, South Carolina, "to Shepherd Spencer, who took her to Neshoba County, Mississippi."[40] Most advertisers had less information than Amanda Allison, whose mother, Ann Roscoe, "formerly lived near Gallatin, Tenn. Belonged to a Mr. Patton, but was purchased by Thos. Roscoe, was left with a trader named John Taylor, who is said to have sold her to South Carolina."[41] Far more typical was Marshall Williams, who knew that Catherine Massey lived in Clarke County, Virginia, "belonged to Dr. Wm. McGuire, and was sold to traders twenty years ago"; or Melinda Smith, whose daughter and four sons were "sold in Richmond at different times."[42] Like many others, Charity Ward counterbalanced the absence of knowledge about where to find her children with details about who they were. She sought three sons, Andrew, Ransom, and George, "who were taken from me and sold when they were very small. Also two others, (twins) one called Martha Ann and the other had no name." The children had lived with their mother, who "belonged to a man in Franklin Co., Ky., by the name of Seth Ward." Charity Ward explained that Washington Kearney was her husband and the father of her children, that he "belonged to" Joseph Kearney, and that he "was killed by a fall from a wagon."[43] Perhaps one of those details, her ad implied, would ultimately bring her children back.

Occasionally news trickled in from the person sold away. Moses Sisseney's mother, brother, and three sisters "were sold from Liberty, Mo., over 30 years ago" to "a man named Francis Benware" and, he noted, "the last time I heard of them they were on Red River."[44] Sometimes the grapevine repeatedly telegraphed news of a far-flung family member. Rachel Davis's daughter Abbie was "born at Wilmington, Delaware . . . [and] was carried to Cuba, by Mr. Guelle, for Mr. Peter Bodway, over thirty-five years ago." Rachel had somehow learned that "since then [Abbie] has been with Mr. Martin, of Texas, and latterly with Mr. A. Bell of New Orleans" and that Abbie's "husband died about 7 years ago" and that "she kept a wash-house in New Orleans, about 1862." Revealing as this information was compared to the stony silence heard by most advertisers, Abbie's "distressed mother" still did not know where to find her.[45]

The Civil War accelerated the antebellum rate of family separations. Some masters tried to maintain control of their slaves by sending them away from Yankee armies. One advertiser sought two daughters and three sons whose masters, "before the first battle of Bull Run, moved them from Fauquier Co., Va., to Mississippi."[46] Hannah Holland's husband "was sent [from Virginia] to Georgia in 1863."[47] George Hamilton Jones hoped to find his three sons and three daughters, whom he had not seen "since Jackson captured Harper's Ferry," when "it is likely" that they and his brother "were sent—to Richmond, or elsewhere."[48]

In all, wartime incidents "parted" about one in four advertisers from their families.[49] Matilda Jones, like many other slaves, became lost in the confusion of maneuvering armies. She sought her husband and two sons, who "were separated [from her] in the woods near a place called Alleywhite [Virginia] in November 1862. I was carried back to Suffolk by Union troops. I have heard nothing of them since."[50] In 1865, Harriet Mayo advertised that she "now thinks" that her daughter and three sons might be "some where within the lines of the Union army" near Petersburg.[51] Fannie Bostick hoped to find her niece Edith Chappel, who "left Columbia, South Caroina, on February 20th, 1865, with the army of Gen. Sherman."[52]

Being with the army, often with a specific regiment, was mentioned by advertisers more frequently than any other wartime incident.[53] Sandy Lynch "was in the army, performing the duties of a servant," when his wife and three children were "carried away from Carolina county, Virginia, by her 'master' Wm. Goodman, in 1862."[54] Edward Stevenson sought his son Henry, "who was taken away from Gundy Moore, Hardin County, Tenn., in Gen. Dodge's Brigade, Col. Corwin's Division."[55] Henry Christian's three children "came from Winchester in General Banks' division."[56] Half of the advertisers who mentioned the army made clear that the missing family member was not just within army lines but was serving in uniform.[57] Fannie Robinson hoped to get word of her son Cayrel, "who left Liberty, Clay County, Missouri, about four years ago to join the Union army at Wyandotte, Kansas; and he has not been heard from since."[58] John Johnson was in a U.S. Colored Troops regiment, as were Daniel Ash, George McCard, John Burton, George W. Burton, and others.[59]

The maelstrom of war also swept tens of thousands of former slaves into the North, an event quietly documented in the northern residence of the great preponderance of *Recorder* advertisers. Several ads mentioned the migration north. Henry Madden was looking for his wife Mary, "who embarked at New Orleans, in the steamer Media, last August, 1863, bound North."[60] Wesley Johnson sought his brother Gideon, who left Shenandoah County, Virginia, "in 1860 or 1861 for Pennsylvania."[61] Washington Roberson hoped to locate his brother

Fountain Bore, "who was born and raised in Springfield, Va., and was taken by the Union army and came to Philadelphia on the U.S. Ship Wartushett and then got his discharge. He told his brother that he was going to the State of Ohio."[62] Hannah Pierson was separated from her son John, who "was about 12 years of age, and resided in Alexandria, Va." when she "was sold to New Orleans." "Nine long and dreary years have passed away since his mother has seen him," Hannah noted, adding that "through the reverses of this war she has made her way to New Bedford, Mass., where she now resides."[63]

While residence in the North made it easier to place an ad in the *Recorder*, it did not make finding lost family members any easier. Elizabeth Williams hoped to locate her daughter, Lydia, and three sons, William, Allen, and Parker, from whom she had been separated twenty-five years earlier, when sold from Franklin County, Tennessee, to Arkansas. Now living in Marysville, California, "she has never seen the . . . children since. Any information . . . will be gratefully received by one whose love for her children survives the bitterness and hardships of many long years spent in slavery."[64] To penetrate the soul-wounding silence, Elizabeth Williams and other advertisers described their lost kin by name and family relationship, intending to prick the ears of listeners in AME churches across the country.

Names are always a less-than-perfect method of identification because different people can have the same name and because the same person can have different names. After emancipation, when many former slaves exercised their newly minted freedom by taking new names, pre-emancipation names—the only names most advertisers knew—were even less likely to identify the person being sought. Two-thirds of the advertisers' family members had been separated ten years or more; nearly one-third had been separated for twenty years or more.[65] The passage of so much time meant that some names would have changed even before emancipation, especially the names of women and children. How likely was it that Emily Helms, sold from Tennessee to Mississippi in 1844, when she was eleven years old, still had the same surname twenty years later?[66] James Bell in Helena, Arkansas, did not venture surnames in his ad to find his "mother Isabella, my sister Sallie, and . . . my grandmother Minna," whom he "left . . . in Georgia about thirty years ago."[67] Martha Tittle's ad for her three sisters—Margaret Norris, Ann Bausly, and Mary Hall—and Emma Monroe's and Millie Johnson's search for their mother, Minnie Mayes, illustrated the mutability of women's surnames.[68] Rendering the rounded contours of a heard and spoken name in the hard-edged orthography of a printed ad introduced even more uncertainties. These difficulties surfaced in Lucy Lee's ads for her daughter "Julia Cranly" in 1867 and "Julia Crawley" in 1870; in Reverend Thomas W. Henry's ad for his son from whom he had been separated for twenty-seven years, "Ashberry or Rosebey Henry"; in Letitia Weathonton's search for her children, Sarah Elizabeth Weathonton, Jane Eithenton, and Delpha Ann Weathonton; and in George Teamoh's ad for his children, "John and Lavinia Teamer, or Teamoh," who fourteen years earlier were, respectively, nine and eight years old when "it was thought they were sold [from Virginia] to Texas."[69] But all these difficulties with names did not change the stubborn reality that advertisers had little else to use to identify their lost kin. And sometimes they did not even have that. Roman Pleasant, for example, wanted to find his brothers Anthony and Isaiah Pleasant and "three sisters whose names are forgotten."[70]

Imagine sitting in the congregation of an AME church a few years after emancipation, listening to the minister read two fairly typical ads, and then trying to remember whether you had ever known or heard of one of the missing people. Eliza Clark's ad asked listeners to juggle five surnames; her name had been Eliza Brooks before she was sold about 15 years ago, and she was trying to find her "mother, Martha Tiles, and my sister Lucy; also . . . my two brothers John Thomas and Lewis Green, and my daughter Ann Brooks."[71] Hagar Outlaw's ad confronted listeners with the challenge of keeping track of very different people who had the same surname. She hoped to find her eight children, who "went from Wake Forest," North Carolina: "Three of them (their names being Cherry, Viny, and Mills Outlaw) were bought by Abram Hester. Noah Outlaw was taken to Alabama by Joseph Turner Hillsborough. John Outlaw was sold to George Vaughan. Eli Outlaw was sold by Joseph Outlaw. He acted as watchman for old David Outlaw. Thomas Rembry Outlaw was taken away by Wm. Outlaw. Julia Outlaw was sold in New Orleans by Dr. Outlaw."[72]

Hagar Outlaw's bewildering recitation of names of slaves and owners, some with the same surnames, reflected a nearly universal tactic used by advertisers to counteract the mutable names of their lost family members with the much more stable names of their former owners. By coupling names of former slaves with names of their former owners, advertisers tried to root the identity of their lost kinfolk. Although advertisers included masters' names for purposes of identification, they never asked former owners to help find their missing relatives. Doubtless part of the reason was that few former masters read the *Christian Recorder* or attended AME churches. The complete lack of requests for information from masters appears, however, to grow out of advertisers' deeper refusal to request help from the very people responsible for their families' separation. Several advertisers openly expressed their rejection of their masters' values by putting in quotation marks the words "property," "belonged," "owner," and "master."[73] But most advertisers simply described their missing loved ones to the best of their ability; their ads expressed a searing indictment of former masters through their substance, not their rhetoric.

The profound difficulty of describing lost kin in ways that would make them recognizable to other African Americans suggests that advertisers engaged in an almost hopeless quest. All of them would probably have echoed Lewis Wade—who sought his wife and three children, whom he had "left" behind in Virginia sixteen years ago—in promising that "heaven will bless the hand that guides the wanderers home."[74] But most likely, few of the wanderers sought by the advertisers ever came home. Robert Buckner was the only advertiser who left unambiguous evidence of partial success. In February 1867, Buckner, now in Indiana, advertised for his daughter, Mary, and sons, Daniel, Reuben, and George, whom he had "left" in Rappahannock County, Virginia. Five months later he placed another ad, announcing, "I found Reuben Buckner in Chilicothe, Ohio," although he was still looking for the others.[75] If other advertisers matched Robert Buckner's good fortune, it remains unknown. On the whole, the ads were less a realistic device for locating lost kin than a sign of the advertisers' desperation, their willingness to try anything to find their loved ones. The ads voiced a heartfelt yearning to knit back together the families masters had torn apart. Even their yearnings bore the scars of slavery.

Parents who placed ads were almost invariably single parents.[76] And three-fourths of the single parents were mothers.[77] Both mothers and fathers yearned to find daughters just as much as sons.[78] And both mothers and fathers described themselves as "sorrowing," "anxious," and "distressed."[79] But why did mothers express their sorrow and anxiety by placing ads in the *Christian Recorder* three times more often than fathers? Why didn't single mothers and fathers place ads in roughly equal numbers? Fathers, after all, were more likely than mothers to have access to the necessary cash, and overall, advertisers were equally divided between men and women.

It is possible that instead of placing ads, fathers took other steps to locate missing children, such as traveling from place to place, a more difficult and dangerous undertaking for single mothers. It is also possible that when single mothers—who presumably were more likely to attend church than single fathers—expressed their heartache about their missing children, their ministers suggested placing an ad. Compelling evidence against this possibility is that single fathers mentioned ministers in their ads more often than single mothers did.[80]

A third possibility is that ads were sometimes a call for help as well as an expression of affection. Mrs. Chamberlain was probably not the only mother who was looking for her children because "I want them to come and help me, as I am unable to take care of myself."[81] Matilda Jones explained that she was "much in want at this time."[82] Hagar Outlaw declared the mixed motives that other mothers probably felt. "I hope they [her eight missing children] will think enough of their mother to come back and look for her, as she is growing old, and needs help. . . . I wish to see my dear ones once more clasped to their mother's heart as in days of yore."[83] Fathers may have needed help too. Lewis Blackwell hoped to locate his son, who had been sold away from Virginia to Mississippi, because "I am an old man and need the companionship of my son." But as a rule, single fathers may have been better able to provide for their needs than single mothers, and that may partially account for the disparity in their ads.

It remains possible, however, that mothers advertised to find their lost kin much more frequently than fathers partly because they felt stronger ties of affection to their children. Slavery stripped many fathers of the opportunity to nourish their relationship with their children. Perhaps the ads reflected that brutal fact. Evidence from ads placed by sons and daughters supports that conclusion. Both sons and daughters were more concerned with locating lost mothers than missing fathers. Almost all sons and daughters sought to find their mothers; only half of them were looking for their fathers.[84] The realities of slavery appear to have corroded the bonds of affection between many children and their fathers.[85]

In the end, all the advertisers refused to accept the amnesia their masters had forced upon them. While they hoped their ads would reunite their families, they longed at least to hear some words of comfort, some news that would assuage their yearning. But the disorienting silence of separation and the hobbling disabilities of slavery handicapped their searches. In AME churches throughout the nation, they expected to receive a sympathetic hearing. Read by ministers in hundreds of congregations, the ads amounted to a collective prayer of remembrance of some of the unhealed wounds of slavery. And they vividly document one of the deepest meanings of freedom for many former slaves: the freedom to try to learn what had happened to lost kin.

Notes

I am indebted to Professor Atina Grossman for generous advice about displaced persons. I am also grateful to Sarah E. Johnson for expert research assistance.

1. See, for example, Leonard Dinnerstein, "The U.S. Army and the Jews: Policies toward the Displaced Persons after World War II," *American Jewish History* 68 (1979): 353–66; Mark Wyman, *DP: Europe's Displaced Persons, 1945–1955* (Philadelphia: Balch Institute Press, 1989); and Alex Grobman, *Rekindling the Flame: American Jewish Chaplins and the Survivors of European Jewry, 1944–1948* (Detroit: Wayne State University Press, 1993).

2. Informative discussions of the AME Church and the *Christian Recorder* include Clarence E. Walker, *A Rock in a Weary Land: The African Methodist Episcopal Church during the Civil War and Reconstruction* (Baton Rouge: Louisiana State University Press, 1982); Stephen Ward Angell, *Bishop Henry McNeal Turner and African-American Religion in the South* (Knoxville: University of Tennessee Press, 1992); James T. Campbell, *Songs of Zion: The African Methodist Episcopal Church in the United States and South Africa* (New York: Oxford University Press, 1995); and Gilbert Anthony Williams, *The* Christian Recorder, *Newspaper of the African Methodist Episcopal Church, History of a Forum for Ideas, 1854–1902* (Jefferson, N.C.: McFarland and Company, 1996).

3. This study includes all of the "information wanted" ads placed by former slaves in the *Christian Recorder* from 1861 through 1870. Some ads appeared only once or twice. Many others were published verbatim in several consecutive issues. I collected one instance of each ad and excluded duplicates. I also excluded thirty-three ads that lacked plausible evidence that the person placing the ad had been a slave. More ads (33 percent) appeared in 1866, immediately after passage of the Thirteenth Amendment, than in any other year. A majority (54 percent) of the ads were published in 1866 and 1867; almost nine out of ten ads (86 percent) appeared after 1865. I am not aware of another study of advertisements of this sort, but other studies of the reconstitution of freed families after emancipation include C. Peter Ripley, "The Black Family in Transition: Louisiana, 1860–1865," *Journal of Southern History* 41 (1975): 369–80; Herbert G. Gutman, *The Black Family in Slavery and Freedom, 1750–1925* (New York: Pantheon, 1976), 363–431; James M. Smallwood, "Emancipation and the Black Family: A Case Study in Texas," *Social Science Quarterly* 57 (1977): 849–57; Barry A. Crouch, "Reconstructing Black Families: Perspectives from the Texas Freedom's Bureau Records," *Prologue* 18 (1986): 109–22; Ira Berlin, Steven F. Miller, and Leslie S. Rowland, "Afro-American Families in the Transition from Slavery to Freedom," *Radical History Review* 42 (1988): 89–121; Marion B. Lucas, "Kentucky Blacks: The Transition

from Slavery to Freedom," *Register of the Kentucky Historical Society* 91 (1993): 403–19; Cheryll Ann Cody, "Kin and Community among the Good Hope People after Emancipation," *Ethnohistory* 41 (1994): 25–72; Barry A. Crouch, "The 'Chords of Love': Legalizing Black Marital and Family Rights in Postwar Texas," *Journal of Negro History* 79 (1994): 334–51.

4. Redelia Jones, *CR*, 16 March 1867. Here and subsequently I have cited ads by the name of the person placing the ad (when known) and the date of publication in the *Christian Recorder*. Height, hair, and eyes were also mentioned in the description of John Allen; William Allen, *CR*, 20 April 1867.

5. John Pembroke, *CR*, 5 August 1865.

6. George Knox, *CR*, 15 August 1868.

7. Jane Morris, *CR*, 15 September 1866.

8. [No name given; identified in the ad as "the brother of Noah Camper"], *CR*, 24 March 1866.

9. Martha Ann Good, *CR*, 2 April 1870.

10. The editor of the *Recorder* constantly solicited new subscriptions and begged current subscribers to pay their bills. A year's subscription cost $2.50 in advance or $3.50 if not paid within three months. Ministers were charged $2 in advance or $2.25 later. Subscription rates appeared in nearly every issue; see, for example, *CR*, 26 January 1867 or 24 October 1868.

11. Membership was put at 225,000 in 1869. "The Work Before Us," *CR*, 23 February 1867; "What Are They Doing," *CR*, 17 April 1869.

12. The *Recorder* listed 707 AME ministers in 1870; 507 (72 percent) were in the South; 113 (16 percent) in the Midwest; and 81 (12 percent) in the Northeast. Some ministers received handsome support from their congregations and could easily afford the *Recorder*. Others, especially those in the South, barely scraped by. Most likely an issue of the *Recorder* was treasured and passed from hand to hand by Southern ministers. "The Work Before Us," *CR*, 23 February 1867; "Our Helpers," 3 December 1870.

13. "Advice from the Editor of This Paper to the Many Freedmen throughout the South," Part 1, *CR*, 9 December 1865; Part 2, *CR*, 16 December 1865; Part 3, *CR*, 23 December 1865. In 1869 the editor proposed distributing the *Recorder* to former slaves without cost, since children in many families could read it to illiterate adults. This venture evidently failed for lack of sufficient contributions. "An Appeal," *CR*, 17 July 1869.

14. Although I read the *Recorder* carefully, it is possible that I overlooked an article or editorial that mentioned the ads.

15. "Advertisements," *CR*, 9 February 1867; *CR*, 24 October 1868.

16. In 1870, 93 percent of African Americans lived in the former slave states and the District of Columbia. Only 26 percent of the advertisers lived there at the time they placed their ads. Information regarding the African American population in 1870 has been drawn from Ninth Census, *The Statistics of the Population of the United States* . . . (Washington: Government Printing Office, 1872), 5.

17. Specifically, 32 percent of the advertisers lived in Pennsylvania; 46 percent lived there or in New York, New Jersey, Massachusetts, Connecticut, or Rhode Island; 22 percent lived in Ohio, Indiana, Illinois, Michigan, Kansas, or Iowa; 3 percent lived in California, Colorado, or Idaho; 3 percent lived in Canada West. By comparison, in 1870, 1 percent of the nation's African Americans resided in Pennsylvania, 4 percent in the Northeast (including Pennsylvania), and 3 percent in the Midwest.

18. Rachel Ann Martienas, *CR,* 23 March 1867.

19. In contrast, just 12 percent of the South's African Americans resided in Virginia (and West Virginia) in 1870. In most cases, the ads make clear where the advertiser had lived while a slave.

20. In 1870 the mid-Atlantic slave states (Virginia, Maryland, Delaware, and the District of Columbia) included 17 percent of the South's African Americans. Of Northern advertisers, 55 percent had lived in these states; of Southern advertisers, 57 percent. The Ohio and Upper Mississippi Valley slave states (Kentucky, Tennessee, Arkansas, and Missouri) included 17 percent of the South's African Americans in 1870 and 22 percent of the advertisers. The lower Atlantic Coast states (North Carolina, South Carolina and Georgia) included 30 percent of the South's black people in 1870, but only 14 percent of all advertisers. The Gulf Coast states (Florida, Alabama, Mississippi, Louisiana, and Texas) included 36 percent of the South's black population in 1870 but only 8 percent of the advertisers.

21. Ephraim Allen, *CR,* 21 October 1868.

22. Amanda Jane Bass, *CR,* 19 August 1865.

23. George Henry Denna, *CR,* 25 January 1865.

24. Phoebe Ann Jackson, *CR,* 11 August 1866.

25. Reverend Cyrus Boey, *CR,* 18 October 1865.

26. Lucinda Johnson, *CR,* 20 July 1867.

27. William Thomas, *CR,* 20 August 1870.

28. In all, 41 percent of the ads did not provide evidence of why family members had become separated. These ads included 38 percent of the people being sought. Most likely, many of these families had, in fact, been separated by sales.

29. In total, 159 advertisers (59 percent of all advertisers) gave evidence of the cause of separation; they were trying to locate 469 family members (62 percent of all persons being sought). Ads stating unambiguously that sale caused the separation numbered 63; these advertisers were looking for 237 relatives.

30. The vast majority of these advertisers (forty-one of fifty, or 82 percent) used "left" to describe their separation.

31. There were fifty such ads; they sought 145 relatives. They represented 31 percent of the ads that gave a reason for separation and 31 percent of the people being sought in those ads.

32. Only two ads explicitly stated that separation occurred because slaves "escaped" before the Civil War. In both cases the slaves who escaped were said

to be in Canada, one with the help of the Underground Railroad. See Sarah Elizabeth Brooks, *CR*, 12 June 1869; Frances Parker, *CR*, 2 July 1870. During the Civil War, a number of other slaves escaped to Union Lines; they are discussed below.

33. For an instance of a master who moved and took a slave with him, see F. Elizabeth Brisco, *CR*, 21 April 1864.

34. That is, 382 of 467 relatives, or 82 percent of those being sought by advertisers who gave some reason for the separation, had been sold or "left" or "taken" away.

35. Somerset Cannon, *CR*, 25 September 1869.

36. Daniel W. Hicks, *CR*, 23 March 1867.

37. The ads mentioned the state that 98 percent of the people (233 of 237) separated by sale were sold from. Virginia, home of both presidents and slave traders, topped the list, with half of all separations by sale. The mid-Atlantic slave states accounted for 63 percent; the Atlantic Coast states, 14 percent; the Gulf Coast states, 2 percent; and the Ohio and Upper Mississippi Valley states, 21 percent.

38. The ads mentioned the state that 32 percent of the people (75 of 237) separated by sale were sold to. The largest fraction of this group was sold to the Gulf Coast states (31 percent), with the Atlantic Coast states close behind (28 percent), followed by the Ohio and Upper Mississippi Valley states (14 percent). The mid-Atlantic slave states accounted for only 2 percent.

39. Richard Henry Croxen, *CR*, 21 October 1865.

40. John R. Scott, *CR*, 22 June 1867.

41. Amanda Allison, *CR*, 11 September 1869.

42. Marshall Williams, *CR*, 1 August 1868; Melinda Smith, *CR*, 4 May 1867.

43. Charity Ward, *CR*, 5 May 1866.

44. Moses Sisseney, *CR*, 2 July 1870.

45. Rachel Davis, *CR*, 5 August 1865.

46. [Advertiser not named], *CR*, 4 April 1866. The advertiser "left" the morning before his or her children were taken away.

47. Hannah Holland, *CR*, 16 March 1867.

48. George Hamilton Jones, *CR*, 7 July 1866.

49. That is, 25 percent (40 of 159) of the advertisers who mentioned how they became separated referred to a wartime event. These advertisers were looking for 18 percent (82 of 467) of the kin lost by this group. Elizabeth Ann Jackson (*CR*, 3 June 1865), who sought her two brothers and two sisters, noted that "the war, however, has parted us."

50. Matilda Jones, *CR*, 22 September 1866.

51. Harriet Mayo, *CR*, 18 February 1865.

52. Fannie Bostick, *CR*, 5 August 1865.

53. Of the forty advertisers who mentioned the war, twenty-one (53 percent) referred specifically to the army.

54. Sandy Lynch, *CR*, 17 November 1866. Charles Metts had not seen his wife, son, and three daughters for ten years, and the last time he heard from them was when he was "in the Rebel Army" but he "could not get a chance to go see them" in Columbia, S.C. Charles Metts, *CR*, 9 June 1866.

55. Edward Stevenson, *CR*, 6 March 1869.

56. Henry Christian, *CR*, 27 December 1862.

57. That is, of the twenty-one advertisers who mentioned the army, eleven referred to service uniform.

58. Fannie Robinson, *CR*, 29 July 1865.

59. Catherine Johnson, *CR*, 30 December 1865; Amelia Jane Spriggs, *CR*, 8 August 1868; Ann Jones, *CR*, 1 August 1868; Catherine Jones, *CR*, 10 September 1864; [Burton's wife; the ad does not give a name], *CR*, 5 May 1866.

60. Henry Madden, *CR*, 9 July 1864.

61. Wesley Johnson, *CR*, 21 April 1866.

62. Washington Roberson, *CR*, 14 May 1864.

63. Hannah Cole, *CR*, 4 February 1865.

64. Elizabeth Williams, *CR*, 10 March 1866.

65. That is, of the 221 family members of advertisers who had been separated by sale or by being "left" and whose ads specified how long they had been separated, 66 percent (146 of 221) had been separated for ten years or longer, 29 percent (65 of 221) for twenty years or longer.

66. William Fletcher, *CR*, 18 June 1870.

67. James Bell, *CR*, 10 December 1870.

68. Martha Tittle, *CR*, 3 July 1869; Emma Moore and Millie Johnson, *CR*, 28 August 1869. Some fifty-seven ads mentioned women who had different surnames from the relatives they were seeking.

69. Lucy Lee, *CR*, 22 June 1867; Lucy Lee, *CR*, 17 October 1870; Thomas W. Henry, *CR*, 3 June 1865; Letitia Weathonton, *CR*, 25 January 1865; George Teamoh, *CR*, 23 March 1867.

70. Roman Pleasant, *CR*, 3 October 1868.

71. Eliza Clark, *CR*, 7 December 1867.

72. Hagar Outlaw, *CR*, 7 April 1866.

73. See, for example, Joanna Whiters, *CR*, 5 May 1866; Henry and Virginia Thompson, *CR*, 26 May 1866; Lucinda Reynolds, *CR*, 31 March 1866; Catherine Rhodes, *CR*, 14 September 1867; Larcenie Mayhoe, *CR*, 5 May 1866.

74. Lewis Wade, *CR*, 14 July 1866.

75. Robert Buckner, *CR*, 2 February 1867; Buckner, *CR*, 20 July 1867. It is possible that Harriet Mayo found the daughter and three sons she advertised for in February 1865. Two years later she placed another ad, this time for her sister who had been sold away from Petersburg, Va., "when about twelve years of age," In the second ad Mayo did not mention her children, perhaps because she had located them. Similarly, Melinda Smith may have found her daughter Amelia, who was one of the seven relatives Melinda was seeking in her May

1867 ad but was the only one of the seven not mentioned again in Melinda's as six months later. Harriet Mayo, *CR*, 18 February 1865; Mayo, *CR*, 20 April 1867; Melinda Smith, *CR*, 4 May 1867; Smith, *CR*, 30 November 1867.

76. Of the 99 ads placed by parents, 93 percent were placed by single parents; only 7 ads were placed by both father and mother.

77. Of the eighty-nine single parents identified as father or mother, sixty-five (73 percent) were mothers.

78. Children accounted for 80 percent of the 167 people sought by mothers and 75 percent of the 81 people sought by fathers. Mothers sought sons (68) and daughters (66) equally; father sought a few more sons (35) than daughters (26).

79. See, for example, George Hamilton Jones, *CR*, 7 July 1866; Melinda Smith, *CR*, 4 May 1867; Alfred and Eliza Ann Lee, *CR*, 19 May 1866; Caroline Willis, *CR*, 25 November 1865.

80. Ministers were mentioned in 46 percent of single fathers' ads and 34 percent of single mothers' ads. Advertisers typically either requested ministers to read ads to their congregations or asked for information about their kinfolk to be sent in care of a minister. Although I have not been able to locate evidence documenting how advertisers got the idea of placing an ad, I suspect that hearing a minister read an ad in church sometimes prompted worshipers to place their own ads.

81. Mrs. Chamberlain, *CR*, 19 May 1866.

82. Matilda Jones, *CR*, 22 September 1866.

83. Hagar Outlaw, *CR*, 7 APril 1866.

84. That is, of the 43 sons placing ads, 38 of them (88 percent) sought mothers, while 18 of them (42 percent) sought fathers (obviously, several sought both mothers and fathers). Similarly, of the 28 daughters who placed ads 27 of them (96 percent) were looking for their mothers, 14 of them (50 percent) for their fathers. Of course, sons and daughters were also searching for siblings and other relatives.

85. The *Christian Recorder* ads provide some support for sociologist Orlando Patterson's recent statement that "slavery was . . . most virulent in its devastation of the role of father and husband." However, Patterson's argument must be carefully qualified; after all, some fathers and husbands did place ads to locate lost kin. Patterson, *Rituals of Blood: Consequences of Slavery in Two American Centuries* (Washington: Civitas/Counterpoint, 1998), 27.

TWO

FOR BETTER OR FOR WORSE

Black Families and "the State" in Civil War Virginia

Michelle A. Krowl

For better or for worse, the Civil War influenced the domestic relations of African American families in Virginia in a variety of ways,
both temporary and permanent. The war threw many aspects of Afro-
Virginians' domestic lives into turmoil. Wartime disruptions of Virginia's social order allowed slaves to escape slavery in untold numbers,
took black men from homes to serve with the military, allowed fugitive slave men to collect theirs wives and families, facilitated family reunions, and created opportunities for African Americans to begin the
transition from slavery to freedom by reconstructing their familial
connections. Only during Reconstruction could they sort out the relationships that would accompany them into the postwar world.

"The State" played an important role in the construction and reconstruction of African American domestic relations. During the war,
"the State" primarily consisted of the federal governments of the
United and Confederate States of America, as well as their military
forces in the field.[1] While Confederate policy and the actions of
Rebel troops certainly affected black domestic relations during the
war, the United States government and the Union army exerted the
most significant influence on the lives of African Americans. Though
black families took control of many areas of their domestic affairs,

governmental policies and the presence of the military frequently helped establish the options available to them.

Government intervention in the lives of black families often produced inconsistent results. While individual Afro-Virginians set domestic agendas with their hopes and experiences in mind, the government dealt with freedpeople in view of its own procedures and objectives. Thus, African Americans, and more particularly black women, occasionally found themselves determining the course of their domestic relationships, while at the same time being held accountable to policies based on a different frame of reference. In addition to active government interference in the lives of black families, circumstances produced by the Civil War also influenced the domestic decisions made by Afro-Virginians themselves. Regardless of the level of intervention or the message its representatives promoted, "the State" became a larger presence in the lives of black women during the Civil War than ever before. The extent to which African American women took advantage of this presence, considered government policies when reordering their family lives, or even followed regulations, however, remained largely a matter of personal choice and the realities of black life.

The secession of Virginia from the United States and the existence of military troops in the Commonwealth disrupted the social order so carefully constructed by white Virginians and created opportunities for free blacks and slaves to exert more control over their familial relationships. Alternatively, the confusion of war further disrupted black families when individual members escaped to freedom or left to serve with the military. Furthermore, the policies enacted by United States civilian and military officials often did not clarify what African Americans could expect from the government, or the consistency with which its policies would be carried out. For much of the war, federal policy left management of "negro affairs" to the discretion of each commander and his subordinates, which meant that the level of assistance offered to Afro-Virginian families by "the State" depended on the sympathies of the authorities with whom they came into contact. Government action toward blacks generally attempted to keep black families together, while also employing black men as military laborers and encouraging self-support among their families. When these sometimes conflicting goals did not overlap, however, the government usually chose "military necessity" over domestic stability in dealing with African Americans and their families.[2]

For some black women, the military service of husbands, fathers, sons, and brothers formed a direct link between "the State" and their families. Throughout the war, impressment of free black and slave men into the Confederate military as laborers and the use of black men as laborers, then soldiers, for the United States military upset familial arrangements by removing black men from their homes, spouses, and children. While Confederate forces more commonly impressed black men than did Union troops, the latter occasionally forced black men to serve the United States. Jane Wallis claimed that soldiers essentially kidnapped her husband, James, on his way to work as a shoemaker. "If they, keep him, they leave me, and 3 children, to get along, the best we can" she protested. In 1863, a missionary complained to General Benjamin Butler that such actions on the part of United States soldiers were not altogether unusual. Forced impressments aroused fear among the loyal black population and caused financial distress among black families dependent on male labor for support.[3]

Whether he was a soldier or a laborer, a black man's service in the military had far-reaching effects for his family, especially if he enlisted in the Union army. Apart from the pay awarded soldiers and laborers, the families of many black soldiers qualified for emancipation under assorted legislation passed by the United States Congress during the course of the war.[4] By the same token, a black man's service with the Union army could make his family the target of abuse if they remained at home while he served elsewhere. Shortly after the war, Benjamin Triplet of Fauquier County refused to allow John Berry of Alexandria to collect his wife and children, saying that "he went to the d——d yankes [sic] to fight against him," and threatened Berry's life if he were to come for his family. White Southerners throughout the Confederacy directed their resentment about African American military service at the wives of black Union soldiers. With their husbands away, these women were particularly vulnerable and had a difficult time protecting themselves and their families.[5]

Black men who were hired as laborers for the Union or Confederate armies or who enlisted as soldiers in the United States Colored Troops (USCT) risked disease or battle-related wounds, and possibly permanent separation from their families. Even nonsoldiering service with the Union army could have grave consequences for Federal laborers and their wives. Mary Cowling's husband, for example, drowned in 1862 while laboring for Union forces at Bermuda Hundred. Regardless of the manner in which it occurred, a man's death as a result of military service took away a vital source of support for his dependents. Rampant inflation in war-torn Virginia meant that black women had to stretch their already meager resources even further to provide basic necessities.[6]

Black military wives suffered emotional hardships as well as financial ones. Just like white soldiers, black enlisted men left worried families behind. White Northern missionary Lucy Chase described the women at a "contraband" camp on Craney Island in Hampton Roads as heartbroken about their circumstances. "Husbands are with the army, they know not where," Chase wrote of the women. "They are alone, with no one to comfort them." While slave women certainly knew the anxiety of having loved ones taken from them through sale or escape, for fugitive black women living in often unfamiliar environments, it must have been particularly distressing to know that their husbands faced dangerous conditions while serving with the military.[7]

To some extent, though, black women may have felt the loss of a husband or son less than white Confederate women did. Slave women whose husbands either lived "abroad" with a different master, or even on the same plantation, rarely depended on their spouses for economic support. If their masters still provided essential goods and services during the war, slave wives and mothers "only" had to cope with the physical separation from a loved one, which was not a new experience for many of them. Women in contraband camps and government farms could also rely on some measure of government support, regardless of the poor quality of provisions. Free black women, however, certainly felt their losses both emotionally and financially. Some women stayed at home and tried to make ends meet, hoping that their husbands both received the pay promised them and felt a responsibility to send a portion of that money to their families. In either case, slave and free black women in Virginia were accustomed to contributing to their family's welfare. Thus, they may have adapted more easily to the hardships produced by separation than their white counterparts whose menfolk were off fighting for the Confederacy, leaving them to run farms and support families, often for the first time.[8]

Other black women chose to follow their husbands' regiments and remain as close to their spouses as possible. While there, some women found employment as laundresses and cooks to supplement their incomes. Mary Hughes met her future husband, March, in Norfolk, where he had enlisted in the Thirty-eighth Infantry, USCT. Soon after their marriage, Hughes's regiment transferred to Deep Bottom, Virginia, and Mary soon followed him as the cook for the regiment's colonel. After March was wounded in battle, Mary cared for her husband in the hospital until the regiment left Deep Bottom. While Julia Custis did not accompany the regiment in which her husband served, illness later forced George Custis into a hospital in Eastville, on Virginia's Eastern Shore. When Julia learned of her husband's whereabouts, she went to the hospital to nurse him for three weeks prior to his death. For the Hugheses and Custises, military service may have made marital relationships more difficult to sustain, but it did not prevent the couples from maintaining contact.[9]

Military authorities had mixed reactions to women following their husbands' regiments and to the presence of black families in and around forts and camps. Some commanders recognized the beneficial effects on African American laborers and soldiers of having loved ones nearby and thought it unfair to turn away their families. One military order, for example, stated that "women and children are received, because it would be manifestly inquitious and unjust to take the husband and father and leave the wife and child to ill-treatment and starvation." Other commanders were considerably less welcoming to black families, especially those requiring government assistance. Since useful work could not be provided to every military wife, many generals found soldiers' families burdensome and sought to remove the families from military posts. Whether the wives and families of black soldiers and laborers were able to stay with their menfolk or had to survive on their own depended on how individual commanders viewed their presence and how much hardship black women were willing to accept.[10]

Military authorities in Virginia generally understood that the families of black recruits had fewer financial resources with which to support themselves than white families did, so they suggested that a "suitable subsistence" be furnished to the wives and children of black enlisted men whose families lived outside military camps or stayed at home. At the same time, officials often gave this support grudgingly, fearing that even minimal aid would make African Americans dependent on government assistance. While the United States government did provide food, shelter, and other necessities to the families of black soldiers, it also encouraged the female recipients to work for their own support and occasionally threatened to find employment for them.[11]

Many black women, though, clearly understood their entitlement to provisions and demanded that the government honor its promise to provide for families until the soldiers returned home. Ann Sumner wrote to General Benjamin Butler in 1864, explaining that "the fowlling order No 49 in your department was orderd that all the

Soljurs wives of collor should be supplied with rations and wood if they ware in the need of it. my husband is in the first U S volunteer Col) cavalry at fort moroe. I have made sevel reports for wood and have bin objectad in Portsmouth at the quartermaster department. Sir you will plase to attend to it as I am in the need of some wood." Other women sought the government's help in resolving problems of domestic finance. Several months after the end of the war, Catherine Massey appealed directly to the secretary of war about her husband's financial neglect. Explaining that William Massey, serving with the First Infantry, USCT, squandered his money and would not take adequate care of her upon his discharge from the army, Massey asked Secretary Edwin M. Stanton to arrange for her to receive his pay directly. "I am his lawful wife and he has neglected to treat me as a husband should," she wrote. "I have toiled and am still striving too earn my bread but as I feel myself declining daily. I think it no more than right than that he should be made to do what he has never yet done and that is to help me to support myself as I helped yes not only helped but naturally did support him before he came in the army." She would not normally ask for assistance in money matters, Massey added, but she feared her husband "to slothfull as to attend to it for him and myself." Few military wives wrote with such directness to government officials, but that some did indicates not only that black women were informed enough regarding policy matters to do so but also that they recognized when they had been unjustly denied their rights.[12]

Not only did the military service of black men separate families during the war, but general wartime disruptions in Virginia also physically divided many slave women from their families. Slave owners, fearing that approaching Union troops would set their slaves free or encourage them to run away, sent their most valuable bondspeople to protected areas, a phenomenon known as "running the slaves." To recover their monetary investment, other masters simply sold their slaves before they had a chance to escape. Still other white Virginians "refugeed" to safety with their own families as well as their slaves. Regardless of the circumstances, slave men and women had little choice about their removal, and the forced separations produced by the war further disrupted the families left at home. In October 1862, the owner of Cornelia McDonald's hired maid Lethea decided to sell the women to prevent her escape with Union troops. While McDonald hated to lose a servant and companion, Lethea mourned having to leave her husband and children behind. Earlier that year McDonald had contributed to the separation of two of her other slaves, Manuel

FOR BETTER OR FOR WORSE 41

and Catherine. Anxious that Manuel would escape to the Yankees, she sent him and his family somewhere safe from Union troops. When Confederate general Stonewall Jackson's forces reoccupied Winchester, however, the slave woman Catherine so feared that Jackson's men would treat blacks cruelly that she fled for safety with her children rather than staying near Winchester with Manuel. The couple likely never reunited, and Catherine was later found on the road from Harpers Ferry, looking the "picture of famine and grief."[13]

Not all black couples who parted company did so as the result of white intervention, though. The disruptions produced by the war allowed some black men to rid themselves of unwanted spouses. Lucy Chase remembered a conversation in which contraband women on Craney Island spoke of their husbands' abandonment of them. "I dont know whether my husband is living or not," one women explained, "he left me in Hampton." With a touch of bitterness, Aunt Nancy then said, "Ive only got *one* man, and he's away; left me here like a rotton [sic] stick to drop down and die." The third and much younger husband of "Mammy," the slave of Charles Friend of Prince George County, simply took the opportunity of her bout of paralysis to escape to Union lines rather than continue living with his disabled wife, a woman apparently unpopular with the other slaves on the White Hill plantation.[14]

While most slaves had a choice in marriage partners, others had been coerced or ordered by their masters to marry certain spouses and thus had little incentive to remain in an involuntary relationship when escape was an option. While much of the existing evidence of abandonment indicates that black men were the instigators, certainly black women also took advantage of upheavals created by the war to escape from husbands to whom they no longer wished to be joined. Thus, despite the seriousness with which most African Americans approached their marital obligations, some men and women took advantage of the wartime opportunities to leave their spouses.

Of course, not all black women confronted the war alone. Many examples can be found of women whose husbands and families remained with them throughout the war. Reuben Pollard, his wife Mary Ann, and their remaining children stayed on a farm in Culpeper County that belonged to Mary Ann's former mistress, who had moved to Louisiana upon the outbreak of hostilities. Until the Union army confiscated the farm in 1863, forcing the family to relocate to Alexandria, the Pollards quietly worked the land together in the face of Confederate threats of arrest and the periodic appearance of troops in their neighborhood. Both Mary Jane Malone and her husband Anderson were blacks, and they remained together at home over the course of the war; Anderson was bothered by Yankee troops only for provisions, not for his labor. Samuel Kenner lived on a different farm than his wife but stayed in the vicinity to work for the support of his sizable family, while his wife hired herself out to neighbors. The owner of the place at which his wife lived recalled later that Kenner visited frequently, thereby maintaining an active presence in his family. Thus, for at least a few Afro-Virginian women, the war may have been a factor in their lives generally, but one that did not detract from their domestic relationships.[15]

Many slaves and free blacks, furthermore, exploited wartime opportunities to reorder domestic arrangements to their satisfaction. Freeborn Betsy Johnson of Fairfax County married Benjamin Johnson before the war but lived apart from him while he remained a slave in nearby Prince William County. When Rebel troops retreated from his neighborhood, Benjamin Johnson escaped from his master, joined his wife, and resided with her for the duration of the war and beyond. Former slave Samuel Ballton reversed this process and brought his wife to him, although the fact that his wife lived in Union-occupied territory made his task a little easier. After a couple of failed attempts to free her, Ballton finally succeeded in bringing his spouse to live with him. He later recalled that "one of the proudest moments of his life was when he said to her, 'Rebecca, I'm going to take you to freedom with me.'" Ballton did not indicate, however, how Rebecca interpreted her husband's action and what psychological impact it had on her.[16]

While many fugitive slaves like Johnson and Ballton escaped independently and reunited with loved ones on their own, other separated black families took advantage of the presence of the Union army, and sympathetic officers, to gather their enslaved members. Union general R. H. Milroy gained a notorious reputation among white residents in Winchester for his assistance in reconstructing black families in the Shenandoah Valley. In 1863, Milroy ordered Mrs. Lorenzo in Clarke County to surrender her slaves to the runaway husband of one of her women. Under the heading "Carrying Out the Emancipation Proclamation," the *Richmond Daily Dispatch* reprinted Milroy's order commanding the mistress to "release to Mr. John Washington his wife and children, and other slaves in your possession, made free by the proclamation of Abraham Lincoln." The *Dispatch* noted sarcastically that "*Mr.* John Washington" successfully reclaimed his family, as well as Mrs. Lorenzo's horses and carriage.[17]

A month later, Sigismunda Kimball of Mount Jackson recorded in her diary that Yankee troops belonging to General Milroy's command assisted two male slaves in claiming their families from her relatives. After collecting William's wife and children, Federal troops escorted the party to Kimball's home to successfully take William's sister-in-law and her child, over the strong objections of Kimball's mother. William and Clifton, the other fugitive, then proceeded to collect Clifton's wife, who, for reasons unknown, refused to leave voluntarily. Over the course of February and March 1863, Kimball's diary entries note a number of black men in the neighborhood returning for their families, often with the assistance of Federal units.[18]

Traditionally, black men were at a disadvantage in terms of being able to protect their families from harm.[19] Slave men could rarely rescue their wives and children from sale, beatings, and other physical or sexual abuse without seriously endangering their own lives. Even during the war, black men could often do little on their own to protect their families or remove them from white control. The presence of the Union army significantly altered the balance of white power in a locality, especially if military authorities expressed a willingness to help black families. Under these circumstances, the proximity of the United States military allowed black men to assume the role of family protector in ways they had rarely been able to before. Interestingly, very few examples have come to light in which black women in Virginia headed military-assisted parties to collect family members who were still enslaved.[20]

Unfortunately, accounts detailing these rescues usually fail to record the views of the women being seized by their husbands. Most probably welcomed the chance for freedom and willingly followed their husbands and military escorts to safety. Others likely feared the unknown perils of escape and paused before committing themselves and their children to flight. For example, Eliza, the slave of Edward Turner of Fauquier County, hesitated to follow her husband Staunton after their reluctant "liberators" from the Union army asked her how she would provide for her large family in the event of her husband's death. Equally uncertain is how marriages between former slaves changed as a result of a man's exertion of patriarchal authority over his family. Whereas military officials viewed helping black men to collect their families as striking a blow at the Confederacy, black men clearly viewed claiming their loved ones as an act of manhood. Not only did a military presence force white slave owners to recognize a black man's authority to seize his family; it may also have had a significant effect on relationships between African American husbands and wives. When husbands assumed their places as heads of their families supported in this role by the United States military, wives may or may not have accepted their husbands' dominance, especially when the military was not present to bolster male authority. While many former slaves welcomed the chance to institute "traditional" gender roles, some black women likely resisted being placed in a subordinate role in the family, thereby creating tension between spouses with differing ideas about dominance within marriage.[21]

The war, of course, also created opportunities for new unions to be formed and for established marriages to be made legal. Justenia Gerad and her fiancé fled to Federal lines to be married legally, rather than submit to a nonbinding ceremony in Confederate Richmond, where the law failed to recognize black marriages. Scores of other Virginia blacks legitimized their unions once they reached Union-occupied regions. Encouraged by missionaries and military authorities to solemnize marriages, whether new or previously established, black couples eagerly engaged the services of military chaplains willing to perform official marriages. As a result, mass wedding ceremonies were not unusual during the war. Reverend L. C. Lockwood married eleven couples at Fort Monroe on 22 September 1861, and another twenty-one couples in the Hampton area on 29 September. In July 1864, Lucy Chase described to friends in the North a mass ceremony she witnessed that involved forty black couples, and she noted that another eighty couples had been married the following week.[22]

High concentrations of African Americans in Union-occupied towns and military installations in Virginia encouraged marriages between local black women and black men serving with the military. In 1863, for example, Elisabeth Turner of Portsmouth married Rufus Wright, a soldier in the First Infantry, USCT, who likely met his future wife while his regiment was stationed in Portsmouth. As with many wartime marriages, troop movements soon forced Wright to leave with his unit, while his wife remained at home. After returning to nearby Hampton, Wright wrote Elisabeth to express his disappointment that she had not yet visited him in camp. Whether or not Elisabeth saw her husband again is not known, but the Wrights maintained their marital bonds through correspondence until June 1864, when Rufus Wright died of wounds received at Petersburg.[23]

What was significantly different about marriages between African Americans living within Union lines, as opposed to those undertaken elsewhere in Virginia, where slavery still remained in force, was the legal stability of these unions after being performed by officials and recorded in some way. Afro-Virginians and governmental authorities both recognized the benefits of converting black marriages into lawful arrangements. Yet authorities also felt responsible for teaching "proper" marital relations to black couples married within Union jurisdiction. In 1863, for example, the American Freedmen's Inquiry Commission (AFIC) urged black men to fulfill their responsibilities as husbands and fathers. "This obligation, and the duties connected with the family relation of civilized life," the commissioners concluded, "should be carefully explained to these people, and, while they remain under our care, should be strictly maintained among them." What "civilized" marital relations actually meant, however, depended on who described them. Regardless of their good intentions, many Northern whites failed to understand that African American spouses adapted their ideas of marriage and family in ways that did not always conform to the male-dominated nuclear family models favored by most white Americans. After the war, agents of the Freedmen's Bureau continued to "advise" freedpeople on proper domestic arrangements and the respective responsibilities of husbands and wives, fathers and mothers. As had been the case during the war, freedpeople continued to follow their own ideas in regard to family life.[24]

During slavery, the master held ultimate command over black couples and their families. Since neither spouse controlled the family physically or financially, slave marriages were based on relative equality between husband and wife.[25] Missionaries and civilian and military authorities, however, continually stressed that black men should assume responsibility as heads of households by providing for their families and exerting patriarchal authority. Under slavery, most blacks could not organize their domestic relations on a "nuclear" model, since family members might be (or were) sold at any time. Thus, black families frequently included a variety of people who may or may not have been related by blood. Though government authorities and missionaries emphasized the importance of male-headed nuclear households, some freedmen and -women followed this advice more willingly than others when given the opportunity to assemble their own family units. Much to the chagrin of Northern civilian and government representatives, not all former slaves abandoned their flexible definitions of marriage or the informality associated with relationships during slavery.[26]

Just as the Civil War and the presence of the federal government in Virginia created opportunities for black women to negotiate their relationships with husbands, it also allowed women to make choices with regard to their children. Although black women had always assumed primary responsibility for child care before the war, wartime circumstances in many cases increased this burden. As black men were impressed into military service or escaped slavery on their own, the women left behind not only had to shoulder additional responsibilities to compensate for lost laborers; they also had fewer sources of assistance in caring for their children. Judging from newspaper advertisements for runaway slaves and journals kept by slaveholders, males very rarely took children with them unless escaping as part of a large group. Slave women, on the other hand, worried about the children they would leave behind, and most often either remained where they were or took their children with them.[27]

While the presence of the Union army in Virginia provided a great incentive for slave escape and frequently provided the destination point for fugitive women seeking freedom with their families, for other black women simply being reunited with family members was incentive enough to escape during the war. Newspaper advertisements suggested that slave owners recognized both that families were important to slaves and that proximity to Union lines encouraged slaves to effect reunions. In January 1864, John Munford advertised for the return of Maria and her teenage daughters, Martha and Emily, who he supposed set out for enemy lines. That Maria's free black husband escaped the week before indicates that the family planned to rendezvous behind the safety of Union lines. In 1865, Charles Rose of Richmond offered a $500 reward for the return of Patty and her five-year-old son, Robert. Patty's husband, Steven, who belonged to another owner, left with them, and the family was suspected of going toward Hanover County and the Yankees. The owner of another fugitive named Maria suspected she had set off for her husband's residence in Petersburg. Clara probably left Richmond to be with her father in Fredericksburg, while Elmira had been seen in the vicinity of the Medical College in Richmond, near the residence of Confederate president Jefferson Davis, her mother's employer.[28]

Of course, not all female slaves fled slavery burdened with offspring. On plantations with slave populations large enough to establish lasting communities, older slaves and preadolescent children assumed many child-care duties, since adult female slaves were expected to work all day. This tradition of communal child care, in addition to the existence of kin networks among nonrelated slaves, may have made it easier and more acceptable for slave women to seek their own freedom, knowing their orphaned children would be cared for by those left behind. When Sophy and Aggy escaped from Edward Tayloe's King George County plantation with troops from New Jersey in April 1862, they left their respective daughters, Anne and Patsy, behind. These children seem to have been adopted by the remaining black community, and when another group fled on 8 May 1863, Tayloe listed Anne and Patsy among the escaped slaves.[29]

Reciprocally, other black women found their families expanded with the addition of children left motherless by the war. Particularly in government refugee centers, where women were expected to perform any work available, black women found ample opportunities to provide temporary child care or assume guardianship of orphans. Lucy Chase recalled a conversation with a woman on Craney Island she described as a "good old, mother-soul." The woman explained to Chase that her husband was with the Rebels and her children had been sold south during slavery or had died. "Oh I should go wild, if I had not any children to look upon," she exclaimed. At that moment a child's cry arose from the woman's bed, and she "took in her arms a young infant, a motherless child, her charge." Similarly, an 1864 runaway slave advertisement suggests that forty-year-old Harriet had assumed responsibility for her granddaughter, Amanda, both of whom escaped with a teenage girl (apparently unrelated) from the farm of Watson Colwell near Campbell Courthouse. The subscriber made no mention of the whereabouts of Amanda's mother. Few slave children ever remained motherless for long in areas where other adult black females resided, as these women took responsibility for caring for orphaned children.[30]

Other black women found themselves childless when their young fell victim to disease, not uncommon in the unsanitary living conditions of the refugee camps to which many women fled. Missionaries noted that a significant number of black women suffered the loss of one or more children after entering government camps. One contraband woman on Craney Island calculated that she had lost six children "since she entered the Army," and Lucy Chase asserted that the lament "All my children have died, since I came into the army," became an all-too-familiar refrain among the women she encountered. Although antebellum mortality rates had always been high among young children, unsanitary conditions in early government camps, frequent movement between camps, rampant disease, and the inferior housing and provisions provided for contrabands all took their toll on the health of black children.[31]

Reactions among white military authorities and missionaries to the parenting habits of the African Americans they supervised, particularly in the camps, were mixed, perhaps reflecting the variety of experiences of the women themselves. Lucy Chase saw one woman beat her child savagely. When Chase complained to the woman about her conduct, she responded, "Reckons I shall beat my boy just as much as I please, for all Miss Chase." Chase then intervened by reporting the woman to the Norfolk provost marshal. Thus, though a master no longer controlled her child-rearing techniques, this woman still found her parenting skills monitored by white authorities. As was the case with white interference in black marital relations, African American mothers often ignored unsolicited parental advice in favor of their own methods.[32]

While the United States government played a varying role in Afro-Virginian domestic life during the war, the relationship between African American families and "the State" expanded in the postwar world, as the Freedmen's Bureau attempted to negotiate the transition of Southern blacks from slavery to freedom. Bureau agents assisted freedpeople in finding loved ones who had been sold away during slavery and arranged transportation for those who wished to be reunited with family members living elsewhere. Bureau officials kept registers of African American marriages, including both new unions and long-standing relationships. In addition to ruling on other matters, Freedmen's Bureau courts heard cases involving domestic disputes between black husbands and wives. The underlying philosophies on which the government based interaction with blacks, though, remained the same. Like their wartime predecessors, Bureau agents and officers continued to urge black men to take control of their families and encouraged their wives to engage in productive labor. In return for assistance and guidance, the government expected black families to conform to Northern ideals, or, in the historian George Bentley's words, "adopt Puritan practices forthwith." As during the war, however, the individuals who comprised black families decided whether to adopt white domestic models or to arrange their households in light of past experiences, current circumstances, and individual preferences.[33]

Notes

    1. Local and state-level authorities also formed part of the larger State that existed in Virginia during the Civil War, and these authorities, too, influenced the domestic relations of African Americans. For the purposes of this article,

however, only the actions of federal governments, and more particularly the United States government, are examined.

2. Martha Mitchell Bigelow, "Freedmen of the Mississippi Valley, 1862–1865," *Civil War History* 8 (March 1962): 39; C. Peter Ripley, "The Black Family in Transition: Louisiana, 1860–1865," *Journal of Southern History* 41 (August 1975): 374, 380.

3. Ripley, "The Black Family in Transition," 372, 374; Jane Wallis to Professor Woodburry, [10 December 1863], and H. S. Beals to Major General Benjamin Butler, 10 December 1863, *Freedom: A Documentary History of Emancipation. Series II: The Black Military Experience* (hereafter cited as *The Black Military Experience*), ed. Ira Berlin, Joseph P. Reidy, and Leslie S. Rowland (New York: Cambridge University Press, 1982), 138–39; Robert Francis Engs, *Freedom's First Generation: Black Hampton, Virginia, 1861-1890* (Philadelphia: University of Pennsylvania Press, 1979), 41. Not only did black men in Virginia face the possibility of being conscripted for military labor, but slave men might also be taken to the front as body servants to masters enlisted in the Confederate army. Either role removed black men from their own domestic circles. See "Grand and Awful Times: Body Servants at War," in Ervin L. Jordan Jr., *Black Confederates and Afro-Yankees in Civil War Virginia* (Charlottesville: University Press of Virginia, 1995), 185–200.

4. In 1862 the United States Congress amended a 1795 militia act to authorize recruitment of black men for military labor, including a provision that freed not only the laborer but his mother, wife, and children as well. In deference to slave states remaining in the Union, this clause only applied to slave women whose owners had either enlisted in the Confederate army or otherwise given assistance to the enemy. Congress eventually broadened familial emancipation through military service provisions to include the wives and children of all black enlisted men, mainly as a means of encouraging enlistment among former slaves. Berlin, Reidy, and Rowland, *The Black Military Experience,* 29–30; Public Act No. 166, extracted in General Orders, No. 91, War Department, 29 July 1862, *The War of the Rebellion: A Compilation of the Official Records of the Union and Confederate Armies,* ser. 3, 128 vols. (Washington: 1880–1901), 2:281 (hereafter cited as *Official Records*); Public Resolution No. 25, extracted in General Orders, No. 33, War Department, 11 March 1865, *Official Records,* ser. 3, 4:1228. See also Secretary of War Edwin M. Stanton to President Abraham Lincoln, 3 March 1865, ibid., 4:1219.

5. Statement of John Berry, 11 August 1865, Berlin, Reidy, and Rowland, *The Black Military Experience,* 799, 29–30, 657; Joseph T. Glatthaar, *Forged in Battle: the Civil War Alliance of Black Soldiers and White Officers* (New York: Free Press, 1990), 70, 216; Catherine Clinton, "Reconstructing Freedwomen," in *Divided Houses: Gender and the Civil War,* ed. Catherine Clinton and Nina Silber (New York: Oxford University Press, 1992), 316; Herbert G. Gutman, *The Black Family in Slavery and Freedom, 1750–1925* (New York: Vintage Books, 1976), 375; Ripley, "The Black Family in Transition," 375; Ira Berlin, Francine

C. Cary, Steven F. Miller, and Leslie S. Rowland, "Family and Freedom: Black Families in the American Civil War," *History Today* 37 (January 1987): 10,12.

6. Summary Report of the Commissioners of Claims, n.d., claim 13131, Mary Cowling, Norfolk, Va., Settled Case Files for the Claims Approved by the Southern Claims Commission, 1871–80, entry 732, Records of the Land, Files, and Miscellaneous Division, Records of the Accounting Officers of the Department of the Treasury, Record Group (RG) 217, National Archives and Records Administration (NARA), Washington, D.C.

7. Lucy Chase letter, 1 April 1863, *Dear Ones at Home: Letters from Contraband Camps,* ed. Henry L. Swint (Nashville: Vanderbilt University Press, 1966), 59. African Americans from the Confederacy who sought refuge behind Union lines during the Civil War were often called "contrabands" after an 1861 decision to confiscate fugitive slaves as "contraband of war." White observers and government authorities applied the term "contraband" very loosely to African American men and women, regardless of their status of freedom. Fugitive slaves who could not be employed in and around Union military camps and who required government assistance were often collected into "contraband" camps or on government farms and supervised by white Northern volunteers or by an officially designated "superintendent of contrabands."

8. Drew Gilpin Faust suggests that as white women within the Confederacy found their situations becoming more desperate, their appeals to their husbands on the front for help prompted increased desertions among Rebel troops, thereby weakening the Confederacy's already strained fighting forces. See Drew Gilpin Faust, "Altars of Sacrifice: Confederate Women and the Narratives of War," in Clinton and Silber, *Divided Houses,* 171–99. While the wives of black soldiers certainly experienced financial hardships, "making do" with few resources was already a part of black life, and little evidence has ever come to light to indicate any comparable situations to that described by Faust.

9. Deposition of Mary Hughes, 9 September 1905, pension file of Mary Hughes, widow of March Hughes, Co. E, 38th United States Colored Infantry (USCI), application 82896, certificate 597603, Records of the Veterans Administration, RG 15, NARA: abstract of deposition of Julia Custis, 12 and 13 April 1901, in J. A. Cuddy to Mr. George C. Stewart, pension file of Julia Custis, widow of George Custis, Co. A, 10th USCI, application 144737, certificate 131242, RG 15, NARA.

10. Leslie A. Schwalm, *A Hard Fight for We: Women's Transition from Slavery to Freedom in South Carolina* (Urbana: University of Illinois Press, 1997), 141; Ripley, "The Black Family in Transition," 373; General Orders, No. 46, 5 December 1863, p. 145, vol. 52 VaNC, General Orders Issued, entry 5078, Geographical Divisions and Departments and Military (Reconstruction) Districts, part 1, Records of United States Army Continental Commands, 1821–1920, RG 393, NARA; Berlin et al., "Family and Freedom," 13; Jacqueline Jones, *Labor of Love, Labor of Sorrow: Black Women, Work, and the Family from Slavery to the Present* (New York: Vintage Books, 1985), 50. In 1864, Speed Smith Fry,

commander of Camp Nelson in Kentucky, evicted black families in response to the escalating female presence in camp. See Gutman, *The Black Family,* 370–74. For more on the black military experience, see Joseph T. Wilson, *The Black Phalanx: African American Soldiers in the War of Independence, the War of 1812, and the Civil War* (Hartford, Conn., 1890; reprint, New York: Da Capo Press, 1994); Benjamin Quarles, *The Negro in the Civil War* (Boston, 1953; reprint, New York: Da Capo Press, 1989); Dudley Taylor Cornish, *The Sable Arm: Black Troops in the Union Army, 1861–1865* (New York, 1956; reprint, Lawrence: University Press of Kansas, 1987); James M. McPherson, *The Negro's Civil War: How American Blacks Felt and Acted during the War for the Union* (New York, 1965; reprint, Ballantine Books, 1991); Berlin, Reidy, and Rowland, *The Black Military Experience.*

11. General Orders, No. 46, 5 December 1863, *Official Records.* ser. 3, 3:1140; General Orders, No. 26, Dept. of Va., 22 February 1865, vol. 21/24, 28 VaNC, entry 5078, pt. 1, RG 393, NARA; Major General E. O. C. Ord to Brigadier General G. H. Gordon, Dept. of Va., 12 May 1865, vol. 13 VaNC, Letters Sent, entry 5046, ibid.

12. Ann Sumner to Major General Butler, 28 February 1864, Berlin, Reidy, and Rowland, *The Black Military Experience,* 721. The editors note that Sumner's letter was eventually forwarded to a superintendent of Negro affairs. Whether she ever received her wood is not stated. Mrs. Catherine Massey to Hon. Edwin M. Stanton, 10 July 1865, ibid., 667. The editors did not state whether or not Catherine Massey's letter was answered or whether she received any of her husband's pay. Massey later applied for a government pension as the widow of William Massey but was rejected for lack of evidence as to her marriage to the soldier in 1862. See pension file for Catherine Massey, widow of William Massey, 1st USCI, application 656074, no certificate issued, RG 15, NARA. William Massey, on the other hand, did receive an invalid's pension until his death in 1883.

13. Ripley, "The Black Family in Transition," 372; Bell Irvin Wiley, *Southern Negroes, 1861–1865* (New Haven: Yale University Press, 1938), 5; J[ohn] B[eauchamp] Jones, *A Rebel War Clerk's Diary at the Confederate States Capital,* ed. Howard Swiggett (Philadelphia, 1866; reprint, New York: Old Hickory Book Shop, 1935), 1:192; *Petersburg (Va.) Express,* 19 April 1862, excerpted in the *Richmond (Va.) Semi-Weekly Enquirer,* 22 April 1862, p. 2; G. W. Randolph to Provost Marshal, Petersburg, Va., 14 May 1862 *Official Records* ser. 1, 11:517; Clarence L. Mohr, *On the Threshold of Freedom: Masters and Slaves in Civil War Georgia* (Athens: University of Georgia Press, 1986), 99, 104; Cornelia Peake McDonald, *A Woman's Civil War: A Diary, with Reminiscences of the War, from March 1862,* ed. Minrose S. Gwin (Madison: University of Wisconsin Press, 1992; rev. ed. of *A Diary with Reminiscences of the War and Refugee Life in the Shenandoah Valley, 1860–1865,* 1935), 82–83, 64–65.

14. Lucy Chase letter, 4 March 1863, Swint, *Dear Ones at Home,* 54; Jennie F. Woodstock, *My Father and His Household, before, during, and after the War,* 22

April 1897, p. 24, unpublished manuscript, Blanton Family Papers, 1818–1961, section 3, Mss1B6117a, Virginia Historical Society (hereafter cited as VHS), Richmond.

15. Testimony in claim 14687, Estate of Reuben Pollard, Fauquier Co., Va., entry 732, RG 217, NARA; deposition of Mary Jane Malone, 13 February 1873, claim 20409, Anderson Malone, Dinwiddie Co., Va., ibid.; deposition of Elias Andrews and Abraham Forney, 10 September 1873, claim 20934, Samuel Kenner, Warren Co., Va., ibid.

16. Depositions of Betsy and Benjamin Johnson, 14 March 1876 and 5 December 1873, claim 10094, Betsy Johnson, Fairfax Co., Va., entry 732, RG 217, NARA; Samuel Ballton interview, 1910, *Slave Testimony: Two Centuries of Letters, Speeches, Interviews, and Autobiographies,* ed. John W. Blassingame (Baton Rouge: Louisiana State University Press, 1977), 545–46.

17. *Richmond Daily Dispatch,* 11 February 1863, p.1; entry of 27 January 1863, Sigismunda Stribling Kimball Diary, 1861–63, Kimball Diary and Scrapbook, acc. 2534, Special Collections, Alderman Library, University of Virginia (hereafter cited as UVA), Charlottesville. In 1864, General Edward A. Wild gained a reputation on the Peninsula similar to that of Milroy's in the Shenandoah Valley. Wild sent a military escort with black government employees attempting to rescue family members in the Smithfield area. Wild also encouraged black refugee women in his camp to whip their former master, who had been brought in by pickets from Wild's command. For this action, Wild faced court martial proceedings. Edward A. Wild to G. F. Shepley, 1 September 1864, *Official Records,* ser. 1, 42:653; Wild to Robert S. Davis, 12 May 1864, *Freedom: A Documentary History of Emancipation, 1861–1867. Series 1, Volume 1: The Destruction of Slavery,* ed. Ira Berlin et al. (Cambridge: Cambridge University Press, 1985),96–97; case file LL-2249, United States Courts Martial General, Records of the Judge Advocate General (Army), RG 153, NARA.

18. Entries for 24, 25, 26, February, 10, 16 March 1863 in Sigismunda Stribling Kimball Diary, 1861–63, UVA.

19. Historian Laura F. Edwards argues that the issue of women's protection from violence and social abuse carried not only a racial component but a class element as well. According to Edwards, poor white women suffered as a result of negative stereotypes regarding their femininity and respectability, and their menfolk found themselves unable to shield them from abuse from members of the dominant white society. Given this prejudice against lower classes, black men, and especially slave men, faced even greater handicaps in exerting male authority on behalf of their women due to their racial status. Edwards further argues that both black and poor white males claimed "patriarchal prerogatives" during and after Reconstruction to close the gap between expectations of masculine protection of females and the obstacles these men had faced due to race and class prejudice in the antebellum period. As the examples cited by Sigismunda Kimball demonstrate, however, some men began laying claim to masculine authority well before Reconstruction. Laura F. Ed-

wards, "Sexual Violence, Gender, Reconstruction, and the Extension of Patriarchy in Granville County, North Carolina," *North Carolina Historical Review* 68 (July 1991): 238–39, 204; Laura F. Edwards, *Gendered Strife and Confusion: The Political Culture of Reconstruction* (Urbana: University of Illinois Press, 1997), 198–217.

20. Brenda E. Stevenson, "Distress and Discord in Virginia Slave Families, 1830–1860," in *In Joy and in Sorrow: Women, Family, and Marriage in the Victorian South, 1830–1900,* ed. Carol Bleser (New York: Oxford University Press, 1991), 121; Deborah Gray White, "Female Slaves in the Plantation South," in *Before Freedom Came: African-American Life in the Antebellum South,* ed. Edward D. C. Campbell Jr. (Richmond, Va., and Charlottesville, Va.: University Press of Virginia, 1991), 119; Elizabeth Fox-Genovese, *Within the Plantation Household: Black and White Women of the Old South* (Chapel Hill: University of North Carolina Press, 1988), 326; Catherine Clinton, "Bloody Terrain: Freewomen, Sexuality, and Violence during Reconstruction," *Georgia Historical Quarterly* 76 (Summer 1992): 326. Clinton notes that after slavery and the end of "white coercion," blacks hoped to institute conventional gender roles within families. During the war, a different kind of white coercion sometimes facilitated traditional gender roles.

21. Schwalm, *A Hard Fight for We,* 90, 96–97; entry of 21 May 1863, Edward Carter Turner Diary, section 9, Turner Family Papers, 1740–1927, Mss1T8596a, VHS. Turner noted that the soldiers accompanying Staunton displayed remorse for their part in the episode once they discovered Turner to be the brother of an Admiral Turner of the United States Navy. My thanks to Richard Holway of the University Press of Virginia for suggesting the power a military escort exerted on the wives being rescued. Despite slavery's subversion of typical gender roles between black husbands and wives, slave women were certainly no strangers to "male domination" at the hands of their white owners. See Fox-Genovese, *Within the Plantation Household,* 299. Asserting patriarchal control over his family, however, might also facilitate a black man's abusing his wife, rather than protecting her female virtue. Both Laura F. Edwards and Susan A. Mann note that a black man's assumption of a patriarchal role often gave him control over his wife and children, but few corresponding limits on his physical power. Freedman's Bureau records do contain complaints from black women about abusive men, but little research has yet been done on the topic of black domestic violence in the context of the transition from slavery to freedom. Edwards, "Sexual Violence," 240; Susan A. Mann, "Slavery, Sharecroppong, and Sexual Inequality," *Signs* 14 (1989): 787–88.

22. R. J. M. Blackett, ed., *Thomas Morris Chester, Black Civil War Correspondent: His Dispatches from the Virginia Front* (Baton Rouge: Louisiana State University Press, 1989), 250; Leon F. Litwack, *Been in the Storm So Long: The Aftermath of Slavery* (New York: Vintage Books, 1980), 240; Peter Bardaglio, "The Children of Jubilee: African American Childhood in Wartime," in Clinton and Silber, *Divided Houses,* 226; "Names of Colored Persons Married by Rev. L. C.

Lockwood," Freedmen's Marriage Certificates, entry 44, Washington Head-
quarters, Records of the Bureau of Refugees, Freedmen, and Abandoned
Lands, RG 105, NARA; Lewis C. Lockwood, *Mary S. Peake: The Colored
Teacher at Fortress Monroe* (Boston, 1863), in *Two Black Teachers during the Civil
War* (New York: Arno Press, 1969), 60–61; Lucy Chase letter, 1 July 1864,
Swint, *Dear Ones at Home,* 121.

23. Marriage certificate of Rufus Wright to Elisabeth Turner, 3 December
1863, and Rufus Wright to elisabeth Wright, 22? April and 25 May 1864,
Berlin, Reidy, and Rowland, *The Black Military Experience,* 661–63; Frederick
H. Dyer, *A Compendium of the War of the Rebellion, Volume 3: Regimental Histories*
(New York: Thomas Yoseloff, 1959), 1723. C. Peter Ripley argued that black
soldiers were among the most eager to have their marriages legitimately registered so that their dependents would have proof of their relationships to the
soldiers in the event of the soldiers' deaths. Ripley, "The Black Family in
Transition," 379. Having her marriage officially documented certainly helped
Elisabeth Wright, who presented her marriage certificate and testimony about
the ceremony when applying for Rufus's back pay and a widow's pension
from the United States government.

24. *Preliminary Report Touching the Condition and Management of Emancipated
Refugees Made to the Secretary of War by the American Freedmen's Inquiry Commis-
sion, June 30, 1863* (New York, 1863), 5–6, series 328 O 1863, Letters Received
by the Office of the Adjutant General (Main Series) 1861–1870 (National
Archives Microfilm Publication M619, Roll 199, frames 5–6), Records of the
Adjutant General's Office, 1780s–1917, RG 94, NARA; Schwalm, *A Hard
Fight for We,* 236, 240.

25. Perhaps no issue has so consumed historians of the African American
family as the question of authority within black marriages and its effect for
both the structure of the black family and the surrounding community. According to Elmer P. Martin and Joanne Mitchell Martin, historical studies of
the black family generally fall under one of four perspectives. The view held
by respective historians further affects their assessment of whether authority
within the family, and especially the slave family, was matriarchal or patriarchal; the relative equality of black spouses within a marriage; and, indeed,
what defines a family. The "pathology-disorganization perspective," most notably advanced by E. Franklin Frazier (*The Negro Family in the United States,*
1939) and Daniel Patrick Moynihan (*The Negro Family: The Case for National
Action,* 1965), argues that black matriarchs controlled the family and emascu-
lated male figures, thereby leading to a breakdown of traditional family structures. Largely in reaction to these studies, the "strength-resiliency perspective"
counters with evidence that historically black families survived against overwhelming odds, and without becoming matriarchal institutions. Herbert Gutman (*The Black Family in Slavery and Freedom, 1750–1920,* 1976) particularly
highlighted the important roles played by men in nuclear-oriented black
families, while Jacqueline Jones (*Labor of Love, Labor of Sorrow,* 1985) pointed to

self-imposed gendered divisions of labor within black households, which countered ideas of black matriarchy. Building on the "strength-resiliency perspective," the "Africanity perspective" suggests that the persistent influences of African kinship traditions explains the resilience of black families. Finally, the "extended family perspective" asserts that defining black families using "matriarchal versus patriarchal" nuclear-family models as the archetype misses the significant influence of extended family in "the black family." Current historians, such as Brenda E. Stevenson (*Life in Black and White,* 1996) and Leslie A. Schwalm (*A Hard Fight for We,* 1997), tend to employ a broad definition of "family" when examining black families. Referring specifically to the slave experience, Stevenson captures the variety of arrangements encompassed within "the slave family" when she states, "Matrifocality, polygamy, single parents, abroad spouses, one-, two-, and three-generation households, all-male domestic residence of blood, marriage, and fictive kin, single- and mixed-gender sibling dwellings—these, along with monogamous marriages and co-residential nuclear families, all comprised the familial experiences of Virginia slaves." Other scholars, like Deborah Gray White (*Ar'n't I a Woman?,* 1985) and Suzanne Lebsock (*The Free Women of Petersburg,* 1984), emphasize the female networks cultivated by black women as supplementing or superseding "traditional" family arrangements such as marriage and nuclear families. Current historiography also often takes into account the demographic factors under which slave and free families lived when evaluating the development of black families. Most historians, however, agree that due to economic, legal, and racial factors, African American spouses enjoyed more equality within their marriages than their white counterparts did. Elmer P. Martin and Joanne Mitchell Martin, "The Black Woman: Perspectives on Her Role in the Family," in *Ethnicity and Women,* vol. 5: *Ethnicity and Public Policy* (Madison: University of Wisconsin Press, 1986), 185–90; Brenda E. Stevenson, *Life in Black and White: Family and Community in the Slave South* (New York: Oxford University Press, 1996), 160.

26. White, "Female Slaves in the Plantation South," 119; Ira Berlin, Steven F. Miller, and Leslie Rowland, "Afro-American Families in the Transition from Slavery to Freedom," *Radical History Review* 42 (1988): 93. Berlin, Miller, and Rowland point out that Northerners "took special interest in formalizing marriage relations," but former slaves also desired official ceremonies to bring their marriages in line with "standards of freedom." While that may have been true for many former slave spouses, by no means all freedpeople rushed to get married. Slave traditions of "taking up with" another person continued well into the late nineteenth century and signified a completely nonmarital relationship even when children were involved. Special Pension Examiner H. P. Maxwell, in referring to William Carney's having taken up with more than one wife prior to the war, asserted that "this course of conduct was quite common among colored people prior to the late war and it prevails largely at this date." The widow of Civil War soldier Andrew Fitchett, furthermore, tes-

tified that although she was usually known as Jane Anderson, had two children by David Anderson, and lived with him for twenty years, she did not consider Anderson her legal husband. Special Examiner H. P. Maxwell to the Honorable Green B. Raum, 28 April 1890, pension file of Phebe Carney, widow of William Carney, Co. G, 38th USCI, application 147047, certificate 268782, Records of the Veterans Administration, RG 15, NARA; Donald Robert Shaffer, "Marching On: African-American Civil War Veterans in Postbellum America, 1865–1951" (Ph.D. diss., University of Maryland, 1996), 129; Deposition of Jane Fitchett, 2 January 1894, pension file of Jane Fitchett, widow of Andrew Fitchett, Co. G, 10th USCI, application 130458, certificate 148009, RG 15, NARA.

27. Bardaglio, "The Children of Jubilee," 224; Deborah Gray White, *Ar'n't I a Woman?: Female Slaves in the Plantation South* (New York: W. W. Norton, 1985), 70; Wilma King, "'Suffer with Them till Death': Slave Women and Their Children in Nineteenth-Century America," in *More than Chattel: Black Women and Slavery in the Americas,* ed. David Barry Gaspar and Darlene Clark Hine (Bloomington and Indianapolis: Indiana University Press, 1996), 160

28. Ripley, "The Black Family in Transition," 371; *Richmond Daily Dispatch,* 21 January 1864, p. 1; ibid., 3 January 1865, p. 1; ibid., 18 May 1862, p. 3; ibid., 16 September 1862, p. 2; ibid., 15 January 1863, p. 3; ibid., 28 August 1863, p. 2.

29. Stevenson, "Distress and Discord in Virginia Slave Families," 107; Mann, "Slavery, Sharecropping, and Sexual Inequality," 781; Edward Tayloe Agricultural Journal, 1850–69, Tayloe Family Papers, 1708–1890, acc. 38-62, UVA. Although Tayloe did not record whether the First New Jersey was a unit of cavalry or infantry, it was more likely the latter. See Dyer, *A Compendium of the War of the Rebellion,* 1353, 1356. The group containing Aggy's and Sophy's children probably left Tayloe's King George County estate due to the presence of Union troops in nearby Spotsylvania County following the battle of Chancellorsville, which took place 1–4 May 1863. White, "Female Slaves in the Plantation South," 114; Lucy Chase letter, 1 April 1863, Swint, *Dear Ones at Home,* 60; Gutman, *The Black Family,* 226.

30. Lucy Chase letter, 1 April 1863, Swint, *Dear Ones at Home,* 60; *Lynchburg Virginian,* 28 March 1864, n.p., contained in Financial and Legal Papers: Civil War Records, 1861–72, box 8, William D. Cabell Papers, acc. 276, UVA; White, *Ar'n't I a Women?,* 128; Schwalm, *A Hard Fight for We,* 51.

31. Lucy Chase letter, 7 February, 1 April 1863, Swint, *Dear Ones at Home,* 42, 59. Conditions in contraband camps only accelerated the high infant mortality rates of black children during the antebellum period. According to Wilma King, the children of slave mothers "died at rates twice that of their white cohorts," thereby conditioning mothers to expect that children would die. Poor to no prenatal care, strenuous workloads for pregnant women, and non-nutritious diets eaten by nursing mothers, in addition to normal factors like disease, increased the death rates of slave infants. King, "Suffer with Them

till Death," 149, 150, 151. Brenda E. Stevenson suggests that the loss of a child also robbed black women of children who would support mothers in their old age, and affected future family history, particularly if a child had been named for an ancestor to perpetuate family connections. Brenda E. Stevenson, "Gender Convention, Ideals, and Identity among Antebellum Virginia Slave Women," in Gaspar and Hine, *More than Chattel*, 175. For more on slave children, see Wilma King, *Stolen Childhood: Slave Youth in Nineteenth-Century America* (Bloomington and Indianapolis: Indiana University Press, 1995).

32. Lucy Chase letter, 1 July 1864, Swint, *Dear Ones at Home*, 123; Myrta Lockett Avary, *Dixie after the War: An Exposition of Social Conditions Existing in the South, during the Twelve Years Succeeding the Fall of Richmond* (New York: Doubleday, Page & Co., 1906), 195; Stevenson, "Distress and Discord in Virginia Slave Families," 116.

33. George R. Bentley, *A History of the Freedmen's Bureau* (New York: Octagon Books, 1974), 86; Jones, *Labor of Love, Labor of Sorrow,* 57–62.

THREE

IN THE SHADOW OF
THE OLD CONSTITUTION

Black Civil War Veterans and the
Persistence of Slave Marriage Customs

Donald R. Shaffer

In 1919, the Civil War pension application of Mary Jane Taylor came under review by federal bureaucrats. She was the widow of Samuel Taylor, who had served during the war in the Forty-fifth U.S. Colored Infantry, a black regiment from Kentucky. Like all widows seeking Civil War pensions, Mary Jane Taylor had to prove a legal marriage to her deceased husband. In evaluating the application, the U.S. Pension Bureau, which administered the Civil War pension program, dispatched Charles G. Townsend, a "special examiner" or field investigator, to interview Taylor. Townsend took depositions from Mary Jane Taylor and other witnesses, then reported his findings to his superiors in Washington, D.C.

The examiner quickly established that Mary Jane was not Samuel Taylor's first wife, nor was Samuel Mary Jane's first husband. Both Samuel and Mary Jane had previous marriages. Samuel married his first wife, Fannie, during slavery. After freedom they separated, and without obtaining a divorce, the veteran married Susan Fountain, who died before Samuel and Mary Jane's 1892 wedding. Mary Jane's first husband was Bill White, whom she married as a slave. The couple had had a stormy relationship; they separated and reconciled three times in the years following freedom before permanently parting.

When Townsend asked Mary Jane Taylor why she had not obtained a divorce from White before marrying Samuel Taylor, she made a trenchant response. "He was not my legal husband," Mary Jane replied. "He and I were married under the old constitution by slave custom and we didn't have to get any divorce at all they said." Her response was legally accurate. Under Kentucky law, a marriage that began under slavery did not become legal after emancipation unless registered with local authorities. Mary Jane and Bill White never took this step. Neither did Samuel Taylor and his first wife. Consequently, Mary Jane and Samuel Taylor had the legal right to marry each other, and Mary Jane was Samuel's legal widow. The federal government approved her application for a Civil War pension.[1]

The case of Samuel and Mary Jane Taylor raises an important question. Why did they, and many other former slaves, decline to formalize their existing marriages when freedom came? The answer lies in Mary Jane Taylor's pension deposition, which identifies a significant reality of black life in the decades following the Civil War. While freedom gave all African American couples access to the privileges and protections of legal marriage, for many years following the war many couples continued to practice what Taylor aptly called the "old constitution": an informal system of marriage that originated in slavery. In other words, many former slaves did not take the symbolically important step of having a new marriage ceremony performed or registering their union with government authorities, acts associated with an acceptance of formal, legal marriage. The belief of some former slaves in the sanctity of informal unions, the prohibitive costs of the legal marriage system, and the continued acceptance of informal marriage in the poorer and more rural segments of the southern black population led them to forgo legal marriages.

Despite its long survival, the old constitution has largely escaped attention by historians. For example, the most influential work on the nineteenth-century black family, Herbert Gutman's *The Black Family in Slavery and Freedom*, all but ignored the continued existence of slave marriage customs after emancipation. Instead, Gutman emphasized the extent to which former slaves embraced legal marriage. He believed that the prevailing sentiment among former slaves was in favor of legal marriage. To substantiate this point, he compared ex-slave marriage registers in Virginia and North Carolina against 1860 census data to get a rough estimate of the percentage of slave couples that legalized their marriages. Gutman calculated that about half of slave couples had legalized their marriages by 1866. From this quantitative data and from other anecdotal evidence, Gutman concluded that most former slaves wanted and obtained legal marriages. Yet Gutman overlooked another obvious inference that could be drawn from his sources. While the marriage registers and census data revealed that at least half of adult freedpeople legalized their slave marriages in the immediate wake of the Civil War, they also suggested as many as half did not.[2]

In the last decade or so historians have begun to pay greater attention to the old constitution, largely because of the growing use of Civil War pension files.[3] Over 178,000 black men served in the Union army during the Civil War. Like other Union veterans, black survivors of the war became the beneficiaries of a generous federal pension system for ex-soldiers and their families. Congress initially intended it to assist soldiers disabled in the war and the dependents of men killed in federal service. Yet in the decades following the end of the Civil War, a politically influential veterans' lobby gradually engineered the transformation of the disability and survivors' pensions into a large-scale old-age pension system. These regular payments to Union veterans and their survivors consumed over 40 percent of the federal budget at their peak in the 1890s.[4]

The eligibility of veterans' widows to collect pensions made marriage a major concern for the U.S. Pension Bureau. Under the nineteenth-century theory of social welfare, government assistance was not a general entitlement but a reward for the worthy. As the Civil War pension system operated, for a man to be worthy he had to have rendered military service. For a widow to deserve a pension she had to have had a legal marriage to a Union veteran. Yet establishing legal widowhood for black women was often difficult. Not only did former slave women generally have difficulty documenting their marriages; also, the standard of deciding the legality of marriages complicated matters. Rather than establish one criterion to test the validity of marriage throughout the United States, the Pension Bureau, in deference to a long tradition of state primacy in marital law, used the marriage codes of the state in which the applicant resided to decide whether or not an applicant was a legal widow. Since the Southern states varied in how they legalized slave marriages, a marriage that was legal in one state might not be legal in another.[5] In any case, to substantiate a woman's worthiness pension bureaucrats felt it essential to determine as precisely as possible the marital history of the widow and her dead husband. Often the proof process included on-site investigations, including numerous depositions, as occurred in the case of Mary Jane Taylor.

The experience of Civil War veterans and their families, as documented in Civil War pension files, conclusively demonstrates that two systems for marriage coexisted in the black community in the decades following emancipation: a formal, legal system and an informal system rooted in slavery.[6] Before the war, of course, slaves had had no choice but informal marriage. Hence, it is not surprising that many veterans or their widows testified in their pension applications that they had legalized slave marriages during the war or soon thereafter. However, despite the availability of legal marriage, the experience of other black veterans and their wives suggests that a substantial percentage of former slaves continued with informal marriages.[7] These couples did not take the symbolically important step of having a new marriage ceremony performed or registering their union with government authorities. In short, while some ex-soldiers eagerly embraced the new system of marriage, others came to it slowly, if at all, clinging to old ways, which had their roots in bondage.

Former slaves later described the old constitution as having several basic characteristics.[8] Generally, a man asked the consent of his owner and his intended's master or mistress. If permission was given, the couple "took up" or started living with one another. No ceremony was necessary to establish a slave marriage, although many slaves had one. Favored slaves might be married by a white minister in their owner's home; other couples "jumped over the broomstick," and some simply set up housekeeping with each other. With or without a ceremony, however, a slave marriage lacked legal existence, and owners could dissolve such unions at any time.[9]

Consequently, legal marriage, perhaps like no other institution, symbolized freedom for the postwar black community. With legal marriages, African Americans gained the assurance—initially from the federal government and later from state governments in the South—that their unions would be respected and protected by law and that they would never be involuntarily separated from their loved ones again. As a black soldier in a Virginia regiment told his comrades at a religious service in 1866, "The Marriage Covenant is at the foundation of all our rights."[10] By this statement he meant that the integrity of marriage, and by implication the integrity of the black family, constituted African Americans' most important gain for from the Civil War. However, the soldier also implied that the black community wished to use legal marriage as the basis for obtaining additional rights. For if they were granted this most basic right, why should they be denied other critical rights, such as suffrage?[11]

However, despite the importance that many African Americans attached to legal marriage, not all black veterans and their wives rushed to embrace it. Some ex-soldiers waited many years or even decades to discard the old constitution and continued to cohabitate with their wives based on their slave marriages. Kitt Mitchell, a South Carolina veteran, and his wife, who had lived together since 1859, did not have a legal marriage ceremony until 1888, nearly thirty years and thirteen children later.[12] Garret Beckley and his wife, married as slaves in Kentucky in 1861, did not register their slave marriage as required by state law until 1904.[13] Some veterans married as slaves never had a new ceremony performed after emancipation.[14]

While one group of veterans proved slow to ratify pre-emancipation marriages with new ceremonies or by registration, other ex-soldiers contracted marital unions after the war in much the same way as antebellum slave marriages. Dispensing with a marriage license and often with a ceremony, they "took up" with women just like before the war. The only difference between these postwar common-law unions and prewar slave marriages was that an owner's permission was no longer needed. A couple's belief that they were married and the community's acceptance of the arrangement cemented a marital union.[15]

The case of Phillip and Josephine Bellfield, who lived in Claiborne County, Mississippi, south of Vicksburg, illustrates the tie between postwar common-law marriage and slave marriage customs. Bellfield joined the Union army in November 1863, as a forty-five-year-old private. After his death in 1890, Josephine applied to the federal government for a widow's pension. Witnesses testified that the couple had begun cohabitating in 1880, well after the death of Bellfield's first wife in 1876. Two of their neighbors, Morgan Black and Glen Willis, stated in an affidavit, "The fact is that he was not legally married to the claimant, but simply married her as was formerly prevalent among slaves. He took her to his house and gave notice to all his friends & acquaintances that she was his wife. Every body, white & black, who knew them, regarded them as man & wife. . . . the claimant was his wife—socially and morally—if not legally."[16]

In instances when either the acceptance of the couple or their community that they were husband and wife was lacking, no informal marriage existed—even if the couple lived together a long time and had children. For instance, Rose Baptiste lived with a New Orleans veteran, Octave Jessie, for nearly two decades but told a U.S. Pension Bureau investigator in 1893, "I lived with him as his wife, but I never went by his name. I would not go by his name as I was not married to him." Although the local community wanted to believe they were married, Baptiste clearly did not consider Jessie her husband. "The people used to call me by his name," she informed the pension examiner, "but I would always correct them and tell them that my name was not Rose Jessie."[17]

The influence and persistence of slave marriage customs extended to the dissolution of marriages as well as their formation. Slave divorce, like marriage, was informal in the antebellum South. Only an owner's consent was necessary for slaves to divorce. Some owners readily gave such permission, while others did not. The experience of black veterans suggests that informal divorce survived among former slaves after the Civil War. For those who practiced it, the end of cohabitation rather than a legal decree constituted the end of a marriage. Of seventy-six documented marriages of black Civil War veterans ending in separation, only twenty-one of the couples went on to obtain a legal divorce. That is, more than 70 percent of these ex-soldiers who separated from their wives never got a formal divorce. Some of those separated but undivorced men remarried while their former wives were still alive.[18]

The case of Tony Alston, a Georgia veteran, illustrates the phenomenon of remarriage without divorce. He wed Katie during slavery, and the couple separated around the time of the Civil War. In December 1866, Alston married Elsie Summers. They moved from Savannah, Georgia, to Goldsboro, North Carolina, and split up about a year later. Alston moved back to Savannah, and in August 1868, without obtaining a divorce from Summers, married Diana Cooper. Their marriage did not last much longer than Alston's previous unions. The couple repeatedly separated and reconciled before permanently parting three or four years later. Shortly before his death in 1895, Alston again remarried, without obtaining a divorce from Cooper.[19]

Tony Alston's marital pattern was not uncommon. Other ex-soldiers remarried after separating from slave wives and women they married in the postwar period.[20] The wives of some veterans also eschewed divorce.[21] Calvin Saulisberry, a Louisiana veteran, and his first wife, Lizzie, separated in the 1880s, and they both subsequently remarried. Saulisberry's second wife, Rebecca Raglin, had separated from the husband she had married just before the end of the Civil War. Neither Calvin Saulisberry nor his first or second wife, divorced before remarrying.[22]

The behavior of these veterans and their wives suggests that just as former slaves wrested the power of marital consent from slaveholders when emancipation came, they also granted themselves the prerogative of choosing when and how to end their marriages. Many former slaves did not consider governmental authority a substitute for slaveholders' authority in the process of ending their marriages, and, once separated from a spouse, they regarded themselves, as in the antebellum period, free to marry again.

White Southerners were aware of the persistence of slave marriage customs in their midst. Mary Conti, the employer of Matilda Johnson, who was the slave wife of Levi Johnson, a Mississippi veteran, alluded to the phenomenon in 1903, when she testified that the couple had separated several years after the end of the Civil War and that Matilda had eventually remarried. "The reason she married another man while Johnson was living is because Johnson left her," Conti stated, trying to explain her employee's behavior. "Being ignorant, she did not think that she was doing anything wrong."[23] Charles G. Townsend, the federal pension examiner who investigated the case of Mary Jane Taylor in Kentucky, put it more concretely. "It is well known in this state," he reported in 1919, "that follwing [sic] Freedom of slaves there was for a time among them a continuance of the same old customs relative to marriage."[24]

As Townsend's statement implies, slave marriage customs persisted in the black community after the Civil War, but these practices did not last indefinitely. There were social and political forces encouraging former slaves to adopt the new system of marriage. And ex-slaves' equating legal marriage with freedom was as important to its adoption as external forces.

Black soldiers were prompted to abandon the old constitution earlier and more intensively than most other African Americans in the South. Union army chaplains tirelessly encouraged black troops to legalize slave marriages. James Peet, chaplain of the Fiftieth U.S. Colored Infantry, reported to Adjutant General Lorenzo Thomas, in September 1864, "I . . . urge marriage upon all those who, already, have families."[25] John Means Thompson, the former chaplain of the Fifteenth U.S. Colored Infantry, echoed Peet's sentiments when he told a Pension Bureau examiner in 1888, "I encouraged all of the colored soldiers to have the ceremony of marriage performed."[26]

After the war, some Southern state governments also exerted pressure on ex-slaves to legalize their antebellum marriages. Kentucky, for example, passed a law requiring freedmen and -women to register their slave unions or to have a legal ceremony performed. Florida was particularly harsh, giving ex-slaves nine months after the passage of its January 1866 law to marry legally and stating that violators would be prosecuted for "fornication and adultery." The illegality of common-law marriage in most of the border states and Louisiana after the war no doubt also discouraged many informal postwar unions.[27]

However, the most potent influence on African American veterans and their wives to abandon the old constitution came from within the black community itself. Churches played a major role within the black community in persuading men and women with informal prewar and postwar marriages to formalize them. Many ministers and congregations disapproved of these unions, seeing the couples as living outside the bounds of religious propriety.[28] They came to see informal marriage as no marriage at all and regarded the people who lived in them as sinners. For instance, Hannah Whittington, the widow of Lewis Booth, a Mississippi soldier who died in 1863, took up after the war with a man named Jerry Turner. Cornelius McCray, a local black minister, later testified to a pension examiner, "Although they appeared to live [as if they were married] . . . there was some talk of expelling . . . [Whittington] from the church on account of her living with this man in adultery."[29] Sometimes black churches made good on the expulsion threat. Mollie Fry, the widow of Philip Fry, an ex-soldier from Kentucky, testified in 1911, "Philip had been a Baptist, but they turned him out of the church because he was living with me without being married." However, if couples gave in and submitted to a religious ceremony, black congregations proved forgiving. For instance, after a minister married Philip and Mollie Fry, the Baptist church in Danville, Kentucky, accepted him back into their fellowship.[30] Sometimes the threat of expulsion was enough to convince a wayward couple to submit to a marriage ceremony. Rosa Farrow, the widow of Volsin Farrow, testified in 1922 that the Mt. Olive Baptist Church in Iberville Parish, Louisiana, "compelled us to marry. We were both members of the church and they took up in church that we were living together that way, and Volsin and I got married rather than be put out of the church."[31]

It must be pointed out, however, that the emphasis of black churches was on marriage in the sight of God, rather than legal marriage. A church wedding was not always a legal marriage, either because the couple did not obtain a license or because the minister did not report the ceremony to the government. Indeed, the lack of a marriage license hurt the pension applications of widows in states like Louisiana that required a license to validate a marriage. The Pension

Bureau rejected the application of Emma Barrett, the widow of William B. Barrett, a New Orleans veteran (and prominent Reconstruction politician), because the couple never obtained a license to legalize their 1875 marriage. It took a special act of Congress to get Emma Barrett on the pension rolls.[32] Still, despite its concentration on religious instead of legal marriage, black churches ultimately contributed to the decline of the old constitution.

For all the forces striving to eliminate it, however, slave marriage customs survived for many decades after the Civil War. While informal marriage was mandatory during slavery, former slaves voluntarily continued the practice in the postwar period for a variety of reasons. The experience of some Civil War veterans and their wives shows that they evidently did not deem a legal marriage necessary to sanctify what years of living together had consecrated. When asked about Wilson and Eliza Fitchett's lack of a legal marriage, their friend Airey Young reported to a Pension Bureau investigator that "they passed as man and wife, 'he owned her and she owned him.'"[33] Clement and Emma Frederick clearly believed they were husband and wife, despite the lack of a marriage license or ceremony. "We lived together happily and he was good to me," Emma stated in 1903. She added, "I called him 'papa' and he called me 'mama.'" During the examination the Pension Bureau investigator asked her, "What agreement did you make with [Clement] when you first began living with him?" Emma replied, "I told him that if he would take me for his bosom wife that I would not allow any man to come between him and me . . . and he promised he would not have any other woman than me."[34]

Economic factors, which encouraged common-law marriage among working-class people throughout the Western world in the nineteenth century, also played a role in the persistence of the old constitution.[35] Some black veterans and their wives found the costs of legal marriage and divorce to be prohibitive. If a marriage license represents the minimum price of a legal marriage, in the postwar South it cost anywhere from fifty cents (Tennessee) to $3.50 (Delaware).[36] Either sum was beyond the means of some cash-poor sharecroppers and day laborers. Divorce was even more expensive. In the post–Civil War period, "no-fault" divorce did not exist, which meant that courts had to find fault with one spouse to justify a divorce. Common grounds included adultery, abandonment, mental and physical abuse, and alcoholism.[37] Hiring an attorney to help prove fault and paying court costs could be an expensive proposition. It was simpler and cheaper for poor persons simply to leave an errant spouse.[38]

Indeed, class played a notable role in determining who supported and opposed the old constitution within the postbellum black community. Informal marriage appears to have survived most strongly among poor and rural African Americans, while formal marriage was most strongly accepted by the black middle class, which embraced legal marriage as a way to prove African American rectitude to skeptical white people. As Laura Edwards has written, "Many middle-class blacks trumpeted the virtues of legal marriage as a way to elevate the race."[39] In short, in the estimation of the black middle class, uplifting the race required African Americans to abandon this morally questionable relic of the past. Informal marriage had been acceptable during slavery, when there was no other choice. Once African Americans had the option, middle-class blacks felt, they should choose legal marriage, and they did if not, the community ought to pressure practitioners of the old constitution to do the right thing.

Disagreement over the basis of marriage in the African American community should also be considered in the context of a larger nineteenth-century debate in the United States about the legitimacy of common-law marriage. Common-law marriages existed among poor whites as well as poor blacks during this period, and among white Americans there was an increasingly tolerant climate toward marital informality in the early nineteenth century. As Michael Grossberg has shown, judges in the early 1800s created the concept of common-law marriage to bring informal unions within the law, so as not to deny informally married women inheritance and other widows' rights, as well as to free Americans from the tight regulation of marriage found under the British system. However, by the late nineteenth century, the legal pendulum swung against common-law marriage; critics argued that it was "misguided and pernicious, and charged it as well with spawning social anarchy and untrammeled individualism."[40] It is likely that the growing intolerance of informal unions among white Americans in the late nineteenth century found its way into the postbellum black community, especially among middle-class African Americans aspiring to Victorian respectability.

Still, the growing hostility toward common-law marriage in the United States did not spread uniformly. Some Southern states, especially those in the Lower South (except for Louisiana), continued to recognize common-law marriages long after the Civil War. In fact, many of these states automatically legalized slave unions after the war and, rather than requiring new ceremonies or registration, simply declared all black couples residing together on a given day to be legally married. The inconsistent manner in which Southern states legalized slave marriages and recognized common-law marriage no doubt created confusion among black couples about whether their marriages were legal.[41]

Indeed, for some ex-soldiers and their wives, dropping the old constitution was motivated less by the sanctity of a legal marriage and more by the fear that a slave or postwar common-law marriage would be treated as invalid. Lucinda Sibley, the widow of Solomon Sibley, a soldier from Arkansas, who had legalized her slave union with him during the Civil War, stated in 1893, "There was a general impression that our old slave marriages were not valid & we were advised to marry again under the United States regulations."[42] Kizzie Sexton, seconded Sibley's opinion, testifying that she and her husband Henry legally married in 1869 because "this second marriage was advised by friends as a protection to myself and the children."[43] Thomasine Stephens, the widow of Peter Stephens, who lived in New Orleans after the war, told a Pension Bureau investigator in 1913 that she and her husband had legalized their nearly forty-year-old common-law marriage in 1907 "to ratify our former relations & for no other reason."[44]

The Sibley, Sexton, and Stephens widows suggest that they embraced legal marriage for the protection it afforded them. Each of these far-sighted women realized that in order to get federal pensions, inherit property, and cultivate middle-class respectability, she would need to prove that she was her husband's legal wife. Yet in adopting the new system they implicitly gave up the advantages of the old, especially its convenience and economy. Under the old constitution, a wife with an errant husband need not spend an inordinate amount of money proving his fault in a court of law in order to obtain a divorce; she could simply leave the offending spouse and take up with another man at a later date. Men, too, benefited from the informality of the old constitution when it came to ending a marriage.

Consequently, it is not surprising that both black men and black women switched between the two systems of marriage when they found one or the other to be more advantageous. Some couples who formalized their slave marriages after the war subsequently separated informally from their spouses and later legally married someone else. In short, they married legally to obtain the protections of that system and divorced informally to avoid the costs of dissolving a legal marriage. Hence, economics encouraged former slaves to re-embrace the old constitution in divorce practices. Many blacks simply could not afford a legal divorce. Yet it is also likely that the informality of divorce during the slave era led to a more tolerant culture in the poorer and rural segments of the postwar black community for those who did not obtain formal divorces in court.

Indeed, it was not only poor African Americans who reverted to the old system when marriages broke down. Marital informality appears in the Civil War pension applications of even middle-class African Americans. The most poignant of these cases involved black ministers. Even as most African American clergymen attempted to suppress the old constitution in their congregations, a few ministers lived in informal marital unions. For instance, Diana Cooper, the third wife of Tony Alston, took up with a black Methodist minister after her separation from Alston.[45] In another case, special examiner R. K. Doe was convinced that Silvy Granville, the widow of a South Carolina veteran, had entered into an informal union with a local black minister, M. C. Singleton. While Granville was ostensibly Singleton's housekeeper, the examiner observed that six people lived in Singleton's house, which had "only two bed[s]." Since four of these six people were children, the examiner doubted the relationship between Singleton and Granville was simply platonic, but he could not prove anything, as all their neighbors denied any knowledge of a sexual relationship. This case suggests that while middle-class African Americans sometimes entered into informal unions, they felt it necessary to be discreet about them and use subterfuge to deflect attention from the true nature of the relationship.[46]

Regardless of the truth about Granville and Singleton, the experience of black veterans of the Civil War, taken as a whole, shows that slave marriage customs did not die with slavery. Instead, they coexisted for many decades with the system of legal marriage that emancipation had opened to former slaves. While some ex-slaves and their wives abandoned the old constitution, during the war or soon after, other couples did so only after many years or not at all. In addition, some veterans continued entering into informal slave-style marriages in the postwar period, separating from wives and remarrying without seeking legal divorces, sometimes to married women undivorced from previous husbands. While ex-soldiers responded to the pressures exerted on them by conservative state governments in the South and black churches to adopt new ways of marriage, the old constitution persisted in the African American community into the twentieth century because of the strength of common-law ties, the prohibitive cost of legal marriage and divorce to the poor, and the tolerance of informal unions in many parts of the South. Indeed, evidence suggests that some men and women used both systems at times, obtaining marriage licenses to gain legal protections but reverting to the old constitution to avoid the prohibitive cost of divorce. Hence, marriage in the post-bellum black community was a complex affair, with old and new systems competing for adherents. However, it is beyond question that for decades after the war an important aspect of slave culture—informal marriage—survived. Hence, even as former slaves embraced the possibilities of freedom, their years in bondage continued to shape their behavior in a significant way even decades later.

Notes

1. Deposition of Mary Jane Taylor, 13 May 1919, Civil War Pension File of Samuel Taylor, 45th U.S. Colored Infantry (hereafter cited as USCI), Record Group 15, Records of the Veterans Administration, National Archives, Washington, D.C. (hereafter cited as RG 15).

2. Herbert G. Gutman, *The Black Family in Slavery and Freedom, 1750–1925* (New York: Vintage Books, 1976), 412–18.

3. James Smallwood, "Emancipation and the Black Family: A Case Study in Texas," *Social Science Quarterly* 57 (March 1977): 850; Noralee Frankel, "Workers, Wives, and Mothers: Black Women in Mississippi, 1860–1870" (Ph.D. diss., George Washington University, 1983), 147, 179; Leslie Ann Schwalm, "The Meaning of Freedom: African American Women and Their Transition from Slavery to Freedom in Lowcountry South Carolina" (Ph.D. diss., University of Wisconsin, Madison, 1991), 341–42; Laura F. Edwards, "'The Marriage Covenant Is at the Foundation of All Our Rights': The Politics of Slave Marriage in North Carolina after Emancipation," *Law and History Review* 14 (Spring 1996): 108–12.

4. Theda Skocpol, "America's First Social Security System: The Expansion of Benefits for Civil War Veterans," *Political Science Quarterly* 108 (Spring 1993): 85–116; Maris Vinovskis, "Have Social Historians Lost the Civil War?: Some Preliminary Demographic Speculations," *Journal of American History* 76 (June 1989): 54.

5. Florida and Missouri demanded a new wedding ceremony for freed couples, and Kentucky, Louisiana, and Maryland required them to register their intent to stay together with a justice of the peace. Alabama, Arkansas, the District of Columbia, Georgia, Mississippi, North Carolina, South Carolina, Tennessee, Texas, and Virginia automatically legalized existing slave unions after the war. North Carolina eventually required registration, and Kentucky dropped its registration law in 1910. Delaware, which had a large free population in the antebellum period, merely applied its prewar statutes regarding free black marriages to its entire African American population after the Civil War. See Congress, Senate, *Letter of the Secretary of War, Communicating . . . Reports of the Assistant Commissioner of Freedmen and a Synopsis of Laws Respecting Per-*

sons of Color in the Slave States, 39th Congress, 2d sess., 1866–67, 170–230; Charles Edward Wright, *Marriage and Divorce: A Collation of the Published Decisions of the Department of the Interior, Rendered on Appeal, Appertaining to the Law of Marriage and Divorce in the United States in Its Relation to Pensionable Status* (Washington: Government Printing Office, 1914), 1–48.

6. Civil War veterans do not perfectly represent the African American population of the late nineteenth century in that a disproportionate percentage of ex-soldiers lived in cities and in the North and they generally were more prosperous than other black people. Used judiciously, however, pension files are still a valuable source on the history of the black family. Despite the advantages some African American veterans enjoyed, most were still poor and lived in the rural South. Hence, pension files document intimately, often over many decades, the experience of tens of thousands of representative black families in the late nineteenth and early twentieth centuries and, to an extent comparable to the WPA Slave Narratives, allow ordinary African Africans of that time to speak about their lives.

7. For the purposes of this study, a formal marriage is a union given sanction by the state or religion and solemnized by a ceremony or a legal declaration. Likewise, an informal union exists where the couple believes they are married but their union has no legal or religious basis and starts with the commencement of cohabitation.

8. Allen Parker, *Recollections of Slavery Times* (Worcester, Mass.: Charles W. Burbank and Company, 1895), 22–27; Pension Files of Charles Barnett (alias Allen), 92d USCI; Lewis Booth, 50th USCI; Stephen Carson, 42d USCI; Andrew Cassaman (alias Jackson), 2d U.S. Colored Light Artillery (hereafter cited as USCLA); Marshall Hamilton (alias Osborn), 123d USCI; Reuben Martindale, 110th USCI; Kitt Mitchell, 128th USCI; Edward Price (alias Ned Waiters), 135th USCI; Solomon Silbey, 63d USCI, RG 15.

9. Margaret A. Burnham, "An Impossible Marriage: Slave Law and Family Law," *Law and Inequality* 5 (July 1987): 187–225.

10. Ira Berlin, Joseph P. Reidy, and Leslie S. Rowland, eds., *Freedom: A Documentary History of Emancipation, 1861–1867, Series 2: The Black Military Experience* (Cambridge: Cambridge University Press, 1982), 672.

11. Edwards, "'The Marriage Covenant,'" 99–101.

12. Pension File of Kitt Mitchell, 12th USCI, RG 15.

13. Pension File of Garret Beckley, 114th USCI, RG 15.

14. Pension Files of Alfred Williams, 107th USCI; Samuel Taylor, 45th USCI, RG 15.

15. Pension Files of Joseph Bell, 12th USCI; Frederick Clement, 70th and 71st USCI; Edwards Gants, 7th USCI; Adam Hayes, 81st USCI (New), 84th and 87th USCI (New) and 95th USCI; George Hibbitt, 14th USCI; Daniel (alias David) Hughes, 27th USCI; Horace Ringgold, 38th USCI; Mack Thompson, 53d USCI; Henry Vass, 2d U.S. Colored Cavalry (hereafter cited as USCC), RG 15.

16. Affidavit of Morgan Black and Glen Willis, 15 May 1891, Pension File of Phillip Bellfield, 63d USCI, RG 15.

17. Deposition of Rose Baptiste, 19 September 1893, Pension File of Octave Colar (alias Jessie), 96th USCI, RG 15.

18. Donald Robert Shaffer, "Marching On: African American Veterans in Postbellum America, 1865–1951" (Ph.D., University of Maryland, College Park, 1996), 130.

19. Pension File of Tony Austin (alias Alston), 21st USCI, RG 15.

20. Pension Files of Walker Bettlesworth (alias Wade), 116th USCI; Peter Bishop, 38th USCI; Jason Brathough (alias Posey), 4th USCC; Henry F. Downing, U.S. Navy; James Flenoy (alias Robinson), 88th USCI (New) and 3d U.S. Colored Heavy Artillery (hereafter cited as USCHA); Hector Friar (alias Jones), 78th and 98th USCI; James Henry Gordon (alias Mabin), 60th USCI; Daniel (alias David) Hughes, 27th USCI; Jacob Overall (alias Hutchinson, alias Abraham I. J. Wright), 4th USCHA, RG 15.

21. Pension Files of George Bird, 110th USCI; James Henry Gordon (alias Mabin), 60th USCI; James Luckett, 50th USCI; Nimrod Rowley, 20th USCI; George Scott, 54th Massachusetts Infantry; Thomas F. Simons, 26th USCI; Isaac Smith, 117th USCI; John Walker, 31st USCI; Wallace Willikey (alias Levi Johnson), 6th USCHA, RG 15.

22. Pension File of Calvin Saulisberry, 51st USCI, RG 15.

23. Deposition of Mary Conti, 12 July 1893, Pension File of Wallace Willikey (alias Levi Johnson), 6th USCHA, RG 15.

24. Charles G. Townsend, Louisville, Ky., to the Commissioner of Pensions, Washington, D.C., 29 May 1919, Pension File of Samuel Taylor, 45th USCI, RG 15.

Even the U.S. Census Bureau indirectly alluded to the phenomenon, in 1909, when it speculated that the divorce statistics of white and black Southerners were not strictly comparable, because it suspected that in many black-majority counties there was a "general disregard" among African Americans for obeying marriage laws. See U.S. Census Bureau, *Special Reports: Marriage and Divorce, 1867–1906, Part 1: Summary, Laws. Foreign Statistics* (Washington: Government Printing Office, 1909). 22.

25. Chaplin James Peet, Vicksburg, Miss., to Brigadier General Lorenzo L. Thomas, Washington, D.C., 1 November 1864, Berlin et al., *Black Military Experience,* 604.

26. Deposition of John Means Thompson, 19 March 1888, Pension File of Green Colyar, 15th USCI, RG 15.

27. Wright, *Marriage and Divorce,* 1–48. Common-law marriage was legal during the postwar period in Alabama, Arkansas, the District of Columbia, Florida, Georgia, Mississippi, Missouri, South Carolina, and Texas. It was illegal in Delaware, Kentucky, Louisiana, Maryland, Tennessee, and Virginia. Informal unions were legal in Oklahoma prior to 1903.

28. Leslie Schwalm also notes this phenomenon. See Schwalm, "The Meaning of Freedom," 340.

29. Deposition of Cornelius McCray, 7 December 1887, Pension File of Lewis Booth, 50th USCI, RG 15.

30. Deposition of Mollie Fry, 18 April 1911, Pension File of Philip Russell (alias Fry), 114th USCI, RG 15.

31. Deposition of Rosa Farrow, 14 January 1922, Pension File of Volsin Brown (alias Farrow), 80th USCI, RG 15.

32. Pension File of William B. Barrett, 74th USCI, RG 15.

33. Deposition of Airey Young, 5 August 1892, Pension File of Wilson Fitchett, 10th USCI, RG 15.

34. Deposition of Emma Frederick, 11 April 1903, Pension File of Clement Frederick, 70th and 71st USCI, RG 15.

35. Common-law marriage was prevalent enough among the white population of the United States during the nineteenth century for its legitimacy to become the topic of debate in legal circles. See Otto E. Koegel, *Common Law Marriage and Its Development in the United States* (Washington: John Byrne and Company, 1922), 54–172; John E. Semonche, "Common-Law Marriage in North Carolina: A Study in Legal History," *American Journal of Legal History* 9 (October 1965): 320–49; Michael Grossberg, *Governing the Hearth: Law and Family in Nineteenth-Century America* (Chapel Hill: University of North Carolina Press, 1985) 69–90. Little if any research, however, has been done on the nature of common-law marriage practices in the United States. Hence, it is difficult to compare the the origins and practice of informal marriage between former slaves and their nineteenth-century white contemporaries. This topic and the extent of common-law marriage among free persons of color in the antebellum period deserves more research.

But there is an extensive literature on the practice of common-law marriage in Europe during the nineteenth century. These studies suggest that while the economic forces encouraging the perpetuation of informal marriage in Western countries—particularly the cost of legal marriage and divorce (often beyond the means of many working-class people)—were similar, the context in which informal marriage institutions developed was quite different from country to country. For instance, common-law marriages in nineteenth-century Germany were often the product of means-dependent marriage laws that prevented poor couples from legally marrying (for fear that they and their children would become dependent on public relief). See William G. Burgin, "Concubinage: Revolutionary Response or Last Resort?: The Attitudes of Town Authorities and of Couples Rejected in Their Marriage Suits in Nineteenth-Century Germany," *Consortium on Revolutionary Europe, 1750–1850: Proceedings* (Tallahassee: Institute on Napoleon and the French Revolution, 1983), 271–87; Lynn Abrams, "Concubinage, Cohabitation, and the Law: Class and Gender Relations in Nineteenth-Century Germany," *Gender and History* 5 (Spring 1993): 81–100. In France and Great Britain, common-law marriage was intimately connected to industrialization and urbanization, a phenomenon outside the experience of most African Americans in the post–Civil War South. See Jeffrey Kaplow, "Concubinage and the Working Class in Early-Nineteenth-Century Paris," in *Vom Ancien Regime zur Französischen Revolution,* ed. Ernst Hinrichs, Eberhard Schmitt, and Rudolf Vierhaus (Göttingen: Vandenhoeck and Rurprecht, 1978), 366–67; Lenard R. Berlanstein, "Illegitimacy, Concubinage, and Proletarianization in a French Town, 1760–1914," *Journal of Family History* 5 (Winter 1980): 369–73; John R. Gillis, *For Better, for Worse: British Marriages, 1600 to the Present* (New York: Oxford University Press, 1985), 190–228.

36. Census Bureau, *Marriage and Divorce,* 200–258.

37. Grossberg, *Governing the Hearth,* 251.

38. In his study of antebellum divorce in Maryland, Richard H. Chused found that attorneys' fees in some divorces amounted to hundreds of dollars and that they constituted the primary costs of divorce. See Richard H. Chused, *Private Acts in Public Places: A Social History of Divorce in the Formative Era of American Family Law* (Philadelphia: University of Pennsylvania Press, 1994), 83n, 91. Postbellum divorces between black men and women were not as expensive. C.Vance Lewis, a black lawyer in turn-of-the-century Galveston, Texas, charged $25 for a divorce. See Maxwell Bloomfield, "From Deference to Confrontation:The Early Black Lawyers of Galveston,Texas, 1895–1920," in *The New High Priests: Lawyers in Post–Civil War America,* ed. Gerard W. Gawalt (Westport, Conn.: Greenwood Press, 1984), 157. However, even $25 was beyond the means of many African Americans in the late nineteenth and early twentieth centuries.

39. Edwards, " 'The Marriage Covenant' " 109.

40. Grossberg, *Governing the Hearth,* 64–102.

41. See note 5.

42. Affidavit of Lucinda Sibley, 18 March 1892, Pension File of Solomon Sibley, 63d USCI, RG 15.

43. Affidavit of Kizzie Sexton, 5 March 1898, Pension File of Henry Sexton, 65th and 67th USCI, RG 15.

44. Affidavits of Thomasine Stephens, 18 January 1909 and 19 May 1913, Pension File of Peter Stephens, 74th and 91st USCI, RG 15.

45. Pension File of Tony Austin (alias Alston), 21st USCI, RG 15.

46. R. K. Doe, Special Examiner, Charleston, S. C., to the Commissioner of Pensions, Washington, D.C., 25 January 1902, Pension File of Washington Granville, 128th USCI, RG 15.

FOUR

"OF NECESSITY AND
PUBLIC BENEFIT"

Southern Families and Their Appeals
for Protection

Amy E. Murrell

I need not tell you of my devotion to my country, of the sacrifices I have made, and of the many more I am willing to make," Margaret A. Easterling of Marlborough District, South Carolina, assured Confederate secretary of war James Seddon in 1862. "Search history and you will see that woman is always true to her country and that there was never an Arnold in the Female world." Easterling was a proud Confederate. But her patriotism did not stop her from asking Southern leaders to take a soldier from the lines of battle and send him home to care for her family. A widow with slaves and children to watch over, Easterling also cared for an aged mother, who herself had fourteen slaves. Boasting that she had set an example to her neighbors by going without an overseer for nearly a year, she wanted the government to understand that she already had made great sacrifices. But as more white men left to fight, she felt less secure in "a neighborhood in which negroes number twenty to one." Willing to keep her seventeen-year-old son Willie, "a brave, hearty lad," in the service, she asked that her "feeble" son Josiah be discharged. For this she apologized to the secretary of war and explained: "I know our cause is worthy of any and every sacrifice . . . but I am not mistress of my fears."[1]

Southern families such as Easterling's did not enjoy a natural alliance with the Confederate war effort. Every man drawn away by conscription laws was one less man at home to care for his family's economic and emotional needs. Some families found their situations eased by legislation in 1862 that authorized the automatic discharge or exemption of overseers on large plantations and of men who could afford to purchase a substitute. But these and other provisions still did not address the concerns of a wide segment of the Southern population—the small slaveholders and yeomen, who found that writing to the president and the secretary of war for a special exemption or discharge was their only hope for protecting their families.[2] Some of these petitioners owned slaves, while others owned none at all. Some owned acres of land, others lived on rented plots of land, and still others shared homes with relatives. Small slaveholders, yeomen, and poor laborers comprised this group of Southern families that appealed to their leaders for protection during the war.

It was a rare Southern family that could remain isolated from the death and suffering of the Civil War. About this most historians agree. But some go further, suggesting that this caused disaffection with the Confederate cause and contributed to the South's defeat. As women grew helpless with the loss of their husbands, and as soldiers became resentful of the poor living conditions of their families, public protests by women and desertions by men became common. These men and women were frustrated with a perceived lack of government support for their welfare. Their frustration, some historians conclude, represented disillusionment with the war on the part of Southerners and undermined any chance of cultivating a common identity or purpose among them. Nationalism could not prevail amid criticism of the government and its policy toward families. The interests of the family and the nation had become incompatible.[3]

Petitions such as Margaret Easterling's are among the sources used to suggest that Southern families gave up on the Confederate cause. Statements of family distress are to these scholars evidence that the people had grown angry at the Confederacy: by writing to their leaders, they indicated that they were willing to abandon the fight. These writings were protest documents, these historians suggest, and the end of a long road of distress and the beginning of the Confederacy's demise. Margaret Easterling, however, would probably take issue with this characterization. She may not have been "mistress of her fears," but she was also emphatic that she was no "Arnold" either. She was not about to give up. Her family's interests and those of the Confederate army had come into conflict, but in her mind a single discharge would reconcile those conflicting interests. Easterling's letter did not signal abandonment of the cause, nor did any of the other 205 petitions surveyed here. A rereading suggests instead that these were narratives of negotiation rather than of protest.[4]

Far from giving up on the cause when their leaders appeared to neglect them, Southern families exhibited a more profound willingness to bargain with their leaders. They wrote with an understanding of the wartime sacrifices required of the Southern people, and in turn offered suggestions for how the government could most equitably deal with Confederate families. Writing was to them a means of opening a dialogue with government leaders; as a result, their relationship with their leaders appears more giving and less adversarial than previously portrayed. Not every individual family received the help it requested, of course. But the government did heed the thousands of petitions and respond with new laws that generally benefited soldiers' families. Over the course of the war, soldiers' families and government leaders actually appear to have grown closer to an agreement about how to reconcile the interests of families and the greater nation. As active participants in this dialogue, these Southern families had every reason to maintain their support for the greater Confederate cause even as the war became more disruptive.

Four years of war took a toll on Southern families. Most experienced the loss of a husband or a son to battle, leaving women and children on their own to provide for themselves. These families were lonely, and they were fearful. They feared slave revolts and worried about not having enough food. Crops went unharvested, and the inflated Confederate currency made obtaining provisions all the more difficult. Disease and "epidemicks" made life even more precarious, and an unreliable postal service unwillingly forced some family members to lose contact with their kin. Southern families who took the time to petition the government were deeply discouraged about their conditions. They were probably most frustrated that the Confederate Congress had written exemption laws that, in the interest of the greater cause, inadvertently favored the wealthier classes and left poorer families—the kin of common soldiers—to bear the brunt of the war effort. For that reason, one might expect the tone of their letters to be forceful and demanding of an immediate end to this inequity. In reality, these writers were far more deferential and wrote for assistance with trepidation.

"I am sorry that i have to trouble you with these few lines," Amy Arnott of Persia, Tennessee, wrote to the secretary of war. A sixty-year-old widow, Arnott assured the secretary that she would not have bothered him "iff it was not a case of need cesity." Arnott wanted her son discharged, but like so many other petitioners, she was wary of presenting her case before a new government with new laws and new leaders. Would the government even care about her situation? Was she being too forward in asking for aid? Arnott and other petitioners probably had never given much thought before to the national government's duty to their families. And few knew how to talk about the private despair that made their petitions necessary. Some responded by writing formalized petitions authorized by their local justices of the peace. Others wrote petitions that were much more informal, akin to a personal letter. Their writings, like Arnott's, are filled with awkward attempts to introduce themselves and their private matters to their leaders.[5]

"I am now about to do what at the commencement of this war I should have blushed to have thought of but am now reduced to the necessity of doing," admitted Sallie Robertson of Albemarle County, Virginia. She may have blushed because she felt it necessary to tell the secretary of war about her "helpless" family. Her mother was dead, her oldest brother had been killed in battle, and her father was ill, with a "large tumour" on his face. This left Robertson, the eldest of four daughters, the sole support for her family—unless her remaining brother could be discharged. She hesitated to ask for that discharge, though, because she feared becoming a burden to the government. This was a fear held in common by a number of petitioners who claimed to have tried living on their own without government support. Desperation, they explained, was the only reason they broke down and wrote for help. A Whitfield County, Georgia, woman thus acknowledged writing "with a trembling hand and all most broken heart" in asking for the discharge of one of her sons to care for her, after her five other sons were killed in the war. Explaining that she had no one left to lean on, she asked the president: "Will you bee my friend?"[6]

Writing to their leaders was an especially uncomfortable task for women, who were the majority of the petitioners. It meant becoming an outspoken advocate for their families' welfare, an unfamiliar role. It also meant dealing in the public arena of policy makers and politics, an arena not normally inhabited by women. This made women such as Evaline Turner of Alabama apprehensive. She explained that child-bearing had left her deathly ill and she had no relatives in her "poor" community to help care for her small children. Her husband's return from the service was an urgent need. Despite her seemingly desperate condition, however, Turner did not feel assured that her case would be heard. "Kind sir do not pass this unnraised as a womans whim," she pleaded to the secretary of war, expressing what likely crossed other women's minds when they wrote. One South Carolina woman admitted that her letter was written "in an awkward, womanish manner," as if to apologize for her boldness in writing. Others appealed to Davis as a father and husband to sensitize him to the condition of Southern women. These women were well aware of their new, quasi-public role as family advocates and shaped their requests accordingly.[7]

Uncertainty about writing to government leaders, exhibited by male writers as well as females, also derived from a murky special exemption and discharge process. Laws passed in 1862 and 1863 gave the secretary of war and the president wide latitude in determining who would be dismissed from service outside of existing exemption regulations. They could do so, as one law put it, when they thought it "essential to the good of the service or the general interest of the country."[8] Citizens were left to guess what qualified as the country's "general interest."

T. T. Tredway of Prince Edward County, Virginia, addressed this issue by explaining that he wrote "without any personal interest other than that of a friend & fellow citizen." He wrote to obtain a discharge for a teacher, but said little about himself and gave no information about why he was requesting the discharge. Instead, he stressed that his intentions were disinterested. Such denials of personal, private interest are echoed in petition after petition. It seems a curious admission, particularly when each man and woman who wrote likely did have a personal interest in their request. In Tredway's case, for example, a census record reveals that he had a school-age child, who perhaps would have benefited from a discharged teacher. But considering the political setting in which Tredway petitioned, his disavowals of self-interest may not have been so disingenuous.[9]

The leaders of the new Confederacy proclaimed that their government was to embody the purified republican ideals inherited from the founders of the United States.[10] They believed the Confederacy would replace an antebellum society corrupted by the excesses of democracy and would therefore demand that each citizen suppress individual interest for the good of the greater public. Politicians, clergymen, and newspaper editors alike trumpeted this theme, one that would have been particularly resonant in a society embroiled in war.[11] These appeals were heard by the masses of Southern citizens and may explain why a soldier serving in the Ninth Virginia Cavalry wrote so clearly about his selfless intentions: "Selfishness does not prompt me to make this request . . . but [rather] the interests and welfare of a widowed mother and seven sisters." Rather than admit a personal stake in his exemption, he preferred to acknowledge the Confederate leaders' expectation for a society in which individuals subsumed their personal interests in those of the people around them. In that sense his denial of selfishness, just like that of other petitioners, was a nod to the country's "general interest."[12]

Others similarly claimed to write on behalf of family and neighbors. Mrs. S. M. Evatt of Catoosa County, Georgia, explained that her brother's discharge would at once serve "the interest of the family at home . . . and the greater interest of the whole community." Evatt's father had died just months before, compounding the troubles her family already had faced following the death of her son-in-law at the Second Battle of Manassas. The losses left Evatt the sole support for her widowed mother and daughter, another daughter, and a grandchild. She sought the return of her brother, who, she argued, could also help her neighbors by producing apparel in his mechanical shop. Those neighbors, she explained, had been denied this necessary apparel since being cut off from "foreign supply" at the start of the war. Her brother's return would thus serve interests beyond those of her immediate family. Other petitioners made similar cases for the benefits to be enjoyed by an entire community from an individual's discharge, including one doctor in Mississippi who promised to practice "gratis" for the families of "poor volunteers."[13]

Such promises may not have been merely clever attempts at covering up self-interest. The petitions suggest instead that families did work closely with their neighbors to survive the war. Some letters tell of separate families moving in together. Others describe the steps taken by neighbors to find a substitute blacksmith among them when their old one was conscripted. Still others tell of neighbors coming together to form patrols when a new threat entered their lives, such as Yankee soldiers luring slaves away. They refer to "neighborhoods," "settlements," and even "communities," networks formed within towns and among scattered rural populations. Some of these had established names—such as the Steam Mill Neighborhood of Decatur County, Georgia—while others appeared to be new networks formed in the exigencies of war.[14] When writing on behalf of such communities, petitioners explained why they needed just one more person to ensure that local relief efforts could continue unabated. They thus wrote as if being a good Confederate meant working locally with neighbors to adapt to wartime changes.[15]

Certainly a discharged soldier could contribute something to his community and help his neighbors survive the war. But another reason why a man's discharge or exemption petition would go to lengths to testify to his usefulness at home was so that he avoided appearing as if he was shirking military duty.[16] These writers were undoubtedly aware that they could be met with charges of "skulking" if they were at home, that they could be criticized for not making the same sacrifice for war as did the men who donned Confederate uniforms. That may explain why few men wrote on their own behalf, and why their neighbors instead wrote testimonials to their usefulness and potential contributions to their communities.[17]

The appeal written by one group of Alabama citizens was typical. "We are all doing what we can for the cause of our country and would rather increase the number of its soldiers than take one from its ranks," explained the petitioners from Shelby and Bibb Counties in Alabama. But they needed their family physician, Dr. S. M. Doak. The doctor had volunteered for service at the beginning of the war, and while he was gone his neighbors had to travel roughly fifteen miles to see a physician. This proved impossible for some men and women, and they initiated the proceedings to have Doak return a year later. There was no question that his discharge would serve the community, they argued; it was an urgent necessity. "We feel that the lives & health of our families should be protected as far as human means can do it and that the services of Dr. Doak are absolutely necessary to that end." As if to reinforce Doak's selflessness, they noted that "this is done by ourselves without his request or knowledge."[18]

These Alabamians were not alone in insisting that a soldier did not know about the petition. Mrs. J. E. Anderson of Cuthbert, Georgia, was quite open about her decision to write without her husband's knowledge. He was too "proud" to write for himself, she explained, so when his health deteriorated, she decided to take action. "He can not stand camp life," Anderson admitted, "but [he] scorns to be exempted by a board of physicians—so many able bodied men are exempted that way." Anderson wished to distinguish her husband from the men who had previously cheated their way out of the service. But even as she protected his honor and dignity as a soldier, she also made it clear that he was in "feeble health" and could not be doing much good for the army. Instead, she argued, by coming home he could support his family, which recently had been driven from its home by the "hated invader."[19]

Women writers such as Anderson were especially helpful to men who wanted to avoid accusations of self-interest. Indeed, because the duty of serving in the military was not hanging over their heads, women were less likely to be seen as acting out of selfish motives. This may be why petitioners for a cap-maker in Forsyth County, Georgia, noted at the bottom of their letter that "the undersigned ladies particularly need his work." Or why still other petitions separated women's signatures into a separate column, as if to emphasize the numbers of women participating in the request. Women in general may have been uncertain and uncomfortable as petitioners, but they were useful. The specter of starving women and children could hardly fail to have an effect on the Confederacy's leaders who were undoubtedly humbled by their pleas.[20]

Some men wisely asked women to write for them. Jane Elliott of Red Bank, Virginia, for example, explained that her soldier-husband had requested that she write for his discharge. She then proceeded to tell the secretary of war all about the trouble she had with the "ten infameley" now dependent on her. She could not survive without her husband anymore, she explained, emphasizing that this was the only reason her husband would leave the army. Men in Madison County, Mississippi, apparently felt that their female neighbors would be more effective in seeking the discharge of their coffin-maker. After failing to hear a response to their petition, they asked women to write an identical one. And in doing so, the women of this county wrote that they hoped their effort "may have the influence we so earnestly desire."[21]

Men may have relied on them, but some women were less than confident about their influence and felt it necessary to have the endorsement of their community when they wrote. Sarah Dicky of Scriven County, Georgia, provides a clever example. Her petition began with the statement that "the Soldiers Wifes of Scriven County do request of you to hav Privet David Dicky . . . discharged." David Dicky was her twenty-one-year-old son, one of ten children in the Dicky family, and the one who could be most helpful in the absence of their father. Dicky repeated three times in the petition that it was the "Soldiers wifes" who asked for his discharge. But no other women in her county signed the petition with Sarah Dicky. Perhaps other women had given her their consent, but maybe not. Certainly, Dicky did not explain why any other soldier's wife would want David Dicky discharged. What her wording suggests, perhaps, is that Sarah felt uncertain about her influence and was hesitant to appear to act on her behalf alone.[22]

If Dicky had thought only of herself, some of her neighbors might have stopped her. Members of other communities took it upon themselves to police the requests of those they deemed selfish. One Alabama man wrote after hearing of a neighbor's petition: "The widow H.M. ferel alrede has agood over seer and agitenon very wel with her bisne," this writer explained. Her request that her son-in-law be discharged as her overseer should be turned down, he explained, for "I thank you wold doo wel to ceep him as you hav got him" as a member of a Virginia regiment. Another writer deplored the fact that her rich neighbors were not doing enough to share their food with her. "It is folly for a poor mother to call on the rich people about here," Almira P. Acors of Spotsylvania County, Virginia, complained to the president, "there hearts are of steel they would sooner thow what they have to spare to their dogs than give it to a starving child." Acors's family consisted primarily of laborers who worked for several more prosperous households in their county. When the war became difficult for their family, however, those employers did not appear sympathetic. Acors thus was forced to seek from the government what she did not receive from her neighbors.[23]

The selfishness that Acors deplored was to some degree behind every petition, though few writers would admit it. Their eagerness to hide self-interest suggests that these Southerners wrote with a different sense of themselves and their place in the nation than is generally assumed. Historians who write of Southerners' disaffection with the war base their arguments on the premise that southern men and women maintained a strong belief in their individual rights and that it was this belief that pushed them to protest on behalf of their own private needs.[24] As these testimonies indicate, however, the republican ethos of sacrificing self-interest for the good of a greater whole was just as operative in the petitions. Framing their requests accordingly, writers could claim to serve the nation's "general interest," rather than abandoning it, and thus the government would have to respond to their petition.

Government officials did respond to the neighbors of widow Mary Adkins in Sussex County, Virginia, who succeeded in obtaining a discharge of one of her five sons in 1863. They had explained to the secretary of war why she could not manage her farm. "She is in very delicate health," they wrote, and "entirely unable to supervise her farming operations," which included overseeing her slaves. With an eye to the larger war effort, Adkins and her neighbors selected her "most feeble" son, one who suffered from a back injury, and promised that "she would not ask even this boon, if she were not fully convinced that the interest of the Confederacy would be promoted." After reading about Adkins's case, the secretary of war scribbled the words "allow discharge" at the bottom of the petition, without further explanation. Other discharges found in this selection of petitions included one for the husband of a "deranged" woman who needed help at home. There was no consistent reason for these discharges, nor were such discharges common. Only 7 percent of the special exemption requests in this sample were granted—roughly half the rate at which Confederate laws automatically exempted overseers and large plantation owners.[25]

In most cases, the war department took no action at all. The secretary of war simply wrote the word "file" on most requests. Apparently, however, war department officials came to realize in 1862 that they needed to at least explain their decision to reject a petition. When a new secretary of war, James S. Seddon, took office that year, the petitions received notes such as "decline for usual reasons" next to Seddon's initials, or "Kindly decline for the usual reasons." Those "usual reasons" were probably explained by another notation: "Ack. & regret that the department is not authorized by law to perform what would be a grateful task, that of returning the brother to his family at home." As the war progressed and the Confederacy suffered from inadequate manpower, Seddon instructed his clerk to reason with petitioners: "No soldier can be spared in this supreme struggle," he wrote on one letter, while on another he directed, "Answer: The exigencies of the service do not allow the detail."[26]

Despite receiving discouraging replies, or none at all, civilians did not stop writing to their leaders. They may have derived hope from the fact that their own leaders were quite conflicted about their duties to the Southern people. Indeed, Confederate leaders hardly agreed on how to create a government that fulfilled both the ideological and the practical needs of the Confederacy, and they disagreed in particular about the ideal relationship between the Southern government and its people. Some resisted the centralization of the Confederate government and criticized the development of conscription and impressment policies as somehow inconsistent with the Confederacy's proclaimed allegiance to states' rights. Others argued that the Confederacy's viability demanded such programs. These competing forces naturally clashed. Their clash was rooted in a greater dispute over what the Confederacy stood for, a debate over the South's identity and values.[27]

Published proceedings of the Confederate Congress reveal that the soldier's family was at the center of this debate. Just as some members rejected any legislation that would expand the size of the national government, others considered the needs of soldiers' families a paramount concern. In offering a bill in 1862 to increase the pay of privates and noncommissioned officers, one Texas representative declared that the government was bound to support the family of any man who was taken away from his home by the conscription act. A Virginia representative likewise supported the bill and called it a "sacred duty" of the Congress to make provisions for soldiers' families. Laws exempting men from service who could afford to purchase substitutes also inspired a discussion about soldiers' families. Countering arguments that substitution served to protect poor families by sending men home to guard communities, a Mississippi representative asked about his poorer constituents: "If I should tell them the rich were permitted to stay at home to guard the families of the poor, would they not at once reply that they had much rather entrust the protection of their families to their own presence?" He concluded that each family deserved to have its own "natural protector" at home.[28]

Members of the Confederate Congress channeled this debate into a variety of legislation benefiting soldiers' families. In 1862, a South Carolina representative offered a bill making hospitals more accessible to relatives, while an Arkansas representative offered legislation to support soldiers' widows. General relief bills for families of noncommissioned officers and privates were offered in 1863, as were various versions of the exemption bill that would allow skilled workers to return to their communities. Legislation considered in 1863 to protect families from impressment specified that "in no instance shall any individual be deprived of the amount of provisions required for the comfortable support of his family." Another bill proposed that soldiers' families be permitted to buy provisions at "cost prices of the Government." Most of this legislation, however, never made it to the president's desk; it fell victim to critics of centralization and was instead implemented on the state level, as state governments began assuming greater responsibility for needy families with laws of their own. Yet this dialogue about the national government's duty to soldiers' families never stopped, and through petitions citizens continued to offer their own ideas for how the government could do its part for their families.[29]

Petitioners had paid close attention to their leaders' actions. In its most specific attempts to establish guidelines for discharges, the Confederate Congress declared several times in laws passed between 1862 and 1863 that special discharges could be granted when required by "justice, equity, and necessity," or when important to the "public interest." Subsequent petitions from citizens reflect a very deliberate effort to speak the language of their leaders and to engage politicians on these terms. For twenty-seven citizens of Abbeville District, South Carolina, simply stating that their doctor's petition "falls under the law of *'necessity & public benefit'*" was apparently enough in their minds to address the government's guidelines.[30] Eliza Adams, a widow in Montgomery County, Georgia, argued likewise in a petition signed by her four daughters: "I think Equity, justice and necessity would say that my son Matthew B. Adams should be exempted from the Service of the Confederate States." Without elaborating, she explained that she needed the oldest of her five sons to manage the family estate.[31] This language of equity allowed Adams and others like her to address their common dilemma: how could one ask for a soldier's discharge and still claim to support the Confederacy's interests?

Petitioners argued that "equity" and "justice" meant giving each family and community an equal chance to survive the war. For this reason fifty-nine men and women of Henry County, Alabama, were optimistic about their chances of obtaining a discharge in 1863. "Ever believing that the true policy of all governments consists in a proper appreciation of the wants and comforts of its different communities," these petitioners wrote, "bids us hope that our prayers for the discharge of said Elliot may be granted us." In their view the government should democratize wartime sacrifice by granting their request and distributing burdens equally. To them, this meant allowing their wool carder to return, which would make it possible for the community to continue producing wool on a large scale. By defining the Confederacy's values in this way, they were easily able to view the protection of an individual family or community as inextricably linked to the larger good of the Confederacy. Making that case convincingly, however, was another matter.[32]

Some writers were careful guardians of an equitable distribution of wartime sacrifice. Petitioners from Nash County, North Carolina, for example, pointed out that collectively they had done enough to benefit the Confederacy and for that reason deserved their requested discharge. They claimed to have already sent one thousand men to serve in the army, and they needed a doctor to attend to those who remained. In making their request, they assured the government that they acted "without any intention or desire to injure the cause in which he is now engaged." Likewise, citizens from Lewisburg, Tennessee, pointed out that their hometown had contributed eighty soldiers. They, too, asked for their physician's discharge and suggested that their petition should be given serious consideration "in as much as this community has already done for our military service." Even more common were the appeals of soldiers' mothers, who expressed a willingness to give up to the service all but their "last" son. In all these cases, negotiations with the government read like a balance sheet: the government could take men away until the point at which a family or community detected an imbalance detrimental to its livelihood.[33]

"He can do the country infinitely more good by staying here than by going," twenty-nine citizens of Randolph County, North Carolina, wrote of their blacksmith. Because Randolph was a "great agricultural county," these petitioners foresaw severe food shortages for the entire South if no smith was around to make their farm implements. "He will be doing the Government more good by being here, than where he is," another set of petitioners similarly explained about their wheelwright. This artisan had become quite ill while in an army camp and, according to these writers, represented a "burden" to the military effort.[34] The suggestion that the military effort could benefit from sending a soldier home was repeated in petition after petition. "We ask you not to discharge our sons and husbands," fourteen women offered in 1863. Instead they suggested that a "nearly blind" man could serve as their overseer, since "he cannot be of little service to the Confederate army."[35] These women consciously sought a fair balance with their request; like other petitioners, they took it upon themselves to choose a disabled soldier over their own kin. Others seemed to suggest, as citizens of one Virginia county did of their neighbor's "delicate" son, that a particular soldier "is now only an expense to the government . . . but if at home he could manage to produce on the farm crops not only sufficient to supply the wants of the family but aid in subsisting others too."[36]

Other letter-writers offered deals with the government. "If you can not discharge my youngest boy," Kitty Daughtry of North Carolina asked of President Davis in 1863, then "can you detail him for a short time?" Concerned about harvesting her crops in the absence of her five sons, Daughtry proposed allowing just her youngest son to return to work her land for the three summer months. "If my son could only be sent home to us until fall until my crop was harvested it would save us from want and assist in providing something for the needy soldiers families in our neighborhood," she argued. In exchange for his discharge, this seventeen-year-old son would provide food to her neighbors and help the Confederate government feed its people. Apparently the government was taken by requests such as hers. By 1864, the Confederate Congress passed legislation authorizing discharges to soldiers to return to their farms as long as they sold their surplus to the soldiers' families around them.[37]

Men and women used petitions to educate Confederate leaders about the circumstances that they thought made them unique. "No community has stronger claims on the government for a special exempt than this," one North Carolina neighborhood explained of their circumstances. In truth, however, the district was not that unusual. As the entire collection of petitions demonstrates, people throughout the South faced similar threats of illness, loneliness, family disruption, slave uprisings, or economic ruin. Still, local communities could hardly see these as a widespread phenomenon. This blindness enabled them to feel justified in seeking special attention for their family or community, on the grounds of "believing that you will give each and every family justice," as one mother explained. Granting the exemption or discharge would promote justice and, thus, the greater interests of the Confederacy.[38]

Other petitioners emphasized that the Confederacy's interests were in view using simple patriotic flourishes. "Am still a friend of southern independence," noted a Russellville, Tennessee, man asking for his son's discharge. "It is nessary for every man that can be spared From hom shold be cept in the field to beet back the hords of Abolishists that now thretens our rites and country," declared forty-five wives of soldiers from Franklin County, Mississippi, when seeking a discharge. These writers promised Confederate leaders that they were on their side, even as they requested a miller to "save the distress that now preevails in the neighborhood." Amy Arnott of Persia, Tennessee, also made clear her family's longtime loyalty to the cause. "My sons have been for the south all the time when the question came up for convention," she explained of their pro-South views, but without one of them "I can not stay by myself." Mary Evans of Tennessee, on the other hand, did not have to spell her views out. Without actually discussing her thoughts about the Confederacy, Evans asked for her husband's discharge on stationery imprinted with the stars and bars and a patriotic verse.[39]

Even the handful of petitioners most outspokenly critical of government policies in the latter years of the war did not extrapolate this criticism to a general disillusionment with the Confederacy. In their minds, the two could be separate. One Virginia man complained of the "crying evil" of healthy men allowed to work in comfortable government offices; but he channeled his outrage toward pressing the government to change its laws. "I know you to be a just man," he wrote in an appeal to flatter Secretary Seddon, "and that it is only necessary to bring this thing to your attention." Hopeful that the secretary would listen, this man argued that the Confederate army would be more formidable if it also conscripted government workers. Also dismayed by the presence of healthy men in government jobs while her three sons fought, Martha Nelson foresaw the Confederacy's doom without a change in the laws: "If we are finally beaten it will be done more by those class of men than our enemies the yankees." Both of these writers expressed disappointment when the government failed to make sacrifices equitable and, in their minds, instituted policies that betrayed the greater cause in which they still believed.[40]

By venting their frustration at the government specifically, even the most desperate of families could profess to support the South by the war's end. Take the case of Elizabeth Patterson of Albemarle County, Virginia, who wrote in March 1865. Hers was "a record of misfortune probably unsurpassed in the Confederacy," according to her local justice of the peace, and whether this was true or not, Patterson believed that her situation was grim. "In every conceivable way, my family have striven to benefit the Confederacy," she argued, noting that her husband and three sons "sealed their devotion with their lives" when they were killed in the service. Her two infant sons died from being in a house in which sick soldiers were treated, and other members of her extended family suffered in impoverished circumstances. In March Patterson found herself without anyone to help her seed oats and pitch crops. For that reason she asked for a temporary discharge of her remaining son and was frustrated that he had not been able to return home yet. "Ought not I be allowed that privilege for my only remaining adult son?" she exclaimed. The government's laxity in caring for her circumstances still would not erode her support for the cause to which her male kin had already devoted themselves: "My record of misfortune has been unparalleled, but I am willing to sink or swim with my country and to do my part towards attaining our independence."[41]

Letters such as Patterson's did not go unheard even in the last year of the war. The Confederate Congress passed a new series of laws in 1864 and 1865 that favored small slaveholders' and yeomen's families. "We must not only have an army, but food and clothing for it and for their families," one member of the Confederate Congress reasoned before passing this legislation. These laws included the elimination of substitution, except in cases where a discharged soldier promised to grow food for needy soldiers' families. The overseer exemption law also was tightened up, a measure meant to democratize wartime sacrifice. A new tax bill in 1865 further promised that families of soldiers would be exempt from tax-in-kind, which had been a huge burden during the war. Additional legislation put women to work in government jobs, allowing them to support their families. But these provisions did not bring men home. In fact, at the same time these laws were passed, new conscription laws widening the eligible draft age took men away from their homes in greater numbers. Most of these families would not see their husbands and brothers again until the end of the war. Yet this general wave of new laws at least suggests that the government was growing sensitive to the needs of common soldiers' families and that during the war, the government and its petitioners had moved closer together in their dialogue about the interests of the family and of the nation. Each and every family was more likely to receive "justice" at the end of the war than at the beginning.[42]

In the aggregate, the Southern war effort might have collapsed even earlier had Confederate leaders granted all the discharges and exemptions sought by Southern families. The passage of new laws instead had to substitute for a general acceptance of the petitioners' discharge requests. But rather than dismiss the petitioners' attempts as somewhat futile, however, we can see an ironic result in their efforts. The petitioning process in and of itself may have given Southerners hope that the Confederacy could and should become a viable nation.

Men and women wrote to their leaders because they believed the government could help them. They would not have kept writing in 1865 had they not. Improvements in government policy toward families, and the growing tendency of its leaders to reply in writing to each petition, probably only encouraged petitioners to make their appeals as the war progressed. Even if the government had appeared to neglect Southern families, it at least demonstrated a potential for change. Writing, then, opened up necessary channels of communication between the people and their government. Citizens informed the government of their condition and made suggestions for how they and the nation could be better served. They were writing not to protest—a tempting assumption for historians trying to explain the South's loss—but to negotiate.

This negotiation took place alongside and even encouraged continued professions of allegiance to the greater Confederacy. This was possible because, in the minds of these writers, the Southern cause and the cause of their misfortune were not one and the same. Their misfortune had been brought on by Yankee aggression and was only exacerbated by the Confederate government, which had not made it possible for all their families to retain needed protectors. So it was to the Yankees and the Southern government—and not to the entire Confederacy—that petitioners directed their frustration. This made it possible for Southerners to be frustrated with their families' condition and still profess to be devout Confederates.

The nation and the family thus merged in the petitioners' writings.[43] Their families' interests and that of the Confederacy did not have to conflict or simply coexist. The petitioners suggested instead that the two were intimately bound, that the nation could not survive without the foundation provided by healthy and stable families. By equalizing the war's burdens on Southern families and allowing them to survive, these men and women argued, the government could guarantee viability of the nation. A request that a soldier be returned from the service therefore was not a sign of self-interested protest; it expressed instead a willingness to strike a deal with the government that would protect both the nation and its families. That willingness—as played out in the petitioning process—may explain how Southerners had at least some incentive to remain loyal to the Confederate nation *and* to their families, even as the war became increasingly difficult.

These narratives of negotiation therefore suggest that historians should rethink common assumptions about the nature of Southerners' Civil War loyalty. To argue that family ties had eroded national allegiance by 1865 overlooks a far more complex connection between those two loyalties, a complexity illustrated by the petitions. Loyalty was not something with clearly defined limits or easily restricted to either the family or the nation alone. Southerners apparently viewed their loyalty as far more flexible—or elastic—and resilient enough to withstand the hardships of war while remaining supportive of the Confederate cause.[44] To view loyalty in this way perhaps makes it possible to understand not why Southerners lost the will to fight, but why they made it possible for the outmatched Confederacy to hold on for four long years.[45]

Notes

1. Margaret A. Easterling and neighbors to President Davis, 17 November, 20 December 1862, Letters Received, Confederate Secretary of War, RG 109,

M-437, Roll 45, National Archives, Washington, D.C. Since these petitions are drawn entirely from this one collection, I will cite the rest of the petitions according to the writer's name, date, and roll number only.

2. Petitioners asked for either an "exemption," which would prevent a man from being conscripted, or a "discharge," which would allow a man already conscripted to leave the service. Under Confederate laws passed in October 1862, men automatically exempted were: overseers on plantations with over twenty slaves; doctors who had worked in the profession for at least five years; artisans "habitually engaged in working for the public"; and mechanics involved in contract work with the government. In terms of discharges, legislation in 1861 authorized the dismissal of any soldier with a significant medical disability—a determination to be made by the army's surgeons and commanding officers. When men or their families felt that they deserved an exemption or discharge although they were not eligible under these guidelines, they then appealed to the national government. President Jefferson Davis and the secretary of war were the only leaders given the authority to grant such a special reprieve. General Order 9, Adjutant and Inspector General's Office, 25 June 1861, *The War of the Rebellion: A Compilation of the Official Records of the Union and Confederate Armies* (hereafter cited as *Official Records*) (Washington: Government Printing Office, 1880–1901), ser. 4, 1:398–99; General Order 58, ibid. ser. 4, 2:51; General Order 82, 11 October 1862, ibid., ser. 4, 2:160–62.

3. Historian Paul Escott argues that lower-class families turned away from the Confederacy, while George Rable and Drew Gilpin Faust tell the story of women who became disillusioned with the Southern cause. Escott, *After Secession: Jefferson Davis and the Failure of Confederate Nationalism* (Baton Rouge: Louisiana State University Press, 1978); Rable, *Civil Wars: Women and the Crisis of Southern Nationalism* (Urbana: University of Illinois Press, 1989); Faust, *Mothers of Invention: Women of the Slaveholding South in the American Civil War* (Chapel Hill: University of North Carolina Press, 1996). For a recent revision of this line of argument, see William A. Blair, *Virginia's Private War: Feeding Body and Soul in the Confederacy, 1861–1865* (New York: Oxford University Press, 1998). Although "nationalism" is by nature an ambiguous term, I am defining it here as the way Confederates defined themselves and their commitment to their common existence. This definition comes from Faust, *The Creation of Confederate Nationalism* (Baton Rouge: Louisiana State University Press, 1988), 2.

4. In a section specifically on letters from women to the government, George Rable argues, for example, that as they detailed their woes, "women became more protective of their families and less concerned about the future of the Confederacy." Rable, *Civil Wars,* 80; see also Escott, *After Secession,* chap. 4.

5. Amy Arnott to Secretary of War, 17 October 1862, Roll 30.

6. Sallie Robertson to Secretary Breckinridge, 26 February 1865, Roll 150; Mary Earnest to President Davis, 3 March 1862, Roll 45. Another example is the petition of Mary E. Acree to Secretary of War, 20 March 1862, Roll 29.

7. Drew Gilpin Faust calls women's participation in the petitioning process "a more explicit and bolder claim to a public voice and a political identity." Their uneasiness in writing, she suggests, arose from an acknowledgment of this new position. Faust, *Mothers of Invention*, 162–63. Evaline Turner to Secretary Randolph, 1 August 1863, Roll 75; Margaret A. Easterling to President Davis, 8 December 1862, Roll 45. Another example: Mary Early to President Davis, 14 September 1862, Roll 30.

8. Law published in the Proceedings of the Confederate Congress, House of Representatives, 20 January 1863, *Southern Historical Society Papers* (Wilmington, N.C.: Broadfoot Publishing Company, 1991) 47:160–61.

9. T. T. Tredway to Secretary Randolph, 26 July 1862, Roll 75; U.S. Population Census, Prince Edward County, Va., 1860, p. 919.

10. Two historians of Confederate nationalism have highlighted this call for a return to the virtuous eighteenth-century society of the founders. George Rable argues that Southerners developed and embraced a political culture that rejected antebellum party politics in favor of a unified political system promoting virtue over self-interest. He goes on to say that appeals to republicanism were used effectively to bind slaveholders and nonslaveholders together, concluding that with "denials of personal ambition, warnings of corruption and conspiracy—Southerners well understood the language of republicanism." Rable, *The Confederate Republic: A Revolution against Politics* (Chapel Hill: University of North Carolina Press 1994), 13. Drew Faust likewise suggests that republican ideals were a source of Confederate nationalism. Politicians condemned self-interest and market values, she notes, and were joined by evangelical clergymen who decried Yankee materialism. Together their calls for virtue created a basis for Confederate unity (even if, as Faust argues, that basis proved to be weak). Faust, *The Creation of Confederate Nationalism*.

11. As David Potter once suggested, "War harnesses the motives of self-interest, which ordinarily pull in various directions, and causes them all to pull in the same direction and thus to reinforce the spirit of nationalism." Potter, "The Historian's Use of Nationalism and Vice Versa," *American Historical Review*, vol 67, no. 4 (July 1962): 937. I would suggest that in the case of the Confederate South, these centripetal forces of war—which no citizen could deny required everyone's help and sacrifice—would have made Southerners more receptive to appeals to republican virtue.

12. R. S. Ryland to Secretary Seddon, 16 December 1862, Roll 30; U.S. Population Census, King William County, Va., 1860, 568.

13. Mrs. S. M. Evatt to Secretary of War, 17 February 1863, Roll 90; Citizens of Neshoba County, Miss., to Secretary Randolph, 24 August 1862, Roll 30.

14. For more on the centrality of neighborhoods to Southern society, see Robert Kenzer, *Kinship and Neighborhood in a Southern Community: Orange County, North Carolina, 1849–1881* (Knoxville: University of Tennessee Press, 1987), and Robert McMath Jr., "Community, Region, and Hegemony in the Nineteenth-Century South," in *Towards a New South?: Studies in Post–Civil*

War Southern Communities, ed. Orville Vernon Burton and Robert C. McMath Jr. (Westport, Conn.: Greenwood Press 1982), 281–95.

15. Confederate officials—at least on the state level—recognized local communities' ability to take care of themselves and even relied on that ability. In Virginia, for example, the General Assembly voted in 1863 to give county governments the right to levy a tax-in-kind and to impress goods for families of soldiers. For more on the case of Virginia, see Blair, *Virginia's Private War,* 95.

16. Historian Paul Escott, in his study of these same petitions, did find evidence of soldiers scheming for their own discharge through the petitions. He cites two examples of this, but I found no concrete evidence of it in my survey of these petitions. Escott, *After Secession,* 107.

17. Proceedings of the Confederate Congress reveal what a source of insecurity not serving may have been for men. In a debate over a conscription bill, several legislators launched into tirades about all the "skulkers" who remained at home rather than fighting. Those men at home probably could not help but feel this pressure. Proceedings of the Confederate Congress, House of Representatives, 21 January 1863, *Southern Historical Society Papers,* 47: 173–75.

18. Citizens of Shelby and Bibb Counties, Ala., to Secretary of War, [?] October 1862, Roll 30.

19. Mrs. J. E. Anderson to President Davis, 20 September 1864, Reel 118.

20. Citizens of Forsyth County, Ga., to the Secretary of War, 25 March 1864, Roll 135.

21. The fates of the men referred to in these petitions is unknown; neither of the petitions is clear as to the secretary of war's decision. Jane Elliott to Secretary of War, 30 March 1863, Roll 90; "Ladies of Madison County, Mississippi," to Major General Earl Vandorn, [?] 1863, Roll 45.

22. Sarah Dicky to Secretary Seddon, 17 November 1863, Roll 90; U.S. Population Census, Scriven County, Ga., 1860, p. 133.

23. W. D. Slaton to Secretary Seddon, 27 April 1864, Roll 145; Almira P. Acors to President Davis, 23 March 1862, Roll 29. For more on the Acors family, see U.S. Population Census, Spotsylvania County, Va., 1860, pp. 220, 362, 363, 366, 376.

24. Paul Escott, for example, argues that a "powerful tradition of individualism" endowed Southerners with "an assertive sense of themselves and their rights." This idea propelled Southerners to protect their rights by protesting through means including petitions to the government. Escott, *After Secession,* 102.

25. Of the 205 petitions examined for this study, only 14 clearly received the special discharge or exemption directly from the president or secretary. This was certainly fewer than the general rate at which Confederate laws automatically exempted men. In Virginia, for example, by 1864 Confederate laws made it possible for 25,063 men (14 percent) to receive exemptions, while 153,876 served in the army. Likewise, in North Carolina, 38,166 (or 30 per-

cent) were exempted, while 88,457 served. Report of the Bureau of Conscription, 25 January 1864, *Official Records,* ser. 4, 3:103; Mary Adkins and citizens of Sussex County, Va., to Secretary Seddon, 4 November 1863, Roll 57.
For more on Mary Adkins and her family see U.S. Population Census, Sussex
County, Va., 1860, p. 410.

26. In 1862, 81 percent of the petitions in this sample went unanswered.
That figure declined to 7 percent by 1864. Mrs. C. J. Dungan to Secretary Seddon, 28 September 1863, Roll 90; Maggie Edmondson to Secretary Seddon,
12 June 1863, Roll 90; Citizens of Edgefield District, S.C., 24 May 1864, Roll
145; Rebecca Miller and Neighbors of Shenandoah County, Va., 8 February
1864, Roll 135.

27. George Rable, in *The Confederate Republic,* outlines this conflict most
clearly. Confederate leaders may have been united in their allegiance to abstract republican principles, but they could not agree on the application of
these principles to the reality of war. Some leaders identified with Jefferson
Davis and emphasized the central nation as the focus of republican virtue;
they therefore supported a centralized war effort. Others aligned themselves
more with Alexander Stephens and viewed individual liberty as the most effective means for mobilizing virtue in support of the war. These leaders—
whom Rable labels "libertarian"—opposed policies, such as conscription, that
would expand the national government's power over the people.

28. Proceedings of the House 20, 21, 29 August 1862, *Southern Historical
Society Papers,* 45:189, 200, 273; Proceedings of the House, ibid., 46:167.

29. Proceedings of the House, 20, 26 August 1862, *Southern Historical Society Papers,* 45:188, 238; Proceedings of the House, 3, 11 February 1863, ibid.,
48:46, 101; Proceedings of the House, 21 December 1863, ibid., 50:94. The responsibility for families assumed by states as the war progressed is most clearly
described in Escott, *After Secession,* chap. 5. I would not go so far as to argue, as
Escott does, that the states' help encouraged civilians to give up on the national government.

30. Laws published in the Proceedings of the Confederate Congress, Senate, 21 April 1862, House of Representatives, 13 March 1862, *Southern Historical Society Papers,* 44:128–29, 59; see also Escott, *After Secession,* 142–43; Citizens
of Abbeville district, S.C., to Secretary of War, [?] 1863, Roll 90.

31. Eliza Adams and Daughters to President Davis, [?] 1862, Roll 30.

32. Citizens of Henry County, Ala., to Secretary Seddon, 12 June 1863,
Roll 99.

33. Citizens of Nash County to Secretary of War, 27 June 1862, Roll 30;
Citizens of Lewisburg, Tenn., to President Davis, 20 October 1862, Roll 75.

34. Citizens of Randolph County, N.C., to Hon. T. S. Ashe, 5 September
1862, Roll 30; Citizens of [?] to Secretary of War, 7 April 1862, Roll 45.

35. Citizens of [?] Settlement to Secretary of War, 14 October 1863, Roll
45. Such soldiers, however, were probably not severely disabled. If they had
been the government would already have discharged them. Confederate laws

did allow for the automatic discharge of soldiers for health reasons. Grounds for a disability discharge included: "blindness, excessive deafness, permanent lameness . . . confirmed consumption, large incurable ulcers, and chronic contagious diseases of the skin." From General Order 58, Adjutant and Inspector General's Office, War Department, 14 August 1862, *Official Records,* ser. 4, 2:51.

36. Citizens of Chesterfield County, Va., to Secretary Randolph, 5 September 1862, Roll 30.

37. Daughtry requested a temporary leave from the army, or a "furlough," for her son. In most cases furloughs were granted outside the bureaucracy of the national government by a soldier's commanding officer. These officers were known to vary in their inclination to grant furloughs or not. Apparently this legislation would make it possible for farmers to provide such services to their communities without being subject to the whims of a commanding officer. Kitty Daughtry and five neighbors to President Davis, 20 June 1863, Roll 90; U.S. Population Census, Sampson County, N.C., 1860, p. 1028; Proceedings of the Confederate House of Representatives, 30 January 1864, *Southern Historical Society Papers,* 50:347–48.

38. Citizens of Wilson, Nash, and Johnson Counties, N.C. to Secretary of War, [?] 1863, Roll 45; Eliza Adams to President Davis, [?] 1862, Roll 30.

39. D. Alexander to President Davis, 28 September 1862, Roll 30; Citizens of Franklin County, Miss., to Secretary of War, 3 March 1863, Roll 90; Amy Arnott to Secretary Randolph, 17 October 1862, Roll 30; Mary Evans to President Davis, [?] 1862, Roll 45.

40. It is important to recognize that Southerners distinguished between the government and the greater cause. Frustration with one did not mean disillusionment with the other. This bears true what David Potter once suggested: "There is a great difference between the nation and the political state," and historians must not confuse them. Potter, "The Historian's Use of Nationalism," 928; J. T. Wellbourne to Secretary Seddon, 22 September 1864, Roll 145; Martha L. Nelson to President Davis, [?] 1864, Roll 150.

41. Elizabeth Patterson to Secretary of War, 23 March 1865, Roll 150.

42. Historian William Blair has argued that in 1864 Confederate policymakers "began to pay more attention to the needs of small slaveholders, nonslaveholding farmers, and soldiers' families." *Virginia's Private War,* 81. For more on these policies, see Proceedings of the House, 7, 30 January 1864, *Southern Historical Society Papers,* 50:347–48; Proceedings of the House, 23 February 1865, ibid., 52:143, 390; see also Escott, *After Secession,* chap. 5.

43. Historians who argue that Southerners lost the "will" to fight tend to downplay expressions of Confederate loyalty and place more emphasis on statements of family distress as testimony of Southerners' feelings about the war. I would argue that both expressions should be taken seriously because as the petitioners demonstrate, the two could coexist.

44. This view of loyalty follows in the spirit of David Potter's 1962 essay,

"The Historian's Use of Nationalism." In this article he suggests that other allegiances, such as the family and community, can intersect and even potentially bolster one's loyalty to a nation. This is true, according to Potter, because individuals tend to give their loyalty to institutions that "protect" other allegiances, such as family. I am departing from him, however, in that I do not believe Confederates remained loyal to the cause simply because the Confederate government protected their families. That was not always the case. Instead, the relationship between family and the Confederate government was far more ambiguous, as the rejected petitions suggest. Potter, "The Historian's Use of Nationalism," 924–50.

45. Historians Gary Gallagher, William A. Blair, and Anne S. Rubin have recently made strong arguments suggesting that Confederates could maintain an allegiance to the South's larger war goals while still growing weary of the war's impact on their lives. See Gallagher, *The Confederate War* (Cambridge: Harvard University Press, 1997); Blair, *Virginia's Private War*; and Rubin, "Redefining the South: Confederates, Southerners, and Americans, 1863–1868" (Ph.D. diss., University of Virginia, 1998).

✴

FIVE

"HIGH WITH COURAGE AND HOPE"

The Middleton Family's Civil War

Judith Lee Hunt

On 23 February 1865, Union troops arrived at Middleton Place plantation outside Charleston, and slaves greeted them with "numerous demonstrations of joy." After enjoying "their dinner comfortably" in Williams Middleton's "old dining room," the troops pillaged and destroyed the family seat. As the Union officers burned the main house, the flanker building that contained the library, and numerous other outbuildings, some of the slaves chose a different but equally symbolic target: they ransacked the handsome marble mausoleum set in the midst of the elegant garden, opened the caskets, and cast the "decayed remnants of humanity outside."[1]

The slaves' desecration of the crypt is an apt metaphor for the dramatic rise and fall of Low Country South Carolina's plantocracy. Three generations of Middletons rested in the vaults, including Mary Williams Middleton, who brought the plantation into the family; her son, Arthur Middleton, a signer of the Declaration of Independence; and Williams's father, Henry Middleton, state governor and minister to Russia. They had built and maintained the Middleton empire, and they bought and exploited the ancestors of the slaves who took final revenge by destroying the tombs and exercising their newfound freedom. Leaving the big house to the soldiers, the slaves struck at a more personal target, one that represented the pride and prejudice of both their present and past masters. After the flames died and the plantation house fell in "a mass of ruins," the freedpeople "seem[ed] happy" and made "ready to leave for town."[2]

The degree to which the Civil War reshaped the South has been the subject of scholarly debate for decades, but for the Middleton family, the impact of the war is not open to debate. In the past decade, historians of the Civil War have looked beyond the military and economic studies that traditionally dominated the field and have instead called our attention to the social aspects of the war. However, few scholars have studied the war's impact on kinship patterns of elite planters and the consequences of slavery's demise for the idealized conception of the white Southern family. The experience of the Middletons reveals much about the effects of the Civil War on the wealthy elites that had long ruled the South. The relationships within the Williams Middleton family of South Carolina, one of the Low Country's most prominent planter families, shows this process at work. The focus here is on three sets of relationships: that between the Middletons and their brother Edward, a Union naval officer; Williams Middleton and his Low Country brothers, John Izard, Henry, and Oliver Hering; and Williams and his sister Eliza and brother-in-law J. Francis Fisher, elite Philadelphians.

The Middletons used such elaborate kinship networks to exercise their economic, social, and political power. Marriages, births, and deaths defined the processes through which Middleton family fortunes passed from generation to generation. The Middletons worked within and across generational lines to maintain their shared socioeconomic status, to manage estates, and to provide mutual assistance, and thereby created an intricate and highly integrated social economy. Their mutual socioeconomic interests helped maintain, and indeed necessitated, an expansive familial structure, one that stretched into the upper ranks of elite Philadelphia society and even into the European aristocracy.

Extended kinship patterns shaped the structure of the nuclear family of Williams and Susan Middleton and created resilient emotional, economic, and social ties. Their correspondence indicates that their travel and visiting habits, mutual economic concerns, and emotional ties went far beyond the nuclear household and included extended family members and in-laws.[3] These socioeconomic kinship ties played a crucial role in maintaining an elite family's high social status. As Bertram Wyatt-Brown argues, individuals established their own identities within this structure. Middleton kinship networks also served to monitor and control individual behavior, crucial to the maintenance of family honor. The family's public image confirmed their elite status in Low Country South Carolina and Philadelphia and linked the private family to the public sphere.[4] The Middletons' far-flung familial connections cemented their position as part of a national elite.

The Civil War drastically altered these antebellum patterns and contributed to the nuclearization of the Middleton household. As the Middleton's plantation economy faltered during the war, so too did familial ties among the Southern kin. As homefront losses mounted, bonds between the various nuclear households frayed and snapped. Kinship, the plantation economy, and slavery—the century-old institutions that had shaped the lives of the Middletons and their slaves in the antebellum period—disintegrated. Their plantations collapsed into ruin, and their slaves turned against them. Thereafter, individual interests and self-preservation became the chief concern of everyone, both black and white. No longer could the Southern branch of the Middleton family maintain their position as part of a ruling national elite.[5]

Williams Middleton once had extensive economic relationships with members of his extended family. Williams's father, Governor Henry Middleton, had ensured that the cooperative patterns nurtured in the colonial period would continue into the next generation. His complex will and heavy debts guaranteed that the economic livelihood of his offspring would be locked together, fulfilling his belief that their collective self-interest was best maintained through close kinship relationships. In 1846, Williams and his brothers John Izard and Edward were appointed executors and administrators of their father's estate. Although the property was vast and included plantations and slaves, it was encumbered by a debt of over $100,000, much of which had been accrued when Henry Middleton resided in the opulent luxury of Czar Nicholas's court. Rather than sell off part of the estate to settle these debts, Henry attempted to maintain the tangled Middleton family structure by forcing his sons to manage the estate together and pay its debts. Each of the sons—Arthur, Henry, Williams, Edward, John Izard, and Oliver—was to receive $2,000 per year, but only on the condition that there was a sufficient surplus from the estate's income after the allotment of half the net profits to debt payment.[6] The terms of the will also obliged the executors to provide for their sisters, Eliza and Catherine, and their mother, Mary Hering Middleton. The paternalistic requirement to provide for their family's well-being, as well as to ensure individual economic interests, was the chief incentive for Williams and his brothers to be actively involved in the efficient execution of their father's estate.[7]

A major source of dissatisfaction in the family arose from the fact that Henry bequeathed the remainder of his estate, which included Middleton Place plantation, the family seat, to Williams, his youngest child. Williams was his "father's favorite son, & was thus preferred before his elder brothers," but Williams, in an effort to alleviate familial resentment, agreed with his brothers "to make their shares more nearly equal." In this demonstration of concern for familial equity and order, as well as for the economic well-being of his kin, Williams sacrificed an estimated $60,000 in the redistribution of the estate. Although Williams's father had structured his estate to ensure the continuation of a kinship economy, its unequal distribution threatened the network he wanted to foster. If not for Williams's willingness to accommodate his siblings, family strife would certainly have erupted.[8]

Because of the nature of the initial bequest, the restrictions imposed on the estate by the large debt, and the informal reallocation of assets, the individual plantation economies of Williams and his siblings were inextricably linked. All had a vested interest in the well-being of each plantation, and estate management became a "joint venture" among multiple nuclear households. Like other large, prominent planter families, the Middletons sat at the center of the web of a complex "social economy."[9]

Williams assisted by John Izard, had primary responsibility for managing the estate. Both brothers frequently visited each plantation, and they did so together whenever possible. In addition, Williams often dropped by his relatives' plantations and assisted in their management and maintenance, often through financial loans and gifts or labor assistance. In 1849, for example, Williams lent his brother Oliver $867 for the construction of a rice mill. With this loan, and with additional funds and contributions of slave labor from his family, Oliver established a new plantation.[10] As executors, the brothers not only shared the responsibilities of management but also provided for the material needs of these plantations, often by barter. These shared managerial responsibilities also ensured that if one executor was unable or unwilling to perform his duties, another would be ready to step in.[11]

The Middleton family's correspondence indicates that their residence patterns and emotional ties went far beyond the individual household as counted in the census and measured in probate records as husband, wife, and children. How and where they traveled, when they visited, and what they wrote in their letters illuminates the economic and political networks among planter elites and enlarges the reality of the "household." Although planters in eighteenth-century Virginia may have experienced what Jan Lewis called a "cult of individuality," the Middletons of South Carolina did not. They understood themselves and their economic, political, social, and moral interests as being intrinsically linked to a larger whole, a kinship network that cemented their households together for generations.

The Civil War upset these long-standing networks. During the initial months of the war, relations between Williams and his Southern siblings remained stable, and visiting continued to be a regular part of their lives. With little immediate threat of violence in Charleston, Susan and Williams enjoyed a relatively peaceful life in the constant company of their Southern kin. In April and May, Henry and Ellen Middleton and Oliver Hering Middleton's family made a lengthy visit to Williams's and Susan's elegant home in Charleston. Susan's kin, including her mother, Elizabeth Pringle Smith, her brother, J. J. Pringle Smith, and her sister, Emma Smith Pringle, remained in the Low Country during the early months of the war and continued antebellum patterns of visiting. The Middletons, like most Charlestonians, expected a "speedy triumph" and reported that "the spirit of the land was high with courage and hope."[12]

Antebellum patterns of visiting between Northern and Southern kin deteriorated more rapidly. In March 1861, Williams's sister Eliza Fisher came from Philadelphia for a visit to Middleton Place with her children, Sophy and George, for what she correctly anticipated would be "most probably . . . her last visit to her family & friends in the South." Eliza and her children left shortly after the Confederate bombardment of Fort Sumter on 12 April 1861. Eliza's abrupt departure from the Low Country came at the insistence of her husband, Fisher, who worried for the safety of his wife and children. Their decision to return to Philadelphia was extremely disappointing for Williams. In a heated letter to his brother-in-law he wrote, "I should have preferred her remaining here longer & I am even now satisfied that it would have been better for both Sophy and herself to have done so could you have made up your mind to rest satisfied with such an arrangement."[13]

The intensity of combat shattered the tranquility of the initial war months. By July 1861, Williams confided to his sister Eliza that his thoughts were occupied with "the current state of affairs." While he assured her that most of her family and friends remained well and carried on in their "usual routine," he admitted that "sorrowful pangs

have been brought home to the heart of some in their severest form
. . . for two days now our own family were [sic] in grief at the intel-
ligence relating to Henry A[ugustus] M[iddleton], Jr. as one of the
victims of the accursed attempt made upon our liberties." The tragic
news of young Henry's death in battle was followed with the news
that John Middleton was serving in one of the Georgia regiments that
had suffered significant losses, and he was suspected to be among
the casualties.[14] John survived, but Henry's death was only one of the
many wartime hardships and tragedies to befall the Middletons in the
years ahead. It would become difficult for them to provide comfort
and support as the war drove them apart.

By the fall of 1861, many planters began to leave the Low Country
for safer abodes. Williams's brother Henry and his wife moved to the
"pleasant" atmosphere of the North Carolina mountains, John Izard
and his family took refuge in Summerville for a short time before
moving up-country to Darlington, and other kin, too, fled to the relative safety of the up-country. Henry reported on the gay atmosphere
among Low Country sojourners in the mountains, as well as the
luxury of being removed from the daily reminders of the war. Out of
the line of fire, Henry retained confidence in a speedy Southern victory. He assured Williams that "the reign of Terror is never a very long
reign and usually ends [with] both the downfall and destruction of its
principal ministers and most prominent agents."[15]

Such predictions proved false, and by the spring of 1862, correspondence between Williams and his brother John Izard had de-
creased. John Izard only made rare visits alone to Williams, and his
family was unable to travel; therefore, the antebellum patterns of visiting and joint management were disrupted. While extended family
members occasionally resided together in various safe havens, this did
not usually include Williams and Susan. Gradually, the entire nature of
familial communication changed. No longer did the Middletons have
the money and freedom to travel as they pleased. No longer did they
have the luxurious and spacious mansions in the Low Country and
Newport. No longer did they entertain on a lavish scale. Although the
wartime company of kin helped reduce tensions and fears, the festive
atmosphere of antebellum visiting and travel had vanished.[16]

Although Williams and Susan spent much of the war together,
there were periods of long separation. The many months Susan,
Williams, and the children spent virtually alone at Middleton Place
contributed to the nuclearization of their household. With the exception of occasional visits from Williams's nephews, Benti and Tom, who

were soldiers in the Confederate army, Williams, Susan, and their children were quite isolated compared to their convivial life in antebellum days. They no longer summered in Newport or Europe with kin; most of their larger family circle had left the Low Country, making short-term and daily visits far less frequent. Increasingly, the family turned in upon itself.

As the war continued, life for the Middletons became far more complicated, and the hardships that permanently altered the nature of the Middleton family structure began to set in. As diarist Sidney Fisher wrote in February 1861, "One of the evils of civil dissentions is that they produce discord between families & friends & great care should be taken to avoid disputes which may cause ill feelings to arise." This was certainly the case with Edward Middleton, whose service in the United States Navy took him away from Southern kin. Early in the war, their long-standing relationship nearly ended. Edward's reputation had already been compromised by a very public and scandalous divorce in 1850, and his service in the Union navy further isolated him from his family.[17]

Edward tried to explain his position to his Confederate kin. Skeptical of the necessity for and legitimacy of secession, Edward felt bound by his honor and his oath to uphold the Constitution and continue his service in the U.S. Navy. Despite his belief that secession and war were both impractical and unnecessary, he sought a commission in the Pacific so he would not have to fight kinfolk.[18] His explanation and efforts, however, made little difference to his brothers.

Edward's position as a federal naval officer not only disrupted family unity but also jeopardized the Middleton plantation economy. In August 1861, the Confederate Congress passed the Act of Sequestration, which called for the confiscation of "land, tenements, and heriditments [sic], goods and chattel" held within the Confederacy by anyone who was a citizen of the United States. Since Edward was a U.S. citizen, the Confederate government attempted to confiscate Hobonny Plantation, the most valuable of the Middleton estates, and the hundreds of slaves who lived there. Their brother's affiliation forced Williams and John Izard to confront the Confederate officials in order to preserve familial and individual interests.[19]

Although Williams and John Izard successfully protected Hobonny, the episode estranged them from their Unionist brother. For years, they had promoted Edward's naval career, but his alleged betrayal of family and region could not be forgiven. Once again, Edward had disgraced the Middleton clan. Through the war, there is virtually no mention of Edward in Williams' and John Izard's correspondence, and after the war their dealings would become overtly hostile.

The relationships between Henry, Williams, and John Izard also frayed. The Union blockade, the demands of the Confederacy for labor and foodstuffs, the decline in agricultural production, and the inflation of Confederate currency made it extremely difficult for Williams and John Izard to manage the estate. Since all the family members relied upon their annuities to support their families, they were all adversely affected by the estate's economic problems. By 1863, the Middletons, like many Southerners, began to suffer considerable hardships on the home front. Plantation management and operations were devastated. The war was going poorly for the South, the death toll was mounting, and money and supplies were scarce. Inflation soared, to reach a staggering 9,000 percent increase by 1865. The Middletons were unable to pay their creditors and settle the estate, so their debts mounted, and the annuities were not enough to support the large extended family.[20]

Production and management on the Middleton estates faltered as wartime demands and home-front hardships grew. The Union blockade made it especially difficult for the Middletons and other Low Country planters to export rice and to obtain essential imported materials and luxury goods. By November 1861, the Union army had captured Port Royal and occupied the plantations of Hilton Head and St. Helena Islands, from which they launched numerous raids on the South Carolina coast.[21]

Supplying food for the Rebel troops was a vital concern, and even in an agricultural region like the South, that was no easy task. Low Country planters, like those across the region, contributed to the Confederate war effort in large part through the provision of staples. For example, the Middletons regularly supplied rice, corn, and peas to the Confederate army, and as patriotic Confederates, they saw such contributions as their civic duty. Yet Confederate food orders placed enormous strains on their plantation economy. Numerous letters from the Middleton overseers described the difficulties they had in fulfilling the government's insatiable demand for rice.[22]

The Civil War brought a host of new hardships to Middleton Place. Coupled with the routine problems of running the estate, the deterioration of the Middletons' plantations continued year after grueling year. Procuring plantation supplies became difficult. In one report from the summer of 1864, B. T. Sellers, a Middleton overseer, complained that he was unable to buy corn because "the people are not disposed to sell for Confederate money." Adequately provisioning and caring for the large slave population in a collapsing plantation complex became exceedingly difficult, a problem that reached crisis proportions when natural disasters, including a flood in June 1862 and a drought in the summer of 1864, devastated valuable crops and left slave provisions dangerously low.[23]

By the end of the war, the plantation complex built over the course of a century by the South Carolina Middletons was virtually destroyed. The decline of the plantation system fostered a change in family structure and a nuclearization of the Middletons' household. Blockades, Confederate war demands, Union raids, and supply and labor shortages, compounded by difficulties in selling rice and the devaluation of Confederate currency, marginalized productivity and profits. In 1862, outstanding debts against the estate totaled over $110,000, and the devaluation of currency made many creditors unwilling to settle bonds while interest on them mounted. The income of the estate was not large enough or stable enough to support all the family annuities, and as a result, all of those dependent upon the funds suffered economic hardship. None of the Middletons had the material means to maintain the kinship networks of the antebellum years.

Despite the difficulties facing John Izard and Williams, their brother Henry was not sympathetic to the managerial obstacles facing the executors. He was concerned with his growing inability to provide his family with "the ordinary necessaries & comforts of life."[24] Henry wrote to his brothers to complain that before the depreciation of Confederate currency, his annuity would have allowed him "to live not only in great comfort, but in great abundance." By 1863, however, he found himself "quite at a loss to imagine how it will be possible for me to make my limited income, even under the most economical management, pay the expenses of the year." Henry complained that it cost him seven dollars to mend a pair of slave shoes, and that wheat, rice, and corn were all exceedingly expensive. He badgered his brothers for money and insisted, "I cannot help thinking that your legal advisers, if they would ponder a little on these things, would be forced to confess that they gave you very bad advise [sic]" when they recommended investing in Confederate bonds. Henry warned his brothers that "unless something is done, and done soon to change the course which things are going I can not see anything ahead but utter bankruptcy and ruin."[25]

By the summer of 1864, Henry became openly hostile and threatened legal action. Williams and John Izard tried to pay as many of

Henry's debts as possible in hopes of avoiding litigation and improving his condition. But just as Edward's Unionism permanently affected his relationship with his siblings, the dispute between Henry and his brothers continued to damage their relationship long after the war ended. Even though John Izard and Williams remained close throughout the war, out of necessity they, too, began to focus more exclusively on their nuclear households.[26]

Oliver Hering Middleton, with whom Williams had never spent as much time as with the rest of his kin, became still more isolated. After their only son, Oliver Hering Jr., died in battle in 1864, they were so completely devastated that they seemed to lose all interest in maintaining extended familial relationships. As one relative observed, "The poor Oliver Middletons! it is dreadful to see them, it is the first heavy blow they have ever had; the first time their immediate family circle had ever been broken & indeed seems hard for them to bear." Just over a year later, Oliver's wife, Susan, died, deepening his sorrow and isolation.[27]

Unlike the fraying relationships among Southern kin, those with Northern family remained strong. Although Eliza's contact and communication with her Southern kin was extremely limited, her loyalties were with the South. Such a position was not easily maintained. According to diarist Sidney Fisher, "several well-known persons, who had openly expressed secession opinions had been assaulted in the streets." Not only did Southern sympathizers face threats of "mob" violence; even "persons suspected" of such "opinions" needed protection.[28] Eliza found herself torn between the prevailing Unionism of her Northern peers and relations and her Southern family and friends.

Eliza's Philadelphia family and friends made efforts to respect her rather precarious position. Many people excused her support of secession and the Confederacy because she was "a Carolinian and her brothers, relatives, & friends" were "all involved most unfortunately in this unhappy contest." Most of her friends found her position therefore "excusable" and broached the subject of the War "with great forbearance," but not everyone humored her. On at least one occasion, Bet, the wife of Sidney Fisher, could no longer refrain from voicing her opinions about the war. As the conversation continued, Bet became a "good deal excited" and raved "about the outrages of the South." Eliza, offended by her cousin-in-law's statements, rose to the defense of the Confederacy, and the conversation among family and friends quickly turned uncomfortable for everyone. While such unpleasant episodes were eventually forgotten, a cloud of potential conflict hung over such social gatherings.[29]

Other episodes suggest that as Eliza's environment became increasingly anti-Southern, she more consciously identified herself as a Southerner. Her brother-in-law Sidney Fisher noticed this subtle change when Eliza made what would be her last trip to the antebellum South. Her choice of escorts for this journey was Pierce Butler, owner of a vast estate in Low Country Georgia and longtime resident of Philadelphia. That Eliza would travel with Mr. Butler was one "of the oddest" changes in relations. Eliza was an intimate friend of English actress Fanny Kemble, Butler's ex-wife, and Eliza's husband, Fisher, was the trustee of Mrs. Kemble's estate. Eliza's decision to travel with Butler was thus surprising, since she had recently been on bad terms with him and "even went so far as to refuse to speak to him." The travel arrangements were not simply a matter of convenience, for their friendship had been "renewed" in "a bond of sympathy."[30]

Eliza's resolve to support the Confederacy proved difficult, and at times she wished for nothing more than a peaceful reconciliation between the North and the South. Williams refused to let his sister take a position of peaceful neutrality, though, and was determined to keep her from falling under the prevailing opinions of her environment. Whenever he was able to pass correspondence safely to Eliza, he took the opportunity to remind his sister of her Southernness as well as her obligation to support the Confederate cause. Speaking to Eliza, "of course, as a Carolinian," he reminded her that "to speak of peace as you understand it" is "revolting to our feelings." Williams vehemently informed his sister that "extermination" was a better "fate" for the South than the "reestablishment of the union." To strengthen Eliza's resolve, her brother reminded her that "it was never regarded as a compliment to call a man a yankee" and that "to propose to us to assume it &, try to give it respectability among the nations of the earth, is nothing short of insanity." Although Williams expressed regret for speaking "so plainly" to his sister, he assured her it was "better to give you some pain than to leave you & others under delusions which might lead to worse consequences."[31]

Williams seized the rare opportunities to keep Eliza informed of the latest news concerning her friends and family in the war-torn South. Periodically Williams sent her a "present catalogue of the misfortunes of our nearest friends." Cut off from her dearest friends and relations, Eliza endured painful "catalogues" such as "Robert Pringle & Julius Alston have both joined the noble band of martyrs that we have to mourn for."[32] These letters, at the most basic level, provided information and helped maintain contact between family members divided by war, but more subtly, they also worked to reinforce Eliza's Southern identity.

Things were not so clearly demarcated for Eliza's husband, Fisher. Although an anti-abolitionist, he was torn between his national senti-ments, his constitutional views, and the emotional bonds of family. Fisher, a nationalist, and Williams, a signer of the South Carolina Or-dinance of Secession, had carried on a heated debate over secession and slavery in the 1850s, and Fisher's initial commitment to the Union's war aims fueled the debate.

Williams ridiculed his brother-in-law's support of the national government, asking: "Why should you consent to do what you do not approve of & know to be wrong? Why lend your influence to uphold evil deeds? Why refrain from denouncing that mad & malignant crew who have proposed themselves of absolute & unauthorized power at Washington?"[33]

Fisher's commitment to the Union faltered as the war continued. His change of heart was probably motivated by a sense of familial loy-alty and duty.[34] Indeed, as the war dragged on, Fisher became an ar-dent supporter of the South, despite the ostracism he experienced from his Northern kin and fellow Philadelphians.[35] Fisher expressed his views in an 1862 letter to his son, George. He wrote, "God grant this may very soon [be over] but I doubt it as the violent measures of the abolitionists in Congress are likely to drive the slaveholders to des-peration." Even war could not obliterate his admiration for his wife's brothers; "I hope you will always assert that however much mistaken the South may be—however criminal according to [the] view of the Constitution . . . Our friends & relations are still honorable and high minded men." Fisher adopted the Southern line and observed that Southerners were driven to rebel by Northern abolitionists' at-tacks. While he rejoiced at Union military success, he warned that if victory was "followed by the destruction of general confiscation and emancipation, I shall think our success almost as deplorable as defeat would be." In his view, the federal government was duty-bound "to protect slavery & put down northern abolitionists."[36]

Fisher's ironic turnabout was fostered in large part by the hardships his Southern kindred faced. Having always respected the "grandeur" of the Middleton family and their proud history, he was distressed by their precipitous decline. After all, Fisher had quite consciously mar-ried into this prominent family, whose destruction could only ad-versely affect him and his children. The farther Williams sank, the more Fisher came to his support.[37]

By the spring of 1864, both Eliza and Fisher hoped for a Confederate victory and were "thus thorough partizans [sic] of the South: denouncing with unmeasured bitterness, Mr. Lincoln, the government, and the northern people."[38] Much to the dismay and embarrassment of many Philadelphians, both Eliza and Fisher expressed "the hope & belief that the rebels" would "eventually triumph." Fisher, a former Unionist, now described Lincoln as "an ignorant blackguard," the government as "corrupt & tyrannical," and Northerners as "a mere mob." Such opinions were considered "trash" by loyal Philadelphians and deprived Fisher "of all influence among sensible people" and the "respect of his friends." Those close to Fisher lamented this change, and his cousin Sidney sadly remarked that "everyone laughs at him."[39]

As the war came to a close and Williams was increasingly drawn into a "vortex of disaster & ruin," Fisher increasingly assumed the role of family patriarch. By the end of 1863, Williams became incapable of fulfilling familial obligations, and Fisher assumed many of the Middletons' financial responsibilities. He supported Benti's widowed mother, Paolina, provided the boarding cost for Eliza's sister, Catherine, and even paid for the care of Henry A. Middleton's insane son, who was Eliza's second cousin.[40] Williams expressed his gratitude and a "deep sense of obligation" to Fisher for the latter's "affectionate sympathy," his "kind & opportune pecuniary loan & generous proffers of assistance."[41]

A number of generalizations can be hazarded at this point. The Middleton experience suggests that, on the one hand, the Civil War contributed to the nuclearization of the planter household. Throughout the antebellum period, familial relationships among the various Middletons endured and transcended a host of troubles. Yet when the Civil War came and the plantation economy crumbled, the entire Middleton clan faced its most severe crisis. Family structures dramatically altered, ultimately resulting in the fragmentation and nuclearization of the Middletons' extended Southern household. For the Middletons, the war was truly a fraternal war that set one Unionist brother against the rest of his kin and strained relations between Southern siblings. Because of the collapse of their plantation economy, the Southern families were forced to focus on their own immediate needs; they had few means of maintaining the complex kinship networks they had used so effectively before the war. In addition, the antebellum assumption that included slaves as part of the planters' conception of extended family evaporated as slaves deserted the plantations in droves.

Ironically, the war ultimately strengthened ties between the Northern and Southern branches of the family. As demonstrated above, the only relationship that mirrored the antebellum cooperative family pattern was that between J. Francis Fisher and his wife, Eliza Middleton Fisher of Philadelphia, and the Williams Middletons of South Carolina. While the Southern plantation system crumbled, the Fishers' lives remained relatively stable both personally and financially. Thus, they had the means and the desire to remain heavily involved in the lives of their Southern kindred. Although the war sorely strained the relationship between the Northern and Southern branches of the family, Fisher became increasingly sympathetic to the plight of the South, no doubt in part because the destruction of the Southern planter elite threatened the social and financial well-being of his immediate family and the alliance he had forged with one of the South's most prominent clans. If, as many historians have argued, the family was the bedrock of antebellum Southern slaveholding society, it should hardly be surprising that the war that destroyed slavery also fundamentally altered the Southern family, a shift exemplified by the Middleton family.

Notes

1. "Diary of Mr. Henry Orlando Marcy" (hereafter cited as Marcy Diary), 23 February 1865, photocopy in the South Carolina Historical Society, Charleston, S.C. (hereafter cited as SCHS); Williams Middleton to Eliza Middleton Fisher, 6 February 1874, Middleton Place Papers, SCHS (all Middleton correspondence is from this source unless otherwise cited); Marcy Diary, 23–25 1865; Henry Orlando Marcy, "Autobiography of Henry Orlando Marcy" (Mr. Henry Orlando Marcy IV, of St. Johnsbury, Vt., provided transcripts of pertinent references in his great-grandfather's autobiography; copies are at SCHS, Vertical File, Marcy, H.O. 30-4); Hering-Middleton Papers, SCHS, Misc. Folders, 24-62-16 (quotation); Sidney George Fisher, *A Philadelphia Perspective, The Diary of Sidney Fisher Covering the Years 1834–1871,* ed. Nicholas B. Wainwright (Philadelphia: Historical Society of Pennsylvania, 1967), 3 May 1865, p. 497 (hereafter cited as Fisher Diary); Emma Smith Pringle to Susan Middleton, 11 March 1865, Williams Middleton Collection, Caroliniana Library, University of South Carolina, Columbia, S.C.

2. Marcy Diary, 23–24 February 1865.

3. The core of the Middleton family conformed to a pattern historian Joan Cashin described as both "permeable" and "elastic," including "aunts, uncles, nieces, nephews, cousin, and in-laws who were intimate members of the family." Joan Cashin, "Structure of Antebellum Planter Families: The Ties That

Bound Us Was Strong," *Journal of Southern History* 56 (1990): 17; Catherine Clinton, *The Plantation Mistress: Woman's World in the Old South* (New York: Pantheon Books, 1982), 36–38.

4. Bertram Wyatt-Brown, *Southern Honor: Ethics and Behavior in the Old South* (New York: Oxford University Press, 1982), 34, 44, 188–222, 190–91.

5. James McPherson, "Introduction," in *Divided Houses: Gender and the Civil War,* ed. Catherine Clinton and Nina Silber (New York: Oxford University Press, 1992), xiii; James L. Roark, *Masters without Slaves: Southern Planters in the Civil War and Reconstruction* (New York: W. W. Norton, 1977), 36–37; Eric Foner, *Reconstruction: America's Unfinished Revolution* (New York: Harper & Row, 1988), 11; Maris A. Vinovskis, "Have Social Historians Lost the Civil War?: Some Preliminary Demographic Speculations," *Journal of American History* 76 (June 1989): 34–35; Wyatt-Brown, *Southern Honor,* 24–28; Daniel Kilbride, "Philadelphia and the Southern Elite: Class, Kinship, and Culture in Antebellum America" (Ph.D. diss. University of Florida, 1997).

6. For information concerning the rise of the Middleton family as members of South Carolina's Low Country elite, see Langdon Cheves, "Middleton of South Carolina," *South Carolina Historical and Genealogical Magazine* 1 (1900): 247–60. Henry Middleton, "Will of Henry Middleton," 20 June 1846, Middleton Place Papers, Microfiche Collection, SCHS.

7. "Will of Henry Middleton": Fisher Diary, 11 October 1846, pp. 190–91.

8. Ibid., 14 June 1847, p. 196.

9. John T. Schlotterbeck, "The Social Economy of an Upper Southern Community: Orange and Green Counties, Virginia, 1815–1860," in *Class, Conflict, and Consensus: Antebellum Southern Community Studies,* ed. Orville Vernon Burton and Robert C. Nash (Westport, Conn.: Greenwood Press, 1982), 4–5.

10. Correspondence between John Izard and Williams was an important element in the management of the estate. For numerous examples, see the Middleton Place Papers Microfiche, SCHS, especially between 1850 and 1863. Williams Middleton to Oliver Middleton, n.d. [1848]; Oliver Middleton to Williams Middleton, 14 September 1849, Williams Middleton Collection, Caroliniana Library; Williams Middleton to Susan Middleton, 3 October 1849.

11. John Izard Middleton to Williams Middleton, 21 May 1849; Williams Middleton to J. Francis Fisher, 26 April 1854; Williams Middleton to John Izard Middleton, 8 October 1856; Schlotterbeck, "The Social Economy," 17.

12. Alicia Hopton Middleton, *Life in Carolina and New England during the Nineteenth Century as Illustrated by Reminiscences and Letters of the Middleton Family of Charleston South Carolina and the De Wolf Family of Bristol Rhode Island* (Bristol, R.I.: Privately printed, 1929), 127; Malcolm Bell Jr., *Major Butler's Legacy: Five Generations of a Slave Holding Family* (Athens: University of Georgia Press, 1987), 345.

13. Fisher Diary, 26 March 1861, p. 384 (first quotation); Williams Middleton to J. Francis Fisher, 30 April 1861 (second quotation).

14. Williams Middleton to Eliza Middleton Fisher, 26 July 1861: John Middleton was the son of Williams's cousin Motte Middleton.

15. Middleton, *Life in Carolina and New England,* 171; Henry Middleton to Williams Middleton, 17 September 1861 (quotation). Correspondence in the Middleton Place Papers indicates that Susan's mother, brother, and sister resided in Columbia, S.C., in 1862. See also Daniel E. Smith, Alice R. Huger Smith, and Arney R. Childs, eds., *Smith Family Letters, 1860–1868* (Columbia: University of South Carolina Press, 1950).

16. For numerous examples describing multiple households residing together, see Smith, Smith, and Childs, *Smith Family Letters*; Catherine Clinton, *Tara Revisited: Women, War, and the Plantation Legend* (New York: Abbeville Press, 1995), 115; Charles P. Roland, *The Confederacy,* (Chicago: University of Chicago Press, 1960) 71–73.

17. Fisher Diary, 23 February 1861, p. 379.

18. Edward Middleton to Williams Middleton, n.d. [1861], Edward Middleton Papers, Southern Historical Collection, Wilson Library, University of North Carolina, Chapel Hill.

19. Mr. Spratt to John Izard Middleton, 18, 25 January 1862; Bell, *Major Butler's Legacy,* 346.

20. James Ford Rhodes, *History of the Civil War, 1861–1865* (New York: Frederick Ungar, 1961), 383–87; James M. McPherson, "American Victory, American Defeat," in *Why the Confederacy Lost,* ed. Gabor S. Boritt (New York: Oxford University Press, 1992), 36.

21. LeeAnn Whites, "The Civil War as a Crisis in Gender" eds. Catherine Clinton & Nina Silber, *Divided Houses: Gender and the Civil War* (New York: Oxford University Press, 1992) 7, 10, 13; Randall C. Jimerson, *The Private Civil War: Popular Thought during the Sectional Conflict* (Baton Rouge: Louisiana State University Press, 1988), 60; Roland, *The Confederacy,* 36; Archer Jones, "Military Means, Political Ends: Strategy," in Boritt, *Why the Confederacy Lost,* 74–75; Bell, *Major Butler's Legacy,* 352–59; Foner, *Reconstruction,* 3.

22. Clinton, *Tara Revisited,* 109; James M. McPherson, *Battle Cry of Freedom: The Civil War Era* (New York: Oxford University Press, 1988, 616–17; James H. Tuten, " 'Live and Die on Hobonny': The Rise, Decline, and Legacy of Rice Culture on Hobonny Plantation, 1733–1980" (master's thesis, Wake Forest University, 1992), 71.

23. John Hucks to Williams Middleton, 17 June 1862; B. T. Sellers to Williams Middleton, 4 February, 29 June 1864; McPherson, *Battle Cry of Freedom,* 440–42; Clement Eaton, *A History of the Southern Confederacy* (New York: Macmillan, 1954), 140–43; Roark, *Masters without Slaves,* 50; Tuten, " 'Live and Die on Hobonny,' " 72.

24. Henry Middleton to Williams Middleton, 13 December 1863, 2 February 1864 (quotation); McPherson, *Battle Cry of Freedom,* 438–40; Frank E. Vandiver, *Their Tattered Flags: The Epic of the Confederacy* (New York: Harper's Magazine Press, 1970), 166–67, 242–43.

25. Henry Middleton to Williams Middleton, 2 February 1864; see also Henry Middleton to Williams Middleton, 18, 23 February, 23 July 1864; John Izard Middleton to Williams Middleton, 5 August 1864; Roland, *The Confederacy*, 74, 88–89; Roark, *Masters without Slaves*, 49–50.

26. John Izard Middleton to Williams Middleton, 16, 24 November 1864 Williams Middleton Papers, Caroliniana Library; Roland, *The Confederacy*, 174.

27. Oliver Hering Middleton to Williams Middleton, 26 February 1864. Oliver Hering Middleton Jr. died in the Battle of Matadequin 30 May 1864; his mother Susan Matilda Harriet Chisolm, died 18 October 1865. Smith, Smith, and Childs, *Smith Family Letters*, 110. See also George C. Rable, *Civil Wars: Women and the Crisis of Southern Nationalism* (Urbana: University of Illinois Press, 1989), 62; Clinton, *Tara Revisited*, 64, 114.

28. Fisher Diary, 26 March 1861, p. 384; Clinton, *Tara Revisited*, 56–57.

29. Fisher Diary, 23 February 1861, p. 379.

30. Ibid., 26 March 1861, p. 383.

31. Williams Middleton to Eliza Middleton Fisher, 19 December 1862.

32. Williams Middleton to Eliza Middleton Fisher, 17 October 1863.

33. Williams Middleton to J. Francis Fisher, 30 April 1861.

34. Fisher Diary, 8 February 1862, p. 416; Williams Middleton to J. Francis Fisher, 30 April 1861; Rable, *Civil Wars*, 180.

35. Fisher Diary, 25 December 1863, p. 464; ibid., 16 March 1864, p. 468.

36. J. Francis Fisher to George Fisher, 26 February 1862; Fisher Diary, 13 July 1862, p. 431; Bell, *Major Butler's Legacy*, 348.

37. For a detailed discussion of Northern political ideology and the changes in ideology as the war progressed, see George Fredrickson, *The Inner Civil War: Northern Intellectuals and the Crisis of Union* (New York: Harper Torchbooks, 1968).

38. Fisher Diary, 25 December 1863, p. 464; ibid., 16 March 1864 p. 468 (quotation).

39. Ibid., 16 March 1864, p. 468.

40. Ibid., 25 December 1863, p. 464.

41. Williams Middleton to J. Francis Fisher, 1 July 1865, Hering-Middleton Collection.

SIX

"THE WHITE WINGS OF EROS"

Courtship and Marriage in
Confederate Richmond

E. Susan Barber

There is something in the atmosphere on even sulphurous battle days," opined a writer in the Richmond newspaper *Southern Punch* in September 1863, "that makes the white wings of Eros—the pleasantest and the sweetest of the minor gods of Olympus—swift to reach the fair votaries of hymen."[1] Richmonders frequently spoke of a "marriage frenzy" that gripped the wartime capital, propelling large numbers of Confederate brides and grooms down the road to wedded bliss. "There is now a list of *marriage* notices that would brighten the eyes of a spinster," crowed a Richmond soldier in a letter to his sister-in-law in March 1863, "and make her think that her turn would come next."[2] "There seems to be a real marrying mania afloat here," Richmonder Alice Wise wrote on 11 November 1864. "A young lady called to see me a few weeks ago & told me in the course of conversation [that] she knew of 52 weddings to take place this Fall & Winter."[3]

Wise's image of brides and grooms in the Confederate capital rushing to solemnize their vows was echoed in a letter written by another woman two months later, recounting the story of a hapless bride who was prevented from attending her own church wedding. "Christmas has passed off very gaily in Richmond," a woman named Jane wrote her friend Mrs. Guthrie. "I never knew of more weddings or parties. As for marrying, it has become a perfect passion; there were 96 marriages in twenty days. The mania to marry is only equaled by the curiosity to witness the ceremony. An acquaintance of mine was married a few days since, & the crowd at the church was so dense, she could not get in & had to go back and have the ceremony performed at home."[4] One Richmond wag described this craze for attending weddings in a decidedly military tone. "Those near the altar acted as infantry," he wrote. "Those a little further back mounted the benches and pews, while a few guerrillas captured the chancel."[5] Even as late as the desperate winter of 1865, when the Confederacy's hopes had all but vanished, Ordnance Department chief Josiah Gorgas reported that "gaiety continues among the young people, and there is much marriage and giving in marriage," although everyone was "depressed and somber" about the war's progress.[6]

These descriptions of Richmond's marriage mania seem to stand at odds with the pattern found by historians of a flurry of hastily arranged unions in locales facing an eminent battlefield departure followed by long periods of marital drought due to a shortage of marriage-age men.[7] While these observations are no doubt accurate for rural Southern communities, evidence from Richmond, Virginia, suggests that a different dynamic was at work there and perhaps in other Southern cities where the Confederate government established a base of operation. Instead of becoming what Drew Faust has called a "world of femininity," Richmond was actually awash with thousands of Confederate soldiers and male government workers, who provided Richmond women with ample opportunities for courtship and marriage.[8]

One measure of the effects of the Civil War on Confederate marriage is the age at first marriage. If Confederate women in Richmond were, indeed, anxious to avoid an unhappy state of perpetual spinsterhood, then they theoretically might have rushed into marriages at ages earlier than the norm of twenty-one years for women in the antebellum South, for fear their potential partners would be killed in battle. Information derived from a sample of the Richmond marriage register for the period from 1860 to 1880 paints a somewhat different picture, however.[9]

Despite perceptions that a marriage mania was sweeping the city, the Richmond sample reveals that most white Richmond brides continued to make their first trip down the aisle between the ages of twenty-one and twenty-two, slightly older than the ages noted for white slaveholding women in the antebellum plantation South, but consistent with findings in the town of Petersburg, Virginia, between 1784 and 1860.[10] Only twice during the entire eighteen-year period did the median age for the city's white brides rise to the age of twenty-three: once in 1867—a time when white women and men in Reconstruction Richmond had to sign an oath of allegiance to the United States government before a marriage license could be issued—and for a second time in 1873, when a reduction in wages for many workers caused by the Panic of 1873 may have induced some to postpone their weddings (Table 1).[11]

The statistics on age at first marriage for white grooms fluctuated more erratically, ranging from a low of twenty-four years of age in 1877 to a high of twenty-eight years in 1865 (Table 1). The later age at first marriage in 1865 may indeed support the argument that some white Richmond grooms, for whatever reason, had decided to forgo taking a bride until the war was over. However, the difference between

Table 1 Median age at first marriage, white brides and grooms, Richmond, Virginia, 1860–1880

Year	Bride's age	Groom's age
1860	21.0	25.0
1861	22.0	27.5
1862	22.0	26.0
1863	22.0	25.0
1864	—	—
1865	21.0	28.0
1866	—	—
1867	23.0	27.0
1868	—	—
1869	21.0	26.0
1870	22.0	25.0
1871	21.0	25.0
1872	21.0	27.0
1873	23.0	26.0
1874	22.0	26.0
1875	22.0	25.5
1876	21.0	26.0
1877	21.0	24.0
1878	21.5	26.0
1879	22.0	25.0
1880	21.0	27.0

Source: Marriage Register, Richmond, Va., 1860–1880, Library of Virginia, Richmond.

the median ages at first marriage for white brides and grooms continued to range between three and seven years for the entire period
between 1860 and 1880, a figure consistent with white brides and
grooms in antebellum Petersburg. When analyzed on the basis of the
groom's occupation, middle-class professional men tended to marry
somewhat later, around thirty years of age in Richmond as compared
to twenty-eight in Petersburg. For white Richmond artisans, however,
the age differential between brides and grooms narrowed to four
years, a span identical to the one for Petersburg, Virginia, during the
first half of the nineteenth century.[12]

One reason for the small difference among age at first marriage
among white Richmond brides is that wartime Richmond did not
experience the severe shortage in marriage-age men that rural communities sometimes faced. Less than a month after Virginia's secession
from the Union, Richmond became the capital of the Confederate
States of America. As the Confederate Congress began holding ses-
sions in the Virginia Capitol and government departments created offices in the U.S. Custom House, the Monumental Hotel, and the Mechanics' Institute, Richmond was transformed from an Upper South
industrial metropolis into a military and political enclave that was the
heart and soul of the Southern Confederacy. Thousands of men
flocked to the city, either to work in one of the government departments or to train for duty in the Confederate army. The Central Fair
Grounds were converted into a kind of boot camp for new recruits,
and the bugle sounds of reveille and taps echoed throughout the city.

The presence of such large numbers of young men was not lost on
the city's white single women. "Every railroad train that arrived in
Richmond bore its freight of soldiers," Sally Putnam later wrote,
"[and] from every direction around the city, the white tents of the soldiers were seen dotting the landscapes."[13] Of the 222 white marriages
in the sample that were performed between April 1861 and April 1865,
nearly 40 percent involved grooms who identified their occupations
as soldier or sailor, or men who worked in a war-related occupation
that was exempt from field duty—contract surgeons, civilian hospital
workers, government gunsmiths and munitions workers, machinists,
blacksmiths, clerks, telegraphers, or ironworkers.

Letters and diaries written by some of the city's single white
women also point to a surplus rather than a shortage of marriageable
white men. "Between eight and ten thousand men went down Main
St. this afternoon, on their way to Yorktown," wrote a sixteen-year-old
Richmond diarist in April 1862.

They did not march in one connected line, but there was so little distance between them that to an observer it was splendid. It was very tanatalising to me to hear the drum and the cheering and to be able to see nothing but their bayonets and the tops of their heads. It is wicked in me to wish that I had gone out so that I might see them, and not to wish that I had gone to church, but I love the soldiers so much, that I forget almost everything else when I get to thinking about them.[14]

Troops marching through the capital blew kisses to Richmond women who waved handkerchiefs or tossed them pincushions, bookmarks, pocket Bibles, and other mementos. Soldiers stationed in the city paid sometimes nightly visits to girls in the community or took them on walks through Capitol Square. "On Franklin St. on many a fine afternoon during the winter," Louly Wright later wrote, "it was a lovely sight to watch the promenaders going up and down. The officers on leave for a few days made the best of their holiday and the pretty girls were decked out in the best finery they could muster."[15] When a regiment of soldiers marched past Miss Pegram's School for Girls on a snowy winter day, one of the female students tossed a snowball into the marching line, and a snowball battle ensued.[16]

During a three-week period in March 1862, one young woman received six visits from at least four different gentlemen callers—Confederate officers, who often visited in pairs—and made three trips to the campgrounds, where she was entertained with band concerts, dress parades, or company drills. On one of these excursions, she also toured a young officer's private quarters.[17] "Yesterday, we went out to the Carolina encampment with Mr. Ford," she wrote on 22 May 1861. "We had a delightful walk and when we got there the place was so pretty that we did not want to come home untill very late. The tents were fixed in rows under trees, and the soldiers were gathering in groups preparatory to dress parade, we saw that before we came away."[18] Mollie Lyne and Lucy Bowles each received Valentine poems from soldiers from Company G of the First Virginia Volunteers, professing love and inviting them to attend a Valentine's Day party.[19]

Young women who worked in the government departments also encountered admirers—and potential husbands—among their co-workers. A clerk in the Confederate Ordnance Bureau, Mattie Pierce enjoyed the attention of two workplace beaux during early June 1864. Eugene Desdunes, a suitor who worked in the office of the Second Auditor, sent Pierce a basket of cherries. "Please receive these few cherries," he wrote in an attached note. "They cannot be eaten up by a most [sic] lovely mouth than yours."[20] Pierce's second admirer, a post office clerk who signed himself only as "E.C.B.," wrote to her on 10 June 1864, proposing an assignation. "Take the Capital Square on your way home at 3 o'clock," he suggested. "I will be *around*."[21] Lettie Jones, a Maryland refugee and a clerk in the Confederate Treasury office, was courted and later wed by a Confederate soldier from New Orleans, Louisiana.[22]

Constance Cary embarked on a wartime courtship with her future husband, Burton Norvell Harrison, while they were both employed by the Confederate government, Cary in one of the city's military hospitals and Harrison as an aide to Jefferson Davis. After a number of horseback rides to local battlefield sites and walks to Hollywood Cemetery, the couple became engaged; they married in 1867, after Harrison was released from a prisoner-of-war camp in Point Lookout, Maryland.[23] War Department clerk Parke Chamberlayne fell in love with, and married, former Confederate soldier George W. Bagby, a journalist who also worked for the Confederate government.[24] Rosa Young fell in love with her future husband, a doctor, while the two cared for her wounded brother at Seabrook Hospital.[25] David Gaines, a Richmond soldier assigned to Company B of the Thirty-eighth Light Artillery, repeatedly went a.w.o.l. from his Petersburg location during the fall and winter of 1864 to return to Richmond and court cartridge maker Delia Daily. On one occasion, he was forced to sit astride a cold cannon barrel all night long as punishment. They were married on 26 August 1866.[26]

Wartime flirtations occasionally drew naive young women into ill-advised or illicit relationships. Chimborazo Hospital surgeon Stephen Habersham, for example, engaged in simultaneous courtships with three unsuspecting Richmond women—Jinny Pollard, Alice Magill, and Carrie Stuart.[27] Lettie Jones's older sister, Ella, became enmeshed in an affair with an older Confederate officer with a wife and children in Missouri. In March 1865, Ella probably suffered an abortifacient-induced miscarriage in a Richmond boardinghouse.[28] In February 1867, Emily Pitts Phillips was shot in the head and strangled by her husband James Jeter Phillips, a Richmond soldier she married after nursing him back to health on her family's Essex County farm.[29] In 1870, Phillips was executed for his wife's murder.

Far more of these relationships, however, resulted in enduring—if not always blissful—unions. Although their marriage was marked by war-related tensions that often led them to live apart, Parke and George Bagby's marriage survived until George's death in 1883. Constance and Burton Harrison were happily married for more than thirty years. And Delia and David Gaines celebrated fifty years of wedded bliss in 1916 by passing out one-dollar gold pieces to their three oldest grandchildren.

Although Richmond brides appear not to have suffered from a want of eligible grooms, wartime scarcity, the escalating cost of wedding finery, and the proximity of Union armies compelled even affluent couples to improvise on their wedding plans and sometimes to marry "on the fly."[30] For example, the ceremony of Major and Mrs. John Harvie was interrupted when a troop of Union soldiers arrived at the bride's home, Idlewood, hoping to arrest him. While the wedding party hid on a remote section of the plantation, Union soldiers feasted on the ham, turkey, and tropical fruit intended for the reception. The Harvies were wed the following day by a justice of the peace who was summoned to the home by a female slave. The bride wore the traditional satin dress, but one she had borrowed from a "city aunt."[31] Parke and George Bagby courted all through 1861 and 1862, sometimes even sharing the same boardinghouse, although not the same dinner table. They were married at St. Paul's Church on 16 February 1863, and after a brief wedding trip to her "Uncle Faltback's" farm in Lynchburg, the Bagbys returned to their work for the Confederate government and set up housekeeping in a Church Hill boardinghouse.[32]

Once married, Richmond brides—especially those with small children—occasionally became snared in a tug-of-war between the desires of their soldier husbands and their parents' anxieties about their safety. Such appears to have been the case for Leila Turpin Willis, the wife of Larkin Willis, a Richmond tobacco agent and an engineer for the Confederate army.[33] Between July 1861 and January 1864, Leila Willis made at least eight trips—many of several months' duration—between her parents' home in Richmond and the country home north of the city that she shared with her husband and two small children, a toddler named Gertrude and an infant.[34] Leila's mother, Rebecca Turpin, doted on her grandchildren and frequently exerted undue pressure on her daughter to visit, alternately citing loneliness, recurrent migraines, or the nearness of Yankee troops as justifications. "It is with anxious feeling that I attempt to answer your last letter," she wrote in August 1863, when the Richmond papers carried accounts of Yankee renegades in the countryside north of the city. "I am glad you are all well & safe . . . but you may be deprived of your husband & everything else soon. . . . Your father says if you can get home you had better come."[35]

On several occasions during this period, Leila Willis's decisions to accede to her parents wishes created tensions in her relationship with her husband, Larkin. A trip in May 1862, for example, separated the young couple when Leila was beginning her third pregnancy and wanted to be closer to her husband, who was on military maneuvers near the Rapidan River. "I am very sorry you can't get off," she wrote, "for I want to see you so much. I have been right sick since you left and have been in bed part of the time . . . , suffering something like I was last summer, nothing serious you know. . . . I should like to make you a visit, but I am almost too lazy to go into camp, as I have to lie down a good part of the time. . . . I hope it will not be many days before we shall be permitted to see each other. Don't let the Yankees get you."[36] Another trip to Richmond with her father in September 1863 was apparently made over Larkin Willis's objections, as evidenced in a letter Miles Turpin wrote, informing his son-in-law of the family's safe arrival. "We got along very well with the children yesterday," he wrote. "Neither of them cried or fretted the whole way. Leila was quite sad. . . . She feels very anxious & fears she has done wrong in leaving."[37]

Although Confederate women in Richmond appear to have experienced less difficulty finding a mate than their wartime rural sisters, evidence from the marriage register reveals a sadder postwar corollary concerning the ability of war widows to form a second postwar union. And it is here that the data reveals the long-term effects of the war's terrible toll on white Southern manhood.[38] The war's conclusion not only brought an end to the Confederacy; in Richmond it also signaled a contraction in the population and a departure of eligible bachelors. Between 1860 and 1863, Richmond's population swelled from 39,000 residents to more than 100,000. In 1870, after the postwar exodus of white government workers and refugees and the influx of rural blacks, the city's population stood at 51,000. By 1880, the population had reached 63,600, and the ratio of white women to white men had shifted significantly. Although there had been a thousand more white men than women in the Richmond population of 1860, by 1870 white women outnumbered men by more than 4,600.[39]

In the immediate postwar years—between 1865 and 1869—white widows married at a higher rate than white widowers. But beginning in 1874, this trend was reversed. From 1874 to 1880, white widowers remarried with far greater frequency, sometimes at rates that were double or triple those for white widows and usually to never-before-married brides who were considerably younger. Between 1867 and

1880, for example, 12.4 percent of white widowers wedded brides who were twenty or more years their junior, compared with slightly less than 1 percent of white grooms during the period from 1860 to 1865. By comparison, only one white widow for the entire period from 1860 to 1880 married a similarly younger groom (Table 2).

It is impossible to tell from the marriage register data exactly how many of these second unions were dictated by wartime losses. It is clear, however, that for white Richmond widows, remarriage after the war was not always an option, a circumstance that no doubt relegated larger numbers of women to old ages marked by poverty and loneliness.

Disturbed by the plight of elderly female parishoners left penniless by the war, Baptist and Episcopalian women in Richmond devoted a portion of their postwar organizational and fund-raising talents to creating homes for aged women within their denominations. In February 1875, women representing the city's white Episcopal churches

Table 2　White widows and widowers as a percent of all marriages, Richmond, Virginia, 1860–1880

Year	Widows	Widowers
1860	17.2	10.3
1861	2.9	11.4
1862	9.6	18.0
1863	11.0	26.0
1864	—	—
1865	25.0	17.4
1866	—	—
1867	24.7	17.8
1868	—	—
1869	16.5	11.5
1870	9.6	9.6
1871	7.1	13.2
1872	12.7	10.8
1873	17.3	16.3
1874	18.0	21.3
1875	6.6	26.3
1876	6.3	14.4
1877	8.6	17.3
1878	10.5	7.9
1879	8.0	16.9
1880	11.2	9.9

Source: Marriage Register, Richmond, Va., 1860–1880, Library of Virginia, Richmond.

met and formed an association "to provide a home for female mem-bers of the Protestant Episcopal Church . . . who are in reduced circumstances, and unable to procure for themselves an adequate sup-port."[40] A month later, they opened the Protestant Episcopal Church Home for Ladies in a house on Fourth Street provided by Frederick W. Hanewinckel, a wealthy benefactor and St. James's vestryman.

The Baptist Home for Aged Women was opened a few years later on 1 January 1883, the culmination of two years of energetic fund-raising begun after a mass meeting of Baptist women in 1881 at Rich-mond's First Baptist Church. By late September 1882, women from four of the city's white Baptist churches had accumulated more than $6,100 toward the purchase of a suitable building "with ample grounds, situated in the western section of the city," and had engaged the services of matron Sarah Ellett at a salary of $10 per month. In January 1883, the home was consecrated in a ceremony conducted by six of the city's Baptist clergy.[41] In that same year, twenty-five women from Richmond's five Presbyterian churches formed the Exchange for Women's Work, a charitable association for selling the domestic handi-work of needy gentlewomen made destitute by the war.[42] Located at 309 E. Franklin Street, the Women's Exchange took in more than 4,500 handmade items during its first year of operation.

Examinations of the Civil War's impact on Northern and Southern marriages have only just begun, and a great deal more research is needed to create a clear picture of how wartime casualties affected marriage patterns for white women and men in both regions of the country. The difficulty of penetrating the veil of privacy that most nineteenth-century Americans raised around their most intimate rela-tionships complicates the process.

Evidence from the Richmond marriage register suggests that re-ports of a marriage mania were probably overblown. More marriage licenses were issued and marriages celebrated during the wartime years simply because more people were living in the city at the time. Richmond's role as the Confederate capital and a city near much of the fighting in the war's eastern theater partially explains why it did not suffer the same wartime imbalance between men and women that more rural communities experienced. The same may be true for other Southern cities where the Confederacy located a portion of its gov-ernment departments: for instance, Columbia, South Carolina, or At-lanta, Georgia.

Conversely, the postwar period led to a contraction of Richmond's white population. As transient white males departed, the war's effects on the white male population could be seen more clearly in the shift-ing ratio between white women and men. As the number of white marriage-age men declined, white women in Richmond faced a world where a first or second marriage might no longer be an option. Although a few women entered into unions with Northern soldiers occupying the city, most Richmond women—like Confederate first daughter Winnie Davis—eschewed the overtures of their former enemies and chose instead to become the "vestal virgins" of the Lost Cause.

Notes

1. *Southern Punch,* 12 September 1863.

2. Charles Wise, Petersburg, to Jean Whitewell, Richmond, 22 March 1863, Peter and Frank Wise Letters, Special Collections Department, William R. Perkins Library, Duke University, Durham, N.C.

3. Alice Wise, Richmond, to Jean Whitewell, 11 November 1864, Peter Wise and Frank Wise Letters.

4. Alice Wise, Richmond, to Jean Whitewell, her sister-in-law, 11 Novem-ber 1864, Peter and Frank Wise Letters. "Jane," Richmond, to Mrs. Guthrie, 7 January 1865, Thomas H. Gee Account Book, Manuscripts Collection, Alder-man Library, University of Virginia, Charlottesville.

5. *Richmond Dispatch,* 29 December 1863.

6. Josiah Gorgas Journal, Ms. 279-Z, Southern Historical Collection, Wil-son Library, University of North Carolina at Chapel Hill.

7. George Rable, *Civil Wars: Women and the Crisis of Southern Nationalism* (Urbana: University of Illinois Press, 1989), 51, 271; Drew Gilpin Faust, *Mothers of Invention: Women of the Slaveholding South in the American Civil War* (Chapel Hill: University of North Carolina Press, 1996), 139–52.

8. Faust, *Mothers of Invention,* chap. 2.

9. The Richmond marriage register was created in 1853, when Virginia passed an ordinance establishing a bureau of vital statistics. According to this law, ministers solemnizing marriages were required to provide the bureau with information regarding the date the ceremony was performed, the names of the bride and groom and their parents, the respective age and marital status of the bride and groom, their race, and the groom's occupation and city or coun-try of residence.

I compiled this sample by recording the age, race, and marital status for each bride and groom listed in the Richmond marriage register for the months of March, June, September, and December, for each year between 1860 and 1880, with the exceptions of the years 1864, 1866, and 1868, for which no information has survived. June and December were popular months for Southern weddings, so data retrieved from these two months were chosen because they were likely to yield the most marriages of any months in a given year. March and September were selected as a means of balancing the weddings throughout the calendar year.

I also kept a list of clergy performing these ceremonies as a means of verifying that all denominations were represented in the marriage register record. In addition, I collected information on the groom's occupation as a way to see whether the sample couples were from all economic sectors in the population. With the exception of Quaker unions, the Richmond sample includes marriages performed by both white and black clergy from the city's major denominations—Methodists, Baptists, Episcopalians, Presbyterians, Unitarian Universalists, Disciples of Christ, Catholics, German Lutherans, and Jews. A survey of 85 percent of the grooms' occupations demonstrates that the marriage register sample also represents a significant proportion of the occupations available to white and black Richmond men during this period of time and appears to include individuals from almost every sector of the economy.

10. Elizabeth Fox-Genovese, "Family and Female Identity in the Antebellum South," in *In Joy and in Sorrow: Women, Family, and Marriage in the Victorian South 1830–1900,* ed. Carol Bleser (New York: Oxford University Press, 1991), 270, n. 35; Suzanne Lebsock, *The Free Women of Petersburg: Status and Culture in a Southern Town, 1784–1860* (New York: W. W. Norton, 1984), 33.

11. Leslie Winston Smith, "Richmond during Presidential Reconstruction, 1865–1867" (Ph.D. diss., University of Virginia, 1974), 53; Michael B. Chesson, *Richmond after the War, 1865–1890* (Richmond: Virginia State Library, 1981), 161–62. I have chosen to use the median age rather than the mean (or average) age because the median reflects the central tendencies of a particular group and is not distorted by aberrations from the norm. The average age of marriage for white brides during the period ranged from 21.5 to 22.8 for most years in the sample, with later ages of marriage for the years 1862, 1879, and 1880. In those years, the average age of marriage for white brides was 23.8, 23.3, and 23.5, respectively. At this time, no other statistical studies of marriage have been done for other Southern or Northern wartime communities, so comparisons with white women in other locations is currently impossible.

12. Lebsock, *Free Women of Petersburg,* 33.

13. Sally Ann Brock Putnam, *Richmond during the War: Four Years of Personal Observation by a Richmond Lady* (New York: G. W. Carleton, 1867; reprint, New York: Time-Life Books, 1983), 29–41.

14. Entry for 13 April 1862, Diary of an Unknown Diarist, Valentine Museum, Richmond, Va.

15. Louisa Wright [Mrs. D. Giraud], *A Southern Girl in '61: The War-Time Memories of a Confederate Senator's Daughter* (New York: Doubleday, Page & Co., 1905), 118–19.

16. Ibid., 119.

17. Entries dated 7–28 March 1862, Diary of an Unknown Diarist, Valentine Museum, Richmond, Va.

18. Entry dated 23 May 1861, ibid.

19. "To Miss Mollie Lyne" from an unknown admirer, 14 Februrary 1863; E. T. Snead to Lucy J. Bowles, 1 February 1862, Valentines File, Eleanor S. Brockenbrough Library, Museum of the Confederacy, Richmond, Va.

20. Eugene Desdunes to Mattie Pierce, Richmond, 4 June 1864, Dorsey and Coupland Papers, Ms. 39.1 D73, Earl Gregg Swem Library, College of William and Mary, Williamsburg, Va.

21. E. C. B., Post Office, Richmond, to Mattie Pierce, 10 June 1864, Dorsey and Coupland Papers. Emphasis in the original.

22. Diary entries dated 13 November 1864, 9 February, 12 March 1865, Lucy Muse Walton Fletcher Papers, Special Collections Department, William R. Perkins Library, Duke University, Durham, N.C.

23. Constance Cary Harrison, *Recollections Grave and Gay* (New York: Charles Scribners' Sons, 1911), 126.

24. Lucy Parke Chamberlayne Bagby, "The Chronicle of Lucy Parke Chamberlayne Bagby," Bagby Family Papers, Virginia Historical Society, Richmond.

25. Entry dated 17 May 1864, Emma Mordecai Diary, Virginia Historical Society, Richmond.

26. Author's interview with Mrs. Doris Rose Pearson, 3806 Seminary Avenue, Richmond, Va., Thursday, 16 March 1995.

27. Phebe Yates Pember, Chimborazo Hospital, Richmond, to Mrs. J. F. [Lou] Gilmer, 30 December 1863, Phebe Levy Pember Papers, Southern Historical Collection, Wilson Library, University of North Carolina at Chapel Hill, reprinted in *A Southern Woman's Story,* ed. Bell I. Wiley (St. Simons, Ga.: Mockingbird Press, 1959), 112.

28. Diary entries dated 13 November, 11 December 1864, 12, 28 March 1865, Lucy Muse Walton Fletcher Papers.

29. *Religious Herald,* 28 July 1870.

30. By late 1863, a satin wedding gown in Richmond cost approximately $1,000. Fanny F. to Charles Elisha Taylor, [n.d.] 1863, Charles Elisha Taylor Papers, Manuscripts Collection, Alderman Library, University of Virginia, Charlottesville.

31. Nannie Kent's account of an interrupted wedding, n.d., Wormeley Family Papers, Virginia Historical Society, Richmond.

32. Parke's mother did not think it would seem proper for the unmarried couple to dine regularly at the same table. LPCB Chronicle, pp. 133–217, Virginia Historical Society, Richmond.

33. Larkin Willis, Rapidan, to Leila Turpin Willis, 28 December 1862; Miles Turpin, Richmond, to Larkin Willis; 15 September 1863, both in the Larkin Willis Papers, Special Collections Department, William R. Perkins Library, Duke University, Durham, N.C.

34. Larkin Willis, Locust Dale, to Leila Willis, Richmond, 3 December 1865, Larkin Willis Papers.

35. Rebecca Turpin, Richmond, to Leila Turpin Willis, Locust Dale, 10 August 1863, Larkin Willis Papers.

36. Leila Turpin Willis, Richmond, to Larkin Willis, 12 May 1862, Larkin Willis Papers. This pregnancy probably resulted in a miscarriage.

37. Miles Turpin, Richmond, to Larkin Willis, Locust Dale, 15 September 1863, Larkin Willis Papers.

38. Maris Vinovskis, "Have Social Historians Lost the Civil War?: Some Preliminary Demographic Speculations," *Journal of American History* 76, no. 1 (June 1989): 34–58, esp. tables 1 and 2. This essay has been reprinted in *Toward a Social History of the American Civil War: Exploratory Essays,* ed. Maris A. Vinovskis (Cambridge: Cambridge University Press, 1991), 1–30.

39. Richmond censuses for 1860, 1870, and 1880.

40. Constitution and By-Laws of the Protestant Episcopal Church Home, Richmond, Va., Protestant Episcopal Church Home for Ladies Records, Virginia Historical Society, Richmond.

41. William R. L. Smith, *History of the Baptist Home for Aged Women, Richmond, Va.* (Richmond: L. H. Jenkins, 1922), 5–16.

42. *First Annual Report of the Exchange for Women's Work of Richmond, Va. for the Year Ending March 1st, 1884* (Richmond: Whittet & Shepperson, 1884), 5, in Richmond Exchange for Women's Work Papers, 1893–1957, Valentine Museum, Richmond, Va.

SEVEN

"GOOD ANGELS"

Confederate Widowhood in Virginia

Jennifer Lynn Gross

> The widow & the orphan are, far more
> significant terms, than they once were to us.
>
> –David Comfort III to Charlotte
> Comfort, 3 October 1874

In 1848 the Rawlings and Kelly families celebrated the marriage of their children, John and Susan. After the wedding, the newlyweds moved to a rented cottage in the small town of Lawrenceville, Virginia, not far from the North Carolina border. There, John worked as a harness-maker while Susan helped make ends meet by taking in mending and other sewing work. Over the next twelve years, they had three children. But the outbreak of the Civil War in 1861 abruptly shattered their household. Like so many other Southern husbands, John joined the Confederate ranks soon after the firing on Fort Sumter and Virginia's secession from the Union. Fighting with Company I of the Fifty-ninth Virginia, more familiarly known as the Brunswick Blues, John saw only a year of action before he was captured and imprisoned in the notoriously lethal Union prison in Elmira, New York. He died there in 1862 from battle wounds and smallpox. John's sudden death left Susan a middle-aged widow with three young children to support and very few options in a region devastated by the war.[1]

Throughout the South there were tens of thousands of women like Susan Rawlings who were no longer part of traditional households. Such women had to become the moral, social, and economic leaders of their families in a patriarchal society in which women were supposed to be helpmates, not heads of households. In the Old South, the roles that young white women had respectably played were limited to the dependent positions of daughter, wife, and mother. Daughters relied completely on their fathers for their public identities, and this dependence transferred to their husbands upon marriage. A woman's legal, social, and economic identity was always attached to the man in her life. According to white Southern social rules, marriage was the only truly acceptable place for a woman. As one scholar has noted, "Women [who] were neither the wives nor the slaves of white men . . . had no place or function in southern society." There was no place for widows; they were expected to remarry, especially if they were young and still in their childbearing years. Yet many Civil War widows could not avail themselves of the traditional solution to the "widow problem"—remarriage. Too many eligible, white Southern men had died in the war—at least 260,000—and those who had survived generally either were already married or chose to marry younger women who did not bring with them the "emotional baggage" of a previous marriage. Widowed and alone, Confederate widows faced difficult choices in their efforts to define a place for themselves and survive on their own.[2]

Every Confederate widow shared the pain and grief of losing a husband; however, a close study of the social and economic situations of seventy Confederate widows in Brunswick County, Virginia, including Susan Rawlings, reveals that there was no single experience of the emotional and practical realities of widowhood. Factors such as prewar wealth, postwar opportunity, the presence or absence of helpful kin or dependent children, and support from the state and larger societal attitudes toward Confederate widows all affected the way that widows dealt with their widowhood and the strategies they employed to survive. Among Virginia's Confederate widows were women who remarried, women who thrived as *femmes soles*, women who just barely made it on their own, and women who became dependent on friends, family members, or the state.[3]

The drama of Confederate widows' joys and sorrows, struggles and opportunities, and successes and failures is compelling in and of itself, yet Confederate widowhood did not exist in a vacuum. During the war, the absence of fathers and husbands from the home front allowed or forced many women to experience expanded opportunities for autonomy. For the war's duration, wives regularly assumed the role of household head. But upon their spouses' homecomings, most wives returned to their prewar positions of subordination within the home, enabling their husbands to reassert their manly "rights" as household heads within a patriarchal system. By virtue of their "manlessness," however, the thousands of widows who could not remarry continued to have access to wartime liberties. The existence of so many women who could no longer conform to the ideals of traditional Southern womanhood—combined with the South's military defeat and the end of slavery—threw a wrench in elite white Southerners' postwar efforts to build a "New South" in the image of the Old. Southern men, desperate to reassert their elevated prewar social status, which was already threatened by the loss of their authority over emancipated black men, needed to control white women, especially unattached white women. For white men to imagine themselves as proper patriarchs, white women could not be independent, just as African American men could not be equal. As the former slaves had to be controlled through discriminatory black codes, unfair labor contracts, and eventually the infamous Jim Crow system, white women, if not in reality, then at least in theory, had to be ensconced within proper patriarchal homes, provided for and protected by their menfolk. To accomplish this, Southerners had to expand their definitions of Southern womanhood to make room for Confederate widows, and to make this new attitude more palatable, they collectively imagined all Confederate widows as good and noble women who had sacrificed mightily for the cause.[4]

When the Civil War ended in 1865, Susan Rawlings and other widows like her began the often difficult task of rebuilding their lives. For many widows, the shock and grief of suddenly losing their spouses further complicated their efforts to survive on their own. One widow's reaction to the "terrible announcement" of her husband's death in a Petersburg hospital "was as a thunderbolt at [her] very feet," recalled Judith Brockenbrough McGuire in her diary. "Oh, how she made that immense building ring with her bitter lamentations! . . . She could hear no voice of sympathy." Yet it was not grief alone that complicated widows' lives; they also had to face new familial responsibilities even while they were still in mourning. For some women, it was all they could do to get by. "I know it must have been hard for you to keep up & take that interest in your duties which your children & domestic cares call for, & I don't wonder that you yielded to these feelings [of grief]," Mary Louise Comfort wrote sympathetically to her daughter-in-law in Georgia.[5]

For most widows, grief was accompanied by intense economic distress that varied according to the family's financial situation before the death of the household head. Generally, the more real estate a family owned before a husband's death, the better off a widow would be when her husband was gone. Conversely, widows from families with small amounts of property often suffered extreme hardship and deprivation. Although there were extremely wealthy Southerners, most white Southerners fell among the yeoman classes. And before the war almost all of Brunswick's future Confederate widows were married to yeomen—middling farmers and artisans. There were also Brunswick widows who came from poorer, less economically established families. Twenty-five Brunswick women who would become widows were married to men who, though in agricultural occupations, owned no land. Additionally, ten women's husbands were artisans—boot and shoemakers, carpenters, tailors, harness-makers, or wheelwrights. Like the twenty-five landless "farmers," these working-class men rarely owned substantial real estate. A woman whose subsistence depended entirely on her husband's labor suffered a tremendous economic loss upon his death because she no longer had either the income from his labor or the means to perform his job in his absence.[6]

Even if a woman had enjoyed economic stability before her husband's death through the ownership of land, the added complication of an economy devastated by the war could often leave her facing a harrowing economic situation. With the end of slavery, all money invested in human property disappeared. Additionally, because Brunswick lay right in the path of both armies, most cattle, horses, and other livestock, as well as any stored tobacco or cotton, was likely to have been confiscated or impressed for military use. Within five years of the war's end, one-third of the widows, both those whose husbands had owned land and those whose husbands had not, held either less property or significantly depreciated property than they had before their husbands' deaths.[7]

Although the bleak condition of the postwar South and the widows' prewar economic positions certainly contributed to the hardships that Confederate widows faced, the existing legal system could also threaten a widow's economic existence. If a woman's husband died without leaving a will—and most did, because wills were rare during this period except among men of considerable property—Virginia estate law limited a woman's access to and control over the family's possessions. Since 1662 Virginia statute law had provided that when a husband died without a will, his widow was entitled only to a "dower" portion of his property. Dower rights gave a widow only the use of the dower real estate during her lifetime ("life interest"), which meant that she did not have the power to sell or give away the property or to alter it in any way. If a widow altered the dower property, even in an effort to increase profits, the law considered this "wasting" another person's property, and the rightful heirs could sue her. From 1790 until about 1890, dower constituted only a one-third life interest in any real estate and one-third of any personal property that her husband had owned during their marriage. If there were children from the mar- riage, they received equal portions of the remaining two-thirds of the real and personal property. If the couple had no children, the widow still received only a one-third life interest in the real estate, but her share of the personal estate increased to one-half. Virginia law dic- tated that inheritance of the other two-thirds pass as follows: the eld- est brother of the deceased received the entire two-thirds; if there were no brothers, it was divided equally between any sisters of the decedent; if there were no siblings at all, the inheritance passed to the "issue of the decedent's paternal grandfather, the eldest male of the nearest degree succeeding first." For personal estate, the line was iden- tical except that the decedent's parents were considered heirs before the siblings. Under Virginia law, a widow was *never* entitled to all of her husband's estate unless there were no legal kin. Because most Confederate widows were married to yeomen, not wealthy planters, one-third of a husband's property would not allow them to support themselves. Of the seventy Brunswick husbands, only five left wills stipulating how they wished their estates disbursed. Like countless other widows in the South, the other sixty-five Brunswick widows, including Susan Rawlings, found themselves at the mercy of Virginia's estate laws.[8]

The postwar period was trying for many Southerners, but widows faced especially daunting circumstances because inheritance laws dis- criminated against them, and there were few options open to unat- tached women in the traditional South. Those widows who could chose the traditional solution to the widowhood question—remarriage. For these women, a new spouse could provide the emotional support and economic stability that they would perhaps be unable to achieve on their own. Only 30 percent of the seventy Brunswick widows were able to remarry.[9]

A woman's decision to remarry generally reflected "a tangled com- ponent of need, opportunity, and desire." Financial concerns over- whelmingly influenced many decisions to remarry. It was, as one widow said of her decision to remarry, "the only chance I saw for my- self." A widow who did not inherit a significant amount of property after her first husband's death might choose to seek a second husband to gain economic stability. For example, Prudence Dean, a propertyless widow at the age of twenty-one, saw advantage in a marriage to George Lippincott, a Northerner she probably met as the Union army passed through Brunswick. Because Prudence was young and penniless, remarriage was probably her best option. At the time of their marriages to Brunswick widows, over one-half of the second husbands owned real estate and/or significant amounts of personal property.[10]

A woman's age, along with the absence or presence of children from her first marriage and their ages, also affected her decision and opportunities regarding remarriage. Older widows had a much more difficult time finding prospective new husbands. Moreover, if a widow was older and had adult children, she might be less likely to remarry because she could rely on her adult children for support. Mary Epperson, for example, had seven children, two of whom were adults within five years of the war's end. The presence of these adult children, along with her inheritance of a 240-acre farm, probably contributed to her decision to remain single. By contrast, if a widow was young and had small children, she might seek out a new spouse to provide for her family. Mary Jane Wilmoth was a twenty-five-year-old mother of three young children when her husband died, leaving her with only a small inheritance. When Charles Thompson, a prosperous forty-eight-year-old farmer with a 444-acre farm came courting, Mary Jane likely saw not only a possible love interest but also an attractive marriage partner for a widow with three young children to support. Like the presence of young children, childlessness might also compel a widow to choose remarriage. Because motherhood was one of the most important tenets of Southern womanhood, women who were childless might seek fulfillment of their "motherly nature" through a second marriage. Susan Seward, whose first marriage left her with neither great wealth nor children, was probably thrilled to accept the marriage proposal of John Dunn, a prosperous farmer with four children. He represented not only a second chance for love and economic stability but also a chance for her to be a mother.[11]

While remarriage was the most traditional answer to the widow question, it was not always possible. Indeed, even if it was possible, it might not be desirable. During the antebellum period, "the wealthier the widow, the less likely she was to remarry." Similarly, the few Brunswick widows who inherited significant amounts of property generally chose to remain single and retain control of their wealth. Julietta Cheely, for example, likely decided against remarriage because she could support herself comfortably on the property she acquired after her husband's death. When Needham Cheely died in 1863, his will bequeathed his entire estate worth $11,965.35 to his wife, stipulating that she could receive her inheritance only if she remained unmarried. Failing to specifically designate the property as a "life estate," Needham inadvertently left Julietta in outright possession of his entire estate, opening the door for her economic autonomy. Until after 1890, Julietta maintained ownership and management of her inherited estate, hiring laborers to aid her sons in farming the land. Though several of her adult sons resided in her household, the census-taker and the community at large regarded her as the legitimate head of the household. Julietta's postwar success as one of the wealthiest and most successful of the Brunswick widows resulted from a combination of her prewar social position among the upper strata of the yeomen, a flair for financial management probably acquired during the war, and a legal loophole in her husband's will.[12]

A widow might also prefer to remain single because of the advantages provided by her *femme sole* status. According to Virginia law, single women, including widows, were *femmes soles*. Theoretically, they possessed all the same legal privileges as men—they could enter into contracts, bring lawsuits against debtors, sell or convey property by deed, and plan for the distribution of their property by executing wills. A few of the Brunswick widows, like Narcissa Faris, took full advantage of their *femme sole* status after their husbands' death. Although Narcissa's husband, Peter, had owned no real estate and only $100 of personal property when he died, Narcissa assumed the responsibility of administering his estate which was her right under inheritance law. As part of her responsibilities as executrix, on 22 September 1866 she filed a petition with the County Court of Brunswick requiring W. A. Faris to repay a bond to her late husband's estate in the amount of $325.60 plus $97.68 in interest. Though she likely had no experience in collecting debts or petitioning the court, Narcissa succeeded in her efforts and settled her husband's estate to her advantage.[13]

While some widows took advantage of the opportunities offered by *femme sole* status to administer their husbands' estates and execute their own wills, many widows made decisions in concert with advice from male family members, often willingly but sometimes with reluctance. Quite often, relatives or in-laws took it upon themselves to advise a "helpless" widow as to the best course of action after her husband's death. Alice Harrison's mother-in-law counseled her to let her brother take care of her affairs after her husband's death. "Oh you know not enough of human nature to have such to deal with, and your life will become more and more labourious and miserable." Similarly, Mangus Jones admonished his sister-in-law, Frances, of King William County, Virginia, to sell the farm that her husband had left her, taking out only her dower third, as a way to disencumber herself from debt. He advised, "I think you would be benefitted by this course—in fact I don't see how it is possible for you to arrest the sale." Certainly Mangus's advice may have been Frances's most prudent course of action; the remaining evidence does not reveal any further specifics. But while her brother-in-law clearly did not regard her as capable of managing her own financial affairs, Frances's husband obviously had, because he bequeathed her his entire estate, not just her dower third. Such doubts and interference alone could make a widow's efforts to take care of herself all the more troubling. Combined with the difficult environment of the postwar period, they could most certainly take their toll on a woman's ability or desire to make fruitful choices in the future.[14]

Deprived of their husbands' labor and left with almost no land or personal property because of Virginia's estate laws, many widows in the predominantly agricultural South had to make difficult decisions in order to survive. Most found it necessary to enter the paid labor force after their husbands' deaths. Of course, this was not always easy, as there were few jobs open to women, and none of them paid very well. Although women could certainly work in the fields, as many yeoman wives had done on their own farms before the war, most white Southerners considered hiring out for such labor "beneath" them and their children. "How often I wished then that of all the land their father had owned, I had only a few acres on which I could live with my children and try to make a living. That would have been independence, and none of us would have shrunk from labour," lamented Cornelia Peake McDonald. "It almost broke my heart. Others worked, the first young men of Virginia went cheerfully to the plough; but the land was their own, the farms they had been born and bred on, and that was so different." Widows could also obtain work as domestics or washerwomen, but these jobs were generally reserved for African American women because, like hired agricultural labor, they were considered too indelicate for respectable white women. A more acceptable and traditional way for women to earn money was through the sale of food or other homemade products in the marketplace. Just as many yeoman families had undoubtedly benefited from women's labor in the fields before the war, many also profited from women's marketing activities in the prewar period. Even before her husband's death, Marie Hubard of Richmond sold strawberries in the marketplace to supplement her husband's income as a cannon-caster for the Confederacy. Apparently, casting cannons did not pay well enough to support a family, although it eventually cost William Hubard his life.[15]

Though many widows were forced into menial labor just to scrape by, others were lucky enough to find work in a traditionally female "profession." Many Confederate widows, including two from Brunswick County, worked as seamstresses after the war. Additionally, women could find employment in one of the new female professions opened by the war. Such new "professional" opportunities were by no means vast, however; they were essentially limited to teaching and nursing. Even so, two Brunswick widows took advantage of them and the higher pay they provided. Mary Thomas supported her family after her husband's death by working as a teacher, most likely in the new public school system that was established in Brunswick in 1870, while Sarah, the widow of James Maitland, became a nurse.[16]

Despite working, many widows were still unable to support themselves and their children without assistance. Maria Hubard despaired, "It seemed as if there was nothing left for us in the world but to starve or descend to the lowest level by working as labourers; and even then we could expect nothing but squalid poverty." Though almost two-thirds of the Brunswick widows were the heads of their own households in 1870, about one-third of the widows lived in other peoples' households at one time or another after becoming widows. Most of them resided with their parents, in-laws, or adult children. After Napoleon Taylor's death, his wife, Mary Jane, and their nine-year-old daughter, Pocahontas, never lived on their own. At first they shared a home with her in-laws, John W. Taylor, a seventy-three-year-old retired carpenter, and Eliza, his sixty-four-year-old wife. By 1880 the elderly Taylors had apparently died, and Mary Jane and Pocahontas moved in with Bassett Rawlings, Mary Jane's brother, and his family on a 459-acre farm. For other widows like Caroline Nash, dependency on friends and relatives was only temporary. In 1870 Caroline and her young daughter, Nancy, shared Lucretia Rawlings's home, but by 1880 they had established their own household.[17]

Not all widows ended up living with relatives or even had such an opportunity. Many, however, faced pressure from family members who feared that they could not make it as "manless women." Charlotte Comfort received a letter from her father-in-law pleading with her to come live with them: "We . . . often wish that you were near us, that we might aid & encourage you in all your cares & responsibilities." And if a widow could not or would not move to be with family members, they often came to her, even if only for visits. Emma Garnett, the widow of General Thomas S. Garnett, received the news shortly after her husband's death that her mother-in-law would be arriving soon: "Mother will go to you very soon. She loved you as her own child, and will do all she can to give you comfort." Other widows faced well-meaning pleas that they send their children away to live with the families of "more stable" relatives. Cornelia McDonald recalled that after the death of her husband, numerous friends and relatives attempted to convince her to send her children away where they could be better provided for, since her situation was "perfectly hopeless":

> Some days passed and many discussions arose with regard to the future of myself and the children. . . . All thought that the children ought to be distributed among the older members of the family. . . . I listened, but was resolved no matter what happened not to part with my children; but often when pressed, and reminded how hopeless my condition was, and indeed how unreasonable, it was to persist in refusing to do what was the only thing that could be done, as far as any one could see, if my heart was inclined to yield for fear I would not be doing the best for the children, the thought of my poor little lonely ones . . . that thought would nerve me for resistance.

Though they could be intrusive, parents, in-laws, and other family or friends generally thought they were doing what was best for their widowed relative.[18]

Until the 1880s, widows had been limited to finding new husbands, making it on their own, or relying on friends and relatives in their efforts to survive. Beginning in 1888, though, a new option arose: they could turn to the state for support. Such financial aid was not without precedent in Virginia. Almost from the beginning of the war, Virginia's various counties had actively raised and distributed money and food for the poverty-stricken families of soldiers. Eventually, such aid activities grew so expansive that state legislators decided to step in. Although Southern lawmakers and citizens regarded such state-sponsored aid as necessary and legitimate, most aid during the war came from local governments or churches and "ladies' aid societies."[19]

In the years after the war, widows could also obtain assistance from memorial groups like the United Daughters of the Confederacy. Referring to their Home for Needy Confederate Women, they argued, "It is a *sacred duty* . . . to care for these women." (my emphasis). Proponents of widows' aid frequently used phrases like "sacred duty," "no charity is sweeter and saner," "their claim is strong and true, and, above all, just," and "unselfish solicitude" to describe and validate their cause, while the widows themselves were always characterized as "worthy recipients," "noble women," and "good women" to further highlight the rightness of such aid. Southern men and women considered it their inviolable responsibility to care for the widows of deceased Confederate soldiers.[20]

Besides wartime aid, the Virginia General Assembly had since 1874 discussed postwar aid to Confederate widows. In 1880, Virginia legislators for the first time extended a one-time cash payment for the loss of a limb to a Confederate widow. Although it was not a pension, the General Assembly voted to "allow commutation for [an] artificial arm to Josephine Robinson, widow of Walter Robinson, deceased." Apparently, Walter had died before he could receive either the artificial arm or a commutation. This was not an official policy, however, and Josephine Robinson was the first and only widow to receive money from state funds until 1888, when the Virginia Assembly first extended yearly pensions to its former soldiers and their widows.[21]

Though the Virginia Assembly began discussing the extension of yearly pensions to Confederate veterans and widows in 1874, it took fourteen long years before they approved such a measure. The political and economic climate of the postwar period contributed to the delay in awarding pensions to soldiers and their widows. From 1867 to 1871, Republicans, who were not exactly friendly toward the idea of rewarding Confederates for their role in the Civil War, ruled Virginia's General Assembly. Also, the state was still recovering from the economic devastation of the war, and the economic depression of the mid-1870s hit Virginia and the South especially hard.[22]

In 1888, Virginia, "redeemed" by Southern Democrats, enacted its first pension law. According to this statute, any widow whose husband had died while in the Confederate armed forces was eligible to receive a pension if her yearly income was less than $300 and she had no more than $1,000 worth of property. Such limits were high enough that they excluded only elite women. More important than the financial limits, however, a widow had to be unmarried when she applied and remain unmarried to receive a Confederate pension. The 1888 statute, set at $30 per annum, was amended in 1900 and 1902 to increase the amount of payment and to broaden the scope of those who were eligible. In 1900 the General Assembly voted to give $40 to widows who had lost their husbands in the war. Additionally, widows whose husbands had been "true and loyal soldiers" but had not died from their wartime injuries or diseases until well after the war's end were given $25. In both cases, widows could receive aid "only so long as [they] remain[ed] unmarried." In 1902 the law was further expanded to provide for women whose husbands had served in the war but had died from causes unrelated to the war. Even if a husband had died simply from old age, under this law, his widow could still receive a pension.[23]

Although the dire financial situations of many Confederate widows were certainly compelling when Virginians took up the issue of pensions in the 1880s, their marital status was vitally important as well. The 1888 and subsequent laws each required that in order for a widow to receive a pension, she must be unmarried when she applied and remain unmarried to qualify. And Virginia was not the only Southern state to use such language. The pension systems of every other Southern state also required that a widow be unmarried to qualify for aid. Additionally, the Virginia Assembly dealt with specific claims by widows whose husbands had died after the war's end. In every case, the act mentions not only that the widow was destitute and deserving of state aid but also that she was unmarried and had no one else to take care of her. When Virginia lawmakers awarded Emma Guy of Campbell County, Virginia, an annual pension because she was "the widow of Samuel R. Guy . . . who died . . . leaving a widow and infant children in indigent circumstances, who still remains unmarried," the state indicated that it was willing to step into the voids left by the deaths of its veterans and play the role of provider for their widows. But if a widow remarried, she did not need the state to be a substitute patriarch, because she was back in a traditional household with a patriarch of her own.[24]

As Linda Gordon has argued regarding the development of the modern welfare system in the twentieth century, there have always been single mothers and poverty, but it is not until the patriarchal family and community system are perceived as breaking down that they become viewed as a "problem." Single mothers, when measured against the "norm" of the breadwinner husband/father and a domestic, economically dependent wife/mother, come up short. In an effort to buttress the norm, governmental aid is distributed in a way that preserves the status of unemployed men as the breadwinner. Aid to single mothers, on the other hand, is aimed at preventing them from becoming comfortable as single women. Like Gordon's twentieth-century single mothers, Confederate widows who were unable to remarry came up short when measured against the norm of the patriarchal family. In order to incorporate them back into the system, the state had to make sure they did not grow comfortable in their positions as single women. Thousands of Virginia widows, including Susan Rawlings and thirty-two other women from Brunswick, applied for and received pensions. The amount of pensions that widows received was certainly not enough to make a woman excessively comfortable in her widowhood, but for Rawlings and other widows who owned small amounts of property, pensions were an important source of income.[25]

As recent historians have pointed out, the postbellum period was a period in which everything, including gender roles, was up for debate. The emancipation of thousands of slaves, the South's military loss in the war, and the political and economic conditions of Reconstruction, along with some of the war's direct effects—the "creation" of capable, independent women, the increase in the number of single women who could not marry and widows who could not remarry—cast doubt on the validity of traditional white Southern gender roles. In order for white Southern men to reassert their masculinity, they had to restake their claim to power. They did so by reaffirming the inferiority of black men and women and the dependent status of white women who needed protection and provision from white men. Because pensions were based on the premise that the patriarchal family was the norm, offering pensions to widows served to reinforce traditional gender roles in which men provided for women. Confederate pension systems differentiated widows' pensions from veterans' pensions. Unlike in the federal system, where a widow collected a pension based on her husband's military rank, each of the Southern pension systems put widows in their own category, emphasizing the importance of aid for widows as a separate matter from providing for veterans. In a sense Confederate widows "earned" their pension simply by virtue of their widowhood. Setting widows apart in their own category reveals the importance in Southern men's eyes of providing for women, especially those who needed it the most. Through widows' pensions, Southern men could again imagine themselves as proper patriarchs. Although they turned over the antebellum responsibility of provision to the state, Southern men could still see themselves as providing for women because it was their state governments that were doing the providing.[26]

Confederate pensions served not only the practical needs of provision but also the ideological needs of patriarchy. The willingness of state legislators in 1900 to grant pensions by individual legislation to women who did not meet the qualifications specified by the pension laws of 1888 and 1900 with language such as "without property and without means of support, *save from her own labor*," and "*is dependent upon her own labor and exertions for a living*" (my emphasis) indicates an affirmation of the traditional image of white Southern womanhood as too good for manual labor as well as the duty of white men to provide for white women. Moreover, by 1902 the Virginia Assembly was willing to provide for widows of soldiers who had simply died from old age, indicating that, for unmarried widows who had no one to support them, regardless of whether or not their men gave their lives for "the Cause," Southern men were willing to use the state to take on the role of substitute patriarch. Finally, there was the debate surrounding federal pensions for Confederates.[27]

In 1894 several Southern Congressmen proposed a bill in the United States Congress that would have allowed Confederate veterans and widows to receive pensions from the federal government the same way that Union pensioners did. Justification for the bill generally fell along the lines that Southerners had contributed to the federal pension system through indirect taxes for years and therefore should benefit from it. Although several versions of the bill were proposed, it never passed. Even so, it engendered a lively debate among Southerners, producing both proponents and opponents in Virginia and the rest of the South. Not surprisingly, opinions on the bill generally broke down along class lines—elite white Southern men opposed the bill, while yeoman and lower-class veterans supported it. One opponent's position reveals what was at stake for elite Southern men in providing for their own. He states, "The failure of the Government of the United States to provide for our disabled soldiers has resulted most fortunately for the manhood and womanhood of the South. . . . Shall we barter this for gold? . . . No! A thousand times, no!" This bill "is inconsistent with our self-respect, and stains the record, to whose purity we devote and consecrate ourselves, our lives, our fortunes, and our sacred honor." Another opponent concurs, "A Federal pension is worse than Confederate poverty." Of course, when made by someone who does not suffer from poverty, such a statement is not all that convincing. Numerous proponents of the bill noted the hypocrisy in such proclamations, arguing that opponents were "not authorized to speak for the great body of ex-Confederates *who move in the more humble walks of life*" (emphasis added).[28]

Confederate pensions, though ostensibly created for the very practical need of providing for needy Southern veterans and widows, also fulfilled the ideological need of buttressing traditional Southern patriarchy. The "willingness to vote pensions and constantly increase them under those circumstances [the postwar economy] indicates a popular and deliberate approval of the expenditure and a desire to make it," wrote William Glasson, a late-nineteenth-century commentator. Southerners—that is, elite Southerners, those who ran the General Assembly—recognized the value of pensions for Southern society, both practical and ideological, and accordingly supported them.[29]

ON A WINTRY SUNDAY NIGHT, 14 DECEMBER 1924, JUST eleven days before Christmas, Brunswick County residents mourned the loss of their oldest citizen—Confederate widow Susan Rawlings. Known to everyone as "Grandma," Susan had lived out her life, after John's death, in the same tiny cottage they had first rented in 1848. She had never remarried, and she and her children scraped by for years on the meager income that sewing and other odd jobs provided in a small Southern town. In 1888, twenty-seven years after John's death, Susan applied for and received a yearly pension of $30 from the state of Virginia because her husband had given his life for the ill-fated Confederacy. She was beloved by her family, including fifty-nine great-grandchildren and fifteen great-great-grandchildren, as well as countless friends. As one local newspaper reported, she was a woman who had "a very presence that seemed to radiate sunshine and good cheer. . . . No one ever went to her in distress or in need of sympathy without being helped," one member of her church fondly remembered. "The news of her death will be heard with regret by hundreds. . . . She was frequently a 'good angel.'" Even as late as Mother's Day 1941, "Grandma" Rawlings's family and friends memorialized her as the epitome of Southern womanhood, gracing the Mother's Day bulletin of Lawrenceville Methodist Church with her picture.[30]

In the postbellum period, Southern society had to come to terms with the tens of thousands of Confederate widows who, like Susan Rawlings, could not remarry and therefore fell outside the traditional definitions of Southern womanhood. Eventually, Southern society solved this dilemma by collectively imagining them as noble women or, as in Susan Rawlings's case, "good angels," who sacrificed tremendously for "the Cause." They thereby expanded the boundaries of appropriate womanhood to include women who were legally autonomous as long as they were socially and economically dependent. In a New South trying to rebuild itself in the image of its past, the existence of so many manless women could have challenged the reestablishment of traditional gender assumptions. In providing wartime and postwar assistance and pensions with the justification that it was a "sacred duty" to "worthy recipients," elite Southerners effectively ensconced widows like Susan Rawlings under the banner of "good angels," thereby mollifying their potential as a threat to traditional Southern gender roles.[31]

Notes

1. Compiled Confederate Records, Eighth Census, 1860, Brunswick County, Virginia Schedule I (Free Inhabitants), Bureau of Vital Statistics, Marriage Bonds, 1853–1935, Brunswick County, Va., all housed at Library of Virginia, Richmond (hereafter cited as LV).

2. A woman could also be a sister, but it was not a primary identifying role. For a discussion of Southern womanhood, the ideal and the reality, see Elizabeth Fox-Genovese, *Within the Plantation Household: Black and White Women of the Old South* (Chapel Hill: University of North Carolina Press, 1988); Catherine Clinton, *The Plantation Mistress: Woman's World in the South* (New York: Pantheon Books, 1982); Jean E. Friedman, *The Enclosed Garden: Women and Community in the Evangelical South, 1830–1900* (Chapel Hill: University of North Carolina Press, 1985); Anne Firor Scott, *The Southern Lady: From Pedestal to Politics, 1830–1930* (Chicago: University of Chicago Press, 1970). For a discussion of deviant behavior—divorce and singleness—among antebellum women and white men's use of the state to control and punish such behavior, see Victoria Bynum, *Unruly Women: The Politics of Social and Sexual Control in the Old South* (Chapel Hill: University of North Carolina Press, 1992). Death statistic from James McPherson, *Battle Cry of Freedom: The Civil War Era* (Oxford: Oxford University Press, 1988), 854. For an in-depth discussion of widowhood and singleness among women in the antebellum South, see Suzanne Lebsock, *The Free Women of Petersburg: Status and Culture in a Southern Town, 1784–1860* (New York: W.W. Norton, 1984).

3. While no Southern community is necessarily representative of the rest of the South, Brunswick County, Va., is rather typical in its demographic makeup, its agricultural structure, and its overall rural character; see U.S. Bureau of the Census, *Statistics of the Population of the United States, Ninth Census, 1870, Compiled from the Original Returns of the Ninth Census* (Washington: Government Printing Office, 1872), 1:68–70.

4. For a discussion of the war's role in expanding women's sphere of activity, see Drew Gilpin Faust, *Mothers of Invention: Women of the Slaveholding South in the American Civil War* (New York: Vintage Books, 1996); George Rable, *Civil Wars: Women and the Crisis of Southern Nationalism* (Urbana: University of Illinois Press, 1989); Scott, *The Southern Lady;* LeeAnn Whites, *The Civil War as a Crisis in Gender: Augusta, Georgia, 1860–1890* (Athens: University

of Georgia Press, 1995). Jean Friedman argues that the war did not greatly change Southern women's sphere of activity; see Friedman, *The Enclosed Garden*. Recently, scholars have brought attention to the gendered nature of the postwar contest for power. See Whites, *The Civil War as a Crisis in Gender;* Nina Silber, *The Romance of Reunion: Northerners and the South, 1865–1900* (Chapel Hill: University of North Carolina Press, 1993); Laura F. Edwards, *Gendered Strife and Confusion: The Political Culture of Reconstruction* (Urbana: University of Illinois Press, 1997); Martha Hodes, *White Women, Black Men: Illicit Sex in the Nineteenth-Century South* (New Haven: Yale University Press, 1997); Rable, *Civil Wars.*

5. Judith Brockenbrough McGurie, "Diary, 28 October 1864," *Women of the South in War Times,* comp. Matthew Page Andrews (Baltimore: Norman, Remington Co., 1920), 389–92; May Louise Comfort to Charlotte Comfort, 22 December 1873, Comfort Family Papers, 1848–1900, Virginia Historical Society, Richmond (hereafter cited as VHS).

6. Linda E. Speth, "More than Her 'Thirds': Wives and Widows in Colonial Virginia," *Women and History* 1 (1982): 5–41. There are numerous studies of the yeoman South, and some of the best include Frank L. Owsley, *Plain Folk of the Old South* (Baton Rouge: Louisiana State University Press, 1949); Stephanie McCurry, *Masters of Small Worlds: Yeoman Households, Gender Relations, and the Political Culture of the Antebellum South Carolina Low County* (New York: Oxford University Press, 1995); Gavin Wright, *The Political Economy of the Cotton South: Households, Markets, and Wealth in the Nineteenth Century* (New York: W. W. Norton, 1978); Steven Hahn, *The Roots of Southern Populism: Yeoman Farmers and the Transformation of the Georgia Upcountry, 1850–1890* (New York: Oxford University Press, 1983); None of the Brunswick widows belonged to Virginia's planter elite before the war, but several of them were from the upper levels of the yeomanry; among the Brunswick husbands there were 22 farmers of small to medium-sized farms (up to 250 acres), 10 farm laborers, 12 overseers, 10 artisans, 2 physicians, 1 unemployed, and 12 unknown (Eighth Census, 1860); for guidelines on class distinctions, see Robert C. Kenzer, *Kinship and Neighborhood in a Southern Community, Orange County, North Carolina, 1849–1881* (Knoxville: University of Tennessee Press, 1987); Eighth Census, 1860; Brunswick County Land Taxes, 1859–63, LV. Only three men owned significant amounts of personal property: John Brewer, $2,300; David Clary, $1,500; and Berry Reed, $5,810 (Eighth Census, 1860; Land Texas, 1859–63; Brunswick County Personal Property Taxes, 1860, LV).

7. One-fifth of the households owned at least one slave. Only two owned more than five. Most of the future widows belonged to families who paid personal property taxes on horses, cattle and other farm animals, wagons, buggies or carriages, furniture and other assorted miscellanies (Personal Property Taxes, 1860). This figure includes only women who did not remarry (Ninth Census, 1870; Brunswick County, Va., Schedule I, LV; Land Taxes, 1865–70; Personal Property Taxes, 1865 and 1870).

8. Under Virginia property laws, a married woman could not own land or other personal property unless it was held in a separate estate. For a discussion of women and Virginia/U.S. estate laws, see Lebsock, *The Free Women of Petersburg*; Marlene Stein Wortman, ed., *Women in American Law*, volume 1: *From Colonial Times to the New Deal* (New York: Holmes and Meier, 1985); Carole Shammas et al., *Inheritance in America from Colonial Times to the Present* (New Brunswick, N.J.: Rutgers University Press, 1987), 37, 64–65; Joan Hoff, *Law, Gender, and Injustice: A Legal History of U.S. Women* (New York: New York University Press, 1991), 107. A widow's portion of the personal estate varied according to the number of children (Speth, "More than Her 'Thirds,'" 8); of the five will-writers, three owned property worth more than $8,000 (Will Book 18, 4 July 1861: 565, 634, 677; Will Book 18, 3 March 1862: 461; Will Book 18, 27 January 1863: 568, 661, 702; Will Book 19, 10 February 1863: 45, 100).

9. Ninth Census, 1870; Tenth Census, 1880; Brunswick County, Va., Schedule I, LV; Marriage Bonds.

10. Speth, "More than Her 'Thirds,'" 27; Memoirs of Martha Jane Evans Quarles, Special Collections, University of Virginia, Charlottesville; Eighth Census, 1860; Land Taxes, 1859–63; Personal Property Taxes, 1860; Marriage Bonds.

11. Younger women more easily attracted new spouses due to their youth and childbearing potential (Ninth Census, 1870; Land Taxes, 1870 and 1875; Personal Property Taxes, 1870; Marriage Bonds). Susan inherited only $210.50 from her first husband (Inventory and Accounting of R. M. Seward Estate, Will Book 18, 19 December 1862: 508, 529). John Dunn owned 920 acres of land worth $2,300 and $540.00 of personal property (Land Taxes, 1875; Personal Property Taxes, 1870); See note 3 for sources on traditional Southern womanhood.

12. Lebsock, *Free Women of Petersburg*, 26. If Julietta remarried, she would receive only one-third of the family's property; although Needham stipulated that after Julietta's death all the property was to go to the children, including an intention to bequeath the property as a "life estate," he never clearly stated it (Will Book 18, 4 August 1862: 563, 630, 632; Land Taxes, 1865 and 1870). At the end of the war, Julietta owned 124.5 acres of land, and within five years, she had added another 90.5 acres. Julietta's personal property holdings also grew during this period. In 1870 she owned one horse, three cattle, two hogs, five dollars' worth of farm implements, and fifty dollars' worth of furniture. Over the next twenty years, she had acquired another horse, four more cattle, nine hogs, two wagons, and five dollars' worth each of gold and guns (Personal Property Taxes, 1870, 1880, 1890; Ninth Census, 1870; Tenth Census, 1880). The five widows whose husbands left wills were often bound by guidelines specifying that upon remarriage they would lose a portion or the entirety of their inheritances, which often acted as a deterrent to remarriage; for more on this topic see Speth, "More than Her 'Thirds,'" 27.

13. Will Book 19, 22 September 1866: nine Brunswick widows executed wills.

14. Janetta Harrison to Alice Harrison, 27 January 1862, Harrison Family Papers, VHS; Mangus Jones to Frances Jones, 1 November 1871, Jones Family Papers, VHS.

15. Between 1860 and 1880, wages in the South were the lowest in the country, and women's wages were about 75 percent that of men's; see Clarence D. Long, *Wages and Earnings in the United States, 1860–1890* (Princeton: Princeton University Press, 1960), 79. Former slaves residing in the country were more attractive employees for agricultural and domestic jobs because employers could pay them lower wages without fear of public sanction; see Cornelia Peake McDonald, "Narrative of Our Refugee Life," in *A Woman's Civil War* (Madison: University of Wisconsin Press, 1992), 238; and Maria Mason Tabb Hubard Diary, 1860–62, VHS. Nearly 80 percent of the Brunswick widows claimed to have no occupation outside the home between 1870 and 1920, yet it is highly unlikely that these women were actually unemployed. More likely, Brunswick's widows considered their jobs outside their households as "nonwork." Arlene Scadron's study of widows in the American Southwest during the postwar period suggests that many women who performed tasks traditionally defined as "domestic"—sewing, cooking, cleaning, or taking in laundry—rarely identified themselves to census-takers as working women because of the nature of their work; see Arlene Scadron, ed, *On Their Own: Widows and Widowhood in the American Southwest, 1848–1939,* (Urbana: University of Illinois Press, 1988), 305. Mary Jane Martin, for example, was a thirty-two-year-old widow employed as a "laborer" with no property and two children, ages fourteen and nine. Ten years later the census-taker identified her as unemployed, a boarder in the home of John and Mary Lucy. Rather than being unemployed, Mary Jane was probably a domestic laborer in Mary Lucy's home, perhaps doing household chores in exchange for room and board (Ninth Census, 1870; Tenth Census, 1880).

16. Though Mary Thomas worked as a mattress-maker in the years immediately after the war, she had become a teacher by 1880 (Ninth Census, 1870; Tenth Census, 1880; Twelfth Census, 1900; Brunswick County, Va., Schedule I, LV). Susan Seward, who married Joseph Dunn in 1873, was also a teacher after 1880 (Tenth Census, 1880). For information about the Brunswick County public school system see Gay Neale, *Brunswick County, Virginia, 1720–1975: The History of a Southside Virginia County* (Richmond, Va.: Whittet & Sheperdson, 1975), 153–54. Before the war, nursing had been largely restricted to men, but the necessity of war often breeds opportunity. Sarah likely learned her profession during the war (Tenth Census, 1880). For a discussion of women's nursing during the war, see Drew Gilpin Faust, "Altars of Sacrifice: Confederate Women and the Narratives of War," in *Divided Houses: Gender and the Civil War,* ed. Catherine Clinton and Nina Silber (New York: Oxford University Press, 1992), 185–86; Faust, *Mothers of Invention,* Rable, *Civil Wars.*

17. Hubard Diary, 239. Thirty-six percent of Brunswick's widows lived with someone else between 1870 and 1920. The number of widows who relied on others for their homes increased as the women aged (Ninth Census, 1870; Tenth Census, 1880; Twelfth Census, 1900; Thirteenth Census, 1910; Brunswick County, Va., Schedule I, LV; Fourteenth Census, 1920; Land Taxes, 1880; Personal Property Taxes, 1880). Caroline's maiden name is Rawlings, so it is possible that Lucretia was a relative, in 1880 Caroline owned 182.5 acres of land worth $421.25 (Land Taxes, 1880; Tenth Census, 1880).

18. David Comfort III to Charlotte Comfort, 3 October 1874, Comfort Family Papers, VHS; letter to Emma S. Garnett, 20 May 1863, Garnett Family Letters, LV; McDonald, "Narrative of Our Refugee Life," 217–18.

19. William F. Zornow, "Aid for the Indigent Families of Soldiers in Virginia, 1861–1865," *Virginia Magazine of History and Biography* 66 (October 1958): 457.

20. *The History of the Home for Needy Confederate Women with the Reports of Officers from October 15, 1900 to October 15, 1904,* United Daughters of the Confederacy Papers, Box 14, Museum of the Confederacy, Richmond, Va., 10–11, 53, 55, 60.

21. In 1866, Virginia began making provisions for soldiers who had lost a limb or an eye during the war; see Virginia, *Acts and Joint Resolutions Passed by the General Assembly of the State of Virginia, 1866–1927,* in Jeffrey Morrison, " 'Increasing the Pensions of These Worthy Heroes': Virginia's Confederate Pensions, 1888 to 1927" (Master's thesis, University of Richmond, 1996), 10. This brief description of Virginia's pension laws is from *Acts of the General Assembly of the Commonwealth of Virginia* (Richmond: Commonwealth of Virginia, 1888), 469–473. The United States government initiated a full-scale pension system for Union soldiers and their families from the beginning of the war, for a discussion of Union widowhood, see Amy E. Holmes, " 'Such Is the Price We Pay': American Widows and the Civil War Pension System," in *Toward a Social History of the American Civil War: Exploratory Essays,* ed. Maris A. Vinovskis (New York: Cambridge University Press, 1990). Confederate pensions never paid as well as Union pensions because they were funded only on the state level.

22. Much has been written about the post-Reconstruction period, but the most complete source remains C. Vann Woodward, *Origins of the New South, 1877–1913* (Baton Rouge: Louisiana State University Press, 1951). See also William H. Glasson, "The South's Care for Her Confederate Veterans," *Review of Reviews* (July 1907): 44–45; Glasson, "The South's Pension and Relief Provisions for the Soldiers of the Confederacy," *Proceedings of the Eighteenth Annual Session of the State Literary and Historical Association* (Raleigh, N.C., 20–21 November 1917), 63–64; M. B. Morton, "Federal and Confederate Pensions Contrasted," *Forum* (September 1893): 70–71.

23. *Acts of the General Assembly,* 1888: 470; *Acts of the General Assembly,* 1900: 1257; *Acts of the General Assembly,* 1902: 472–73. The General Assembly in 1906

and 1918 instituted requirements relating to when a woman married the veteran. According to the 1906 law, they had to have married by 1 May 1866. The 1918 law moved that date back to 1 May 1870 (Morrison, " 'Increasing the Pensions,'" 23, 33; Confederate Pension Records, 1888, Brunswick County, Va., LV). Pension amounts rose every few years; see Virginia Auditor of Public Accounts, *Roster of Confederate Pensioners of Virginia, 1908–1926,* 13 vols. (Richmond: Virginia Auditor of Public Accounts, 1908–26).

24. *Acts of the General Assembly,* 1900: 1328.

25. Linda Gordon, *Pitied but Not Entitled: Single Mothers and the History of Welfare, 1890–1935* (New York: Free Press, 1994). Twenty-one widows remarried, so only forty-nine were eligible for pensions (Confederate Pension Indexes, LV; Pension Records, 1888). Though not all of the Brunswick widows who received pensions were poor, about two-thirds were propertyless.

26. For a discussion of gender roles in the postbellum period, see Hodes, *Black Men, White Women;* Silber, *The Romance of Reunion;* Edwards, *Gendered Strife and Confusion; Acts of the General Assembly,* 1888, 1900, 1902; Morrison, " 'Increasing the Pensions' "; Morton, "Federal and Confederate Pensions"; Glasson, "The South's Care for Her Confederate Veterans" and "The South's Pension and Relief Provisions"; Holmes, " 'Such Is the Price We Pay.' "

27. *Acts of the General Assembly,* 1900: 1198, 1343.

28. "Relief of Confederates by National Appropriation, Hon. P. J. Otey's Bill. R. E. Lee Camp, C. V. Protests against the Consideration of the Bill by Congress," *Southern Historical Society Papers,* ed. R. A. Brock, Secretary of the Southern Historical Society (Richmond: The Society, 1897–1900), 23:840–841; T. S. Garnett et al., "Pensioning of the Confederate Soldier by the United States," ibid., 314; *Congressional Record,* 55th Congress, 3d sess., 3677:5.

29. Glasson, "The South's Care for Her Confederate Veterans," 44.

30. Ninth Census, 1870; Tenth Census, 1880; Twelfth Census, 1900; Thirteenth Census, 1910; Fourteenth Census, 1920; Pension Records, 1888; "Mrs. Rawlings Passed Away," *The Southern Missioner* (1924), 10–11; "Mother's Day," Lawrenceville Methodist Church Bulletin (11 May 1941).

31. "Mrs. Rawlings Passed Away," *The Southern Missioner* (1924), 10.

EIGHT

"A FAMILY OF WOMEN AND CHILDREN"

The Fains of East Tennessee during Wartime

Daniel W. Stowell

The experiences of the Fain family in upper East Tennessee illustrate the challenges that Southern families faced under the stresses of war. A deeply pious Presbyterian and a prodigious diarist, Eliza Fain was the matriarch of a large family.[1] Hardly the plantation mistress of either fact or fiction, she worked hard to sustain her "family of women and children" and directed the labors of a few slaves while her husband and sons fought in the Confederate armies. Eliza viewed everything in her life through the lens of her evangelical religious faith, including marriage, motherhood, women's roles, slavery, death, and the Confederacy. As the war continued to tear Southern society apart, that same faith strengthened Eliza to endure daily challenges, while it also subtly transformed her attitudes about women's proper role in Southern society. Throughout the war and beyond, Eliza took comfort in writing in her diary. "Have felt greatly comforted since writing in my book," she wrote in her entry for 5 June 1863, in the midst of suspense surrounding the siege of Vicksburg, Mississippi, where her son Nick was in the army.[2]

Eliza Rhea Anderson was born in Tennessee in August 1816. Her father died when she was two years old, and she and her mother lived in her uncle's home. As a teenager, she attended the Knoxville Female

Academy. When she was seventeen years old, she joined the Blount-
ville Presbyterian Church and married Richard G. Fain (1811–78) that
same year. An 1832 graduate of the United States Military Academy at
West Point, Richard Fain followed in the footsteps of his father and
became a merchant. He was also a bank officer and a clerk and master
of the Chancery Court. Between 1834 and 1858 Eliza and Richard
Fain had thirteen children at regular two-year intervals, all but one of
whom lived to adulthood.

The Fain family lived on a farm two miles east of Rogersville, the
county seat of Hawkins County, in northeastern Tennessee. Hawkins
County, which bordered Virginia, was deeply divided on the eve of the
Civil War. In the 1860 presidential election, 50 percent of the county's
voters favored Southern Democratic candidate John C. Breckinridge,
but Constitutional Union candidate John Bell ran a close second, with
46 percent of the vote. A well-attended public meeting in Hawkins
County on 29 November 1860 resolved that the "doctrine of secession" was "subversive of all just principles of government." The county
voted against a secession convention in February 1861, and in June 1861,
62 percent of Hawkins County voters disapproved of Tennessee's secession, although the state as a whole voted to leave the Union. In this
county of Unionists and "reluctant Confederates," the Fain family
stood out as zealous Confederates.[3]

When war erupted in the spring of 1861, the Fain household consisted of thirteen adults and eleven children: Richard and Eliza Fain,
their twelve children, and their eight slaves. Bettie Lyon Fain, the wife
of their oldest son, Hiram, also lived with them, as did Caroline, a slave
whom they rented. Eliza Fain frequently referred to their slaves as
their "black family." In September 1860, for example, she noted that
there had been a camp meeting on Sunday with "my family well represented along with all of our black family but the smaller ones."[4]

Shortly after her husband and three of her sons left to join the
Confederate army in May and June 1861, Eliza wrote in her diary,
"My soul is troubled to its greatest depth," but she proudly noted, "my
servants have been so loyal to me ever since these difficulties have
commenced." One of the Fain slaves, Gus, whom they had purchased
in 1854, said to her, "Miss Liza I never have felt so troubled when Master Richard was from home." Fifty-year-old Richard became the
Commissary General for Tennessee troops, and his son Hiram assisted
him. Sons Nick and Sam enlisted in the Nineteenth Tennessee Infantry Regiment. As the war progressed, their younger sons Ike and
Powell also joined the Confederate forces.[5]

Because he was Commissary General for Tennessee troops early in the war and the organizing colonel of the Sixty-third Tennessee Regiment in July 1862, Richard Fain served the Confederacy primarily within the state of Tennessee.[6] Although he was usually in other areas of the state, he had the opportunity to make a number of visits to his home throughout the war. Eliza deeply missed her spouse of twenty-seven years. "This is the second Sabbath since my husband left home," she wrote near the end of May 1861. "How much I miss my darling one." When Richard wrote to Eliza in January 1863 asking her advice about resigning his commission, she urged him to remain. In her diary she wrote, "I do feel could he stand the service I do not want him to resign if he is useful to his country as I hope and believe he is. I feel it is important for everyone to stand firm and unshaken at his post. I do trust that wisdom may be given from God my Heavenly Father to him who is my earthly stay to enable him to do that which is best for him to do."[7]

In her husband's absence, however, Eliza was increasingly forced to manage all of the family's affairs, which sometimes left her unprepared and frustrated. In November 1862, the prospect of obtaining salt from the saltworks was "troublesome": "The more I thought about it the more perplexed I was." She did not want to send her slave Lewis, because he could not "bear exposure," or her slave Gus, because he was "so clumsy and inactive." Her brother-in-law, Hiram Fain, offered to make other arrangements, but she was clearly discouraged: "These are the petty trials of life. How poor how mean they appear to have taken so much thought and so much time but such is earth and they that are earthly." In the spring of 1863, she and Hiram disagreed over the provisions of an agreement "about a field which Richard had consented to take of Brother Hiram." She conferred with her children, who supported her understanding, and determined "in justice to my family to have nothing to do with it." She also conferred in writing with her husband, who replied that she should have the slaves go ahead and "put in" the field and that "if he had made any bargain of that kind he was not particular with him." Clearly perturbed by her husband's lack of business acumen, Eliza wrote, "I received the word but just felt if this is the condition, let me not have anything to do with it." Overcoming her disillusionment, she continued, "But the word of my husband is the law to me so I have nothing to do but just go on and do the best I can. I do hope I may be enabled to do what is right." Perhaps stung by this incident, Eliza Fain wrote a month later: "I often feel so cast down, my family large, my anxiety for their worldly comfort often causes me to feel so depressed feeling ever my great lack as a managing housewife."[8]

In addition to running the affairs of the household, Eliza herself increasingly had to do more physical labor. By July 1863, she confessed that "the labors of the past week," which included directing and helping with the wheat harvest, have "very nearly broken me down." In March 1864, she "determined I would take what force I could muster and went to work making meadow fence" with two of her children and four of her slaves. She concluded that they "did pretty good work considering our force."[9]

Wartime disruptions also multiplied Eliza's duties as a parent; with her husband absent in the service of the Confederacy, all of the parenting tasks fell to Eliza. As a mother, Eliza was stern but loving. On 21 January 1861, she found three of her sons and two of their friends in one of the slave cabins "enjoying as they supposed a game of spotted paper." She confronted them with the "pernicious tendencies" of such games and left. When her sons came to her room later, she "spoke to them of the awful sins which they had committed this night and of the record which has been made. I urged them as we entered on a new year to make resolves that this is their last." She also frequently chided her daughters for dancing during the war, especially while their brothers were away fighting for civil and religious liberty.[10]

When her sons left for the armies, Eliza noted in her diary, "I do not feel I have given my sons to make war upon an enemy but to act in self defense," and wondered, "Have Christian mothers North laid their sons with the same loyalty of feeling upon their countrys altar that we mothers of the South have done[?] I feel it can hardly be possible." Her first concern was for their spiritual welfare: "My sons are in great peril, their souls are of more value than thousands upon thousands of worlds like this with nothing permanent." She prayed, "O my God thou knowest whether or not I have laid my husband and my sons on the altar of Southern Freedom from a right motive." She continually worried over the spiritual state of each of them. After attending church with many of her children, she wrote, "Oh that my dear children would love the Saviour." She feared that sons Sam and Powell had attended the services "with very little impression" and that Sam's "heart is far from God." She hoped that "I may be enabled to pray in faith for my dear, my loved soldier boy," who was "restive under parental restraint."[11]

At home, Eliza had two adult daughters, two teenage boys who would later join the Confederate forces, and four younger children.

She focused much of her attention on her younger children, determined that "my younger children shall be taught the scriptures. I feel I sorely neglected the older ones. My sons know nothing of the Bible." The younger children remained with her almost always, unless she had to go to Rogersville or to a neighbor's home. As she wrote in her diary on a wintry night in January 1862, her young son, Dick, "has just laid himself down on his bed in the corner having drawn out his bed from the bedroom to be as he says company for me."[12]

Her children's physical needs also bore heavily on Eliza. When five-year-old Lillie got her first shoes in the winter of 1863–64, she was "very proud indeed." However, her seven-year-old sister Ella was "still barefooted." Eliza had "felt more about my children being shod this winter than ever before—feel I am as I grow older becoming foolish about my little ones. It may be because they are little girls." During the next winter when "the wind was whistling around our dwelling," she declared, "my ill clad family filled me with care and trouble."[13]

In addition to her roles as wife, household manager, and mother, Eliza Fain was also a slave manager. Her household included nine slaves, of whom three were children—Jim, Lucinda, and Nate. Two slave women—Polly and Caroline—helped Eliza and her daughters with the housework and cooking, and four slave men—Hill, Lewis, Gus, and Ahab—worked the farm. As the war progressed, Eliza wondered, "What is to become of these poor creatures in our midst who are part of our household and for whom we feel such a strong attachment?"[14] Convinced that slavery was a benign institution and part of God's providential plan for the salvation of the black race, she challenged any Northern woman to come into a slave's home and see Southerners "in tender solicitude bending over the sufferer doing all that we can to relieve their sufferings, and then know the great anxiety we are often suffering in regard to their spiritual well being." Then the critic of slavery would, Eliza believed, "turn from the spot and say if this is slavery so let it continue unmolested by me until the great head of the church sees fit to change it if it is his will."[15] For slaves, white Southerners were "the best earthly friends they can have." She prayed, "We know O Father they have precious never dying souls." Although other Southerners were troubled by religious meetings among slaves, Eliza concluded, "If all [slaves] are as these I have around me, I am not afraid of one of Ham's descendants on this side of the Atlantic."[16]

Eliza expressed great concern over the spiritual welfare of her "black family." On the first Sunday in July 1863, after teaching her young daughters to read a psalm, she "spent a while in teaching the little black children. I feel so anxious they shall learn to read so that they may learn from Gods word their duty." By educating her slaves, Eliza defied Southern customs and, in some localities, Southern laws. Later in the war, she wrote, "After I was through reading for Nan I asked my little black ones their [catechism] questions. How anxious I feel for their salvation. I do trust the Lord will work for the moral good of Hams abject sons. Truly they are the greatest sufferers in this terrible war." In March 1865, after reading the Bible to her children, Eliza went out to one of the slave cabins and "read to old Ahab the book of Esther."[17]

Her paternal spiritual concern for enslaved blacks extended beyond her own slaves and shaped how she viewed individual slaves. When the black members of her church sang, she wrote in her diary, "I love to hear them sing on earth and I know I shall love to hear them in Heaven when the spirit shall be disrobed of the clay tenements which they now inhabit and we shall all see Jesus upon the throne. Christ will then make all free. To me this is a delightful thought to meet with the members of my dear family. My husband, my children, my servants at the right hand of God." When Gus told Eliza Fain that her sons had been fighting and swearing, she concluded, "I have confidence in my servant that he told me the truth as I do believe he is trying to be a Christian." A month later, as she listened to Gus sing as he shelled corn "for the use of my children and his," her "heart rose." "I trust in humble and holy gratitude to my God that he has made him, I trust, a Christian."[18]

Eliza worried greatly about the safety of her black family, illustrated one night when Union troops were rumored to be approaching. She thought of sending her adult slaves to a neighbor's and keeping "my own children for my bodyguard," but Polly, one of the Fain's elderly slaves, pleaded with Eliza not to send her because if the Union soldiers "get hold of me they will beat me to make me tell where things are hide and the others have gone," so the Fain slaves remained at home. Ahab, the other older slave, scouted until early in the morning. During the night, nine-year-old Nannie "drew up close" to Eliza and whispered, "Mama they are coming" and "Is that them?" Eliza nursed four-year-old Lillie, and two of her daughters began to cry. Her oldest daughter, Liz, then twenty-six, asked her, "Mama if they shoot us will we go to heaven?" She replied, "Yes my child." "They can't hurt us when we get there," Liz concluded. At last, "the night of suspense past [sic] and the morning came." The Federal cavalry had crossed the mountains and gone a different way.[19]

In September 1863, Federal forces entered upper East Tennessee in force, and they reappeared at times over the next year and a half. Formerly secure in the Confederate interior, during the last eighteen months of the war the Fains lived in what Stephen Ash has termed "the Confederate frontier," a region generally under the control of the Confederacy but subject to sporadic Federal penetration. "Fear was a part of everyday existence on the frontier," Ash rightly argues, "for no matter how infrequently the enemy actually appeared the threat of a raid was ever-present."[20] The Fain family itself was also more separated. Nick Fain, captured in the battles for Vicksburg, was in a Northern prison camp at Johnson's Island in Lake Erie.[21] Ike Fain had already joined his brothers in the army, and Powell, the Fains' fifth son, would soon do likewise.[22] Although Richard Fain and his sons occasionally returned to their home, they could rarely stay for long.

Early in October 1863, "Yankees" made their first appearance at the Fain home and drove off the family's oxen. The next day, two guards arrived at Eliza's house, and soon her meadow was "swarming with the blue coats." Major Brown of the Sixty-fifth Indiana Regiment ate in her home. When the major prayed over the food, Eliza "burst into tears and threw up my hands saying: Oh to think Christian is arrayed against Christian in this struggle almost breaks my heart." He also led family prayer that night, in which "he said nothing offensive." For the next several weeks, every day the Fains would "see blue coats more or less." Federal officers sent guards to the Fain household to protect them from theft. The most frequent guard was Mr. Finley of the Seventh Ohio Regiment, "a noble pleasant Vallandigham man a true Democrat." "For these men," Eliza had "a kind feeling. They love the South and I do believe would rather see her succeed than that abolitionism should gain any stronger hold in the North than it already has." When Confederates reentered the area on 6 November, Eliza and her neighbor and sister-in-law Sarah Fain hid Finley. When the soldier learned that he would be unable to rejoin his command, Eliza introduced him to a Confederate cavalry lieutenant, to whom he surrendered, and she asked the lieutenant "in behest of the pleadings of a Rebel Colonels wife to show mercy to the guard who had been so kind to us."[23]

When Federal troops withdrew, Lewis, the Fains' twenty-four-year-old slave, left with them. Eliza allowed him to go to a neighbor's, and he did not return. "I have ever said and still feel and say," she wrote, "if one I have preferred yankee rule to Southern let them go." Six weeks later, she reflected, "My poor deluded Negro Lewis—I wonder how

Christmas has passed with him. I think of him often when a cold day comes."[24]

As the war and foraging armies increasingly impinged on their food supply, the Fain family struggled to obtain provisions. Fearful that "we must suffer for something to eat," Eliza took comfort in a book that described George Muller's ministry as evidence of the power of prayer. Muller (1805–1898) founded an orphanage in Bristol, England, in 1836 and became famous for supplying the orphans' needs through prayer. Eliza wondered whether "if God in answer to prayer gave to George Muller food and raiment for 700 orphans will he not enable a family of 22 to be provided for when the Father and Mother are believers in Jesus[?]" In mid-May 1864, she was forced to ask a nearby neighbor for meat for her family. The neighbor gave her a "middling" and told her that if her own "black family" did not return, Eliza could have more. A few days later, Eliza went to Rogersville, where she spoke to other acquaintances about obtaining meat and meal.[25]

As Confederate and Federal soldiers passed through, the Fains often gave them meals. Eliza also frequently distributed tracts to those who passed by her home. She told two Federal soldiers that "these tracts were prepared for our Southern soldiers but they too had souls for which I felt very anxious." "Precious messengers of truth," she dubbed the tracts, they "formed an important part of my defensive armor since I came under the power of the enemy." She also used her moral authority to chastise those who failed to act according to her moral standards. When two Confederate cavalrymen passed a neighbor's house with Federal troops in close pursuit, they stopped briefly and told the women, "They are coming as thick as Hell back there." Eliza Fain was shocked at the wickedness of "a man in the very jaws of death as it were giving vent to such language." When their comrade came by soon afterward, "spoke of the cowardice of his pursuers," and swore, she felt "I must reprove him and did."[26]

Illness and death were frequent visitors to Hawkins County during the Civil War, and their arrival revealed much about social relations within this Southern community. When a sick soldier who had been taken prisoner at Gettysburg and exchanged came to a neighbor's home, Eliza Fain had gone to help care for him. After remaining for most of the day, she sent for her oldest slave, Ahab, to come and sit through the night with the soldier, "but he did not want to go and did not until I came home and just had to beg him to go." Ashamed that she had "a servant or anyone else about me who was unwilling to go sit up with a dying person," she "at last after much persuasion" got

Ahab to go. "Had he been a young negro," she later wrote, "I could have told him to go but an old Negro gray-headed has privileges which others do not." When someone died during the war, either as a direct result of the conflict or from the all-too-common nineteenth-century illnesses, only women and slaves remained to mourn and to bury. After slave Peggy Martin died in October 1863, three white women prepared her body for burial, and "she was bourne to the grave by blacks. There was no white man there." When young Jake Tilson was murdered by Unionist bushwhackers in January 1865, Eliza Fain likewise lamented that "we have no male friend tonight to set with us and watch over the lifeless body. But woman, woman is here with all her deep felt sympathy."[27]

By June 1864, Rogersville was subject to "bushwhacking rule," when armed bands of men with only nominal loyalty to either the Union or the Confederacy stole what they wanted from citizens and killed those who challenged them. Eliza wrote, "I tremble for our men when the wicked (such as bushwhackers) rule." In August, some Confederate soldiers formed a line of battle on the Fains' property but retreated without fighting; the Federal soldiers advanced through their meadow, "throwing down fences without compunction." Even before they left, Eliza and her adult slaves worked to get the cornfield fence up and "stock proof."[28]

Although she was a strong Southern partisan and had even stronger religious faith, Eliza sometimes revealed her doubts and fears in her diary. In March 1862, she wrote, "How sad I feel this evening. Tears are falling as I write. The thought has been upon me what if in the providence of God the North shall be successful." In October of that year, she felt "like giving up at times," and "were it not for the thought what is thy duty would sink down." Nevertheless, she wrote, "I am one who says, who believes this mighty conflict has to be waged. It is to do or die." Though Confederates had "not sought this quarrel," they had "no alternative left but to go forward trusting in the God of Abraham, Isaac and Jacob."[29] Her pastor frequently spoke on the issues of the war—especially slavery. "This is a subject of greatest importance to us as a people," Eliza wrote. "Oh let us have Bible truth to sustain us." However, from August 1864 to March 1865, the church had no preaching because the Reverend J. J. Robinson became a refugee.[30]

On 7 September 1864, Eliza confessed to her diary, "I feel this night so oppressed with the cares of life. Have been working so hard to try to get along." Frustrated by her inability to provide for her family, she wrote, "I suppose I have undertaken to do too much. Why my dear friends expect more of me than they seem to of others I cannot tell. My family is large, they have to live and yet they seem to feel I can do all. I feel I am to blame." Rumors that Atlanta had fallen left her troubled: "The news of this evening affects me more seriously than all things else and I do suppose it is one reason why I feel so oppressed." Although distressed about the news, she relied on her faith for strength: "I have listened to my little children praying at my house, have prayed and wept bitter tears myself and now feel so greatly comforted." When she became so feeble that she could "do no hard labor" for several weeks, her daughters took "all the care of the house off of my hands," and she sewed and knitted.[31]

Although the shifting of troop movements brought Richard Fain and several of their sons into the general vicinity, neither they nor other Confederate men could stay at their homes for fear of being captured by Federal troops or killed by Unionist bushwhackers. "He seems to be unwell," Eliza wrote of Richard in the summer of 1864. "I feel so sorry that he cannot stay." Their son Sam Fain, in Virginia with the Sixty-third Tennessee Regiment, also worried about his father's health in a letter to his sister: "I do hope and trust that papa may be permitted to stay at home this winter. If he should have to leave home he will see a hard time. He is getting old."[32] The thought that her husband and sons could not remain at home, even for a short time, distressed Eliza greatly: "I do feel so sorry to see our men coming home when they have not one moment of enjoyment after enduring what they have done for such a long time." When her son Powell and two of his fellow soldiers were home, they slept in Ahab's cabin, Ahab "standing picket for them." The next morning, Ahab said that "he had an uneasy night. The thought of any of them being caught seems to trouble him greatly." When Richard was home a few weeks later, he sat up most of the night and then went to Ahab's cabin to sleep, "determined he will not spend another night at home unless he knows more of the whereabouts of our troops." After learning that bushwhackers had killed two more Confederates, Eliza wrote, "No southern soldier or citizen can remain at home now in much security. Will there be one family when this cruel war shall end in the South who have not tasted the bitter fruits[?]" Ironically—or perhaps providentially—hers was to be one of those very few such families.[33]

By the end of November, Richard was again at home, "permitted to stay day after day unmolested. Our family altar again reared morning and night—delightful seasons." The "delightful seasons" were short-lived, however, as Federal troops again moved into the area. On

Christmas Day 1864, Federal soldiers moving down the valley surrounded and captured three young Confederates, including one of the Fains' nephews, who had been staying with the Fains. Some of the Northern soldiers soon arrived at the Fain home, and the commanding officer threatened to burn it if Eliza did not tell him where the fourth young Confederate, Jake Tilson, had gone. They searched part of the house, took some of her pans, and then left. The next day, they returned to search the house "from garrett to cellar," "the first time my house has been searched since the war began." Although she "had been favored by God with a self possession and calmness" throughout the war, Eliza was "unnerved and shaken" by these events: "Our boys captured, our home threatened, our spirits humbled before the outlaws and barbarians of Lincolns despotism." The worst was yet to come. Four weeks later, young Jake Tilson, on his way to join the Confederate scouts, was surrounded by bushwhackers and murdered near the Fain home. Eliza was one of the first to find the body, "his face so disfigured from blood we could scarcely have known who he was." A week later, she reflected, "This week has been to me one of sorer trials than any I have passed since this unholy, this terrible war began. Never in my life have I been so harrowed by any thing as the murder of our brave noble Jake."[34]

As the war stretched into its fourth year, Eliza began to doubt the loyalty of her dark family. In August 1864, she recorded, "I have gotten so I do not have much confidence in Negro flesh." One of Eliza's sons and several of his fellow soldiers were hiding in a nearby hollow from Union forces, and Eliza feared that one of her sister-in-law's slaves would reveal their hiding place. In December, Eliza and her family spent "a night of suspense" in their home, while Union troops passed through the area. However, she learned from her slave Aunt Polly that her slaves Gus and Caroline had left "to go over and see the finely mounted darkies." The proximity of Federal forces perhaps emboldened Gus and Caroline to go to see the African American cavalrymen. This particular incident did not seem to have a dramatic effect on Eliza, but her relations with her slaves grew more strained as the war drew to a close.[35]

Yet there were exceptions to the growing uneasiness between master and servants. Such an incident occurred on 15 January 1865, a Sabbath day. Amid the uncertainty of Federal troop movements and Unionist bushwhackers' threats, three of the Fain children read from their Bibles. When they finished, Eliza went to the slave cabin and "invited Old Uncle Joe to come into the house and pray with us." When she returned to the house, she "arranged all seating the blacks on the left of the fire place and my white family on the right. I then opened the Bible read the 14 of John, sung 'When I can read my title clear,' Gus raising the tune and we all kneeled while the poor sable son of Africa breathed forth in solemn broken accents his prayer to his Father upon the throne. Truly to me it was a solemn scene. My soul was refreshed. religion was so beautiful so lovely." Remarkably, Uncle Joe was not one of the Fains' slaves; he was a slave from another farm and was the father of Caroline, the slave whom the Fains rented from Henry Watterson.[36]

Despite this brief spiritual respite, Eliza's thoughts soon turned back to the war. When she thought back on four years of "horrible carnage from war with our land laid waste, our dear friends slaughtered and disabled for life, the crys of widows and orphans and of the desolations of Zion, the heart bleeds from every pore." In mid-March 1865, she welcomed home her son Nick, who had been in a Northern prison for many months. For the first time in over two years, she enjoyed "having my 12 children under our roof for their suppers." The joy was again short-lived; Richard and their sons soon left to rejoin their units. "So we are again a family of women and children," Eliza noted in her diary on 23 March.[37]

As East Tennessee descended further into irregular warfare and partisan reprisals, Eliza observed that "our Government and female influence" had restrained Confederate men from attacking Unionists. "Women of the South have generally urged our Soldier to do right," she continued ominously, "but they are beginning to feel entreaty will become useless." On 5 April a "set of outlaws such as I have never seen" came to their house. When she opened the door, their leader, William Sizemore, said, "Good Morning Mrs. Fain, I am here and I intend to tear you up and burn your house down." She warned of retribution, but he said, "I don't care a da———n." They burst in and stole all her silver spoons, all the meat in the smokehouse, the milk and butter from the springhouse, canned fruit from the cellar, and the Fains' old horse George.[38]

As the war neared its end, Eliza began to challenge gender conventions in the name of piety and to take on new roles. As late as January 1865, she was still unwilling to lead her family in prayer and called in an older male slave to do so. However, by the first of April, she "was enabled to bow at the family altar myself for the first time in my life. I have long felt the importance of keeping this duty up in the absence of my dear husband but the cross has always seemed to be too great. I trust I shall from this time forward be enabled to do my duty."[39]

In the first summer of war, women in Rogersville had organized a "female prayer meeting" to support the war effort. Eliza Fain had "thought to go down but have felt so badly for the last two or three days have no desire to go anywhere, but be at my home." Nearly four years later, on 10 April 1865, the day after General Robert E. Lee surrendered the Army of Northern Virginia, an occurrence as yet unknown to her, Eliza lay upon her bed pondering the question, "What will my Master have me to do?" She resolved "under the guidance of the Spirit" to organize "a female prayer meeting." She vowed that "if she lived to see the light of another day," she would go to town and "see the Christian women of Rogersville as to whether it met their approbation." Initially hindered the next morning by rain that seemed to mean "my Father did not approve of my plans," she went to Rogersville when the weather cleared. As she canvassed the town for support for her female prayer meeting, she saw two "rather blue looking men" sitting on the steps of a house. She was saddened to see men "bowing in fear" before "a Lincoln dynasty." "But," she continued, "when I thought of the Christian heart sinking it nerved me and I felt I could almost preach a sermon." Having obtained the support of several women for her female prayer meeting, she drove her ox wagon home, disregarding rumors that "Lee's whole army surrendered."[40]

The next day she awoke to learn that Caroline, her hired slave, had left. "I felt sorry for the poor negro," she wrote, "feeling she had started upon a life of trial such as she had never known before." She insisted that "I feel no feelings of unkindness towards our poor deluded servants." Instead, she blamed "those who would drag God from his throne, if they could, to carry out their great principles of false philanthropy." On Saturday evening of the same week, Gus left without telling her where he was going. When he returned on Monday morning, she lectured him on who his true friends were. Clearly shaken by Caroline's departure, Eliza "told him I did not want him to go away and that I had confidence in him." Even more revealing was her comment to him that "I did not want the last remnant of confidence which I had in the African race destroyed by his leaving us." For his part, Gus "listened attentively but said nothing."[41]

As the news of Lee's surrender became clearer and harder to discount, she mourned, "The saddest sight to me is the Christian heart giving way under it. Christians of the South can you, O will you ever believe that God your Father will give you up[?]" She found it difficult to organize her female prayer meeting because "the right spirit is not pervading the hearts of our people." Not every woman "wore a cheerless face. No, no blessed be God, womans mission to earth seems to be to sustain the heart of fallen man. Well may she do this as she was first in the transgression but she was first at the Sepulchre and may she ever be found first at her post to labor for Jesus is my prayer." Eliza thus adhered to the orthodox religious view that women were by nature weak, while simultaneously carving out a position of moral superiority for women, who in defeat had to "sustain the heart of fallen man." A few days later, when she first heard that her husband might be going to Knoxville to take the loyalty oath, she wrote, "I feel never would I do this, rather would I lose all possessions—yea life itself than take an oath which perjures me before God and man." When Richard actually went a month later, Eliza wrote, "The dreaded hour has come. Oh how my soul has been wrung with anguish as I have looked forward to this sad moment when my beloved husband should say to us, I must leave you and go to Knoxville to take the oath." When she first heard of the oath, she "just felt let me die or go with my family into exile rather than submit."[42]

Eliza Fain was remarkable both because she kept a diary for over sixty years and because she was well educated (for her place, time, and gender) in a Knoxville academy. She and her family were also unusual because of the area in which they lived; many of their neighbors in northeastern Tennessee did not share their devotion to the Confederate cause, and some were actively hostile. Her piety perhaps also made Eliza unusual, but only because of its depth rather than its nature. White women had long been numerically predominant in evangelical Southern churches, and they relied on their religious beliefs to make sense of their world.[43] During wartime, they continued to seek meaning for their experiences from the Bible and Christianity. As the war turned against the South, the faithful remained faithful to the Southern cause. Only near the end did a few come close to questioning the justice of God; most resorted to the inscrutability of God's purposes. Appomattox was unfathomable, and God was loving and just, yet nagging questions lingered.[44] Throughout the spring of 1865, Eliza remained bitter, so bitter at times that she could not write in her diary. Like other Southern women, Eliza perhaps experienced a crisis of faith as the Confederacy crumbled, yet she was too orthodox to commit her murmurings against God to paper.[45]

In many ways, Eliza's experience of the Civil War represents that of thousands of other Southern women whose husbands wore gray. Left alone to care for children and to manage a few slaves, these women endured loneliness, anxiety, heavy physical labor, shortages of food and other essentials, threats from armed bands of irregulars from North and South, and slave unrest. Most, like Eliza, tenaciously supported the Confederate cause, and many lost their husbands and sons in defense of it.

After their emancipation, Ahab, Gus, Hill, and Polly remained in the area and continued to do work for the Fains in return for small payments in money or provisions. Over the next few years, a lack of economic opportunity forced three of the Fains' sons to move out of the area to find work. At the end of 1865, as she thought back over the year, Eliza called upon her deep-seated religious faith to comprehend the meaning of the collapse of the Confederacy and the changes that it had wrought: "We bow submissively and reverently to him who still sitteth as King of Kings and Lord of Lords feeling he cannot err in any thing which comes to pass. And yet our views concerning slavery as an institution of divine origin and one which the Bible recognized are today the same as when in 61, we took our stand in our country's cause. We feel God our Father has not been pleased to perpetuate the system of slavery which then existed. Why we cannot know now but he does and this is all we deserve to know."[46] Eliza Fain, wife, mother, household manager, slave mistress, Christian, and Confederate, no longer owned slaves or dreamed of Southern independence, but she remained convinced that her Bible upheld the righteousness of both slavery and secession. Her faith sustained her during the war as she assumed greater responsibilities as family provider and farm manager; it also emboldened her near the end of war to lead in family prayers and to organize a prayer meeting. Southern evangelical religion proved remarkably resilient for Eliza Fain and for thousands of other Southern women and men, both in sustaining the Confederacy for four long years and in consoling a defeated South.

Notes

1. Eliza Fain kept a diary from 21 June 1835, when she was eighteen years old, to 10 January 1892, nine days before she died at age seventy-five. Approximately 3,750 manuscript pages in twenty-eight volumes of her diary have survived. Eliza Rhea Fain Diaries, John N. Fain Collection, McClung Historical Collection, Knox County Public Library System, Knoxville, Tenn. (hereafter cited as Fain Diaries).

The author wishes to express his gratitude to Dr. John N. Fain for his willingness to share both Eliza Fain's diaries and his own research on their context and contents.

2. Entry for 5 June 1863, Fain Diaries.

For the harsh realities of the antebellum world of elite plantation mistresses, see Catherine Clinton, *The Plantation Mistress: Woman's World in the Old South* (New York: Pantheon Books, 1982), 16–35, and Elizabeth Fox-Genovese, *Within the Plantation Household: Black and White Women of the Old South* (Chapel Hill: University of North Carolina Press, 1988), 37–99.

For transformation and continuity in Southern women's lives during the Civil War, see George C. Rable, *Civil Wars: Women and the Crisis of Southern Nationalism* (Urbana: University of Illinois Press, 1989); Catherine Clinton and Nina Silber, eds., *Divided Houses: Gender and the Civil War* (New York: Oxford University Press, 1992), 134–212; LeeAnn Whites, *The Civil War as a Crisis in Gender: Augusta, Georgia, 1860–1890* (Athens: University of Georgia Press, 1995); Edward D. C. Campbell Jr. and Kym S. Rice, eds., *A Woman's War: Southern Women, Civil War, and the Confederate Legacy* (Charlottesville: University Press of Virginia, 1996), 1–27, 73–111; and Drew Gilpin Faust, *Mothers of Invention: Women of the Slaveholding South in the American Civil War* (Chapel Hill: University of North Carolina Press, 1996).

3. *Knoxville (Tenn.) Whig,* 12 January 1861, quoted in Daniel W. Crofts, *Reluctant Confederates: Upper South Unionists in the Secession Crisis* (Chapel Hill: University of North Carolina Press, 1989), 133; Noel C. Fisher, *War at Every Door: Partisan Politics and Guerrilla Violence in East Tennessee, 1860–1869* (Chapel Hill: University of North Carolina Press, 1997), 188.

4. Entry for 15 September 1860, Fain Diaries. In July 1863 Eliza Fain wrote, "We feel our servants are recognized by God our Father as part of our family." Entry for 14 July 1863, Fain Diaries.

5. Entry for 2 June 1861, Fain diaries. Gus's concerns were "solaces to a troubled heart coming from one, who has been a member of my family many years, and for whom I have such kind feelings." Entry for 2 June 1861, Fain Diaries.

The Fains purchased Gus in 1854 for $900; he was married to Mary, another of the Fain slaves who died in 1858, with whom he had three children (Jim, Cindy, and Nate). Bill of sale, 8 December 1854, John H. Fain Collection.

6. Robert K. Krick, *Lee's Colonels: A Biographical Register of the Field Officers of the Army of Northern Virginia* (Dayton, Ohio: Morningside Bookshop, 1979), 120; entry for 28 October 1862, Fain Diaries.

7. Entries for 26 May 1861, 23 January 1863, Fain Diaries; Faust, *Mothers of Invention,* 114–23.

8. Entries for 2 November 1862, 28 April, 27 May 1863, Fain Diaries. A week later she wrote, "I have been trying to attend to domestic cares but feel every thing so irksome which I undertake." Entry for 2 June 1863, Fain diaries.

9. Entries for 5 July 1863, 31 March 1864, Fain Diaries.

10. Entry for 21 January 1861, Fain Diaries. For Eliza Fain's aversion to dancing, see entries for 21 March 1861, 13 January 1862, 5, 23 January, 19 July 1864, 21 March, 19 May 1865. For the tensions between sacrifice and indulgence on the Confederate home front, see Rable, *Civil War,* 192–96.

11. Entries for 12 May 1861, 5 April 1864, 16 June 1861, 25 February, 28 March 1864, Fain Diaries. When she asked Sam where he had been, "he would not tell me and seemed rather crusty about it. I fear he had not been in good company." Entry for 29 March 1864, Fain Diaries.

12. Entries for 11 September 1864, 13 January 1862, Fain Diaries.

13. Entries for 14 January, 4 November 1864, Fain Diaries.

14. Entry for 18 March 1862, Fain Diaries; Faust, *Mothers of Invention,* 53–74; Rable, *Civil Wars,* 113–21.

15. Entry for 21 April 1861, Fain Diaries.

16. Entries for 29 April, 18 May 1861, Fain Diaries.

17. Entries for 5 July 1863, 2 October 1864, 26 March 1865, Fain Diaries. For the importance of literacy to slaves, see Janet Duitsman Cornelius, *"When I Can Read My Title Clear": Literacy, Slavery, and Religion in the Antebellum South* (Columbia: University of South Carolina Press, 1991).

18. Entries for 25 February, 8 March, 8 April 1864, Fain Diaries. The Fains' three slave children, born between 1853 and 1856, were Gus's children; their mother, Mary, had died in 1858.

19. Entry for 3 January 1863, Fain Diaries.

20. Stephen V. Ash, *When the Yankees Came: Conflict and Chaos in the Occupied South, 1861–1865* (Chapel Hill: University of North Carolina Press, 1995), 77, 92–99 (quotation, 93); Rable, *Civil Wars,* 154–80.

21. Entries for 28 June 1863, 17 May 1864, 17 May 1865, Fain Diaries. Samuel Rhea Gammon, the Fains' nephew, was captured with Nick, and both were imprisoned at Johnson Island until February 1865.

22. Richard Fain was particularly concerned about his son Powell, "fearing he would not be able to stand the soldiers life." Powell felt "there is great glee in being a soldier." Entry for 21 July 1864, Fain Diaries.

23. Entries for 10 October, 26, 27 October, 4 November, 6 November 1863, Fain Diaries.

24. Entries for 19 November 1863, 1 January 1864, Fain Diaries; Faust, *Mothers of Invention,* 74–79. Most of the first runaways were, like Lewis, males between sixteen and thirty-five years of age, and they fled soon after Federal soldiers entered an area or were withdrawing from it. John Cimprich, *Slavery's End in Tennessee, 1861–1865* (University: University of Alabama Press, 1985), 23–24.

25. Entries for 14, 16, 19 May 1864, Fain Diaries.

26. Entries for 21 October 1863, 5 November, 15 June 1864, Fain Diaries. For other examples of her giving tracts to soldiers, see entries for 20, 21, 25, 27, 28 October, 8 November 1863, 1, 5, 16 January 1864, Fain Diaries.

27. Entries for 7 September, 4 October 1863, 22 January 1865, Fain Diaries.

28. Entries for 15, 17 June 1864, Fain Diaries.

29. Entries for 18 March, 21 October 1862, Fain Diaries; Faust, *Mothers of Invention,* 179–95; Rable, *Civil Wars,* 203–19.

30. Entry for 2 August 1864, Fain Diaries. On loss of church services, see

entries for 21 August, 25 September, 6 November 1864, 8 January, 5 March 1865. For sermons on slavery, see entries for 15 May, 12 June, 2 August 1864, Fain Diaries.

31. Entries for 7 September, 5 October 1864, Fain Diaries.

32. Entry for 23 August 1864, Fain Diaries; Sam A. Fain to Sallie Fain, 29 November 1864, John H. Fain Collection.

33. Entries for 3, 7, 27 September, 14 November 1864, Fain Diaries.

By the winter of 1863–64, Eliza Fain was worried that she, like so many others, would lose one of her family members: "I often wonder shall my children all be preserved through the great struggle of the South. When I hear of so many families who have been broken up, their loved ones dying far from home." Entry for 23 January 1864, Fain Diaries.

34. Entries for 29 November, 25, 26 December 1864, 8, 22, 28 January 1865, Fain Diaries.

35. Entries for 25 August, 12 December 1864, Fain Diaries.

36. Entries for 15 January 1865, Fain Diaries.

37. Entries for 7 February, 17, 18, 23 March 1865, Fain Diaries.

38. Entries for 1, 5 April 1865, Fain Diaries. William Sizemore, a Unionist partisan and former member of the Confederate army, was accused of killing at least a dozen men and was labeled "a notorious desperado and bushwhacker—a terror to the southern people." A few years after the war, Sizemore himself was shot and killed by an "old acquaintance." Sheila Weems Johnston, *The Blue and Gray from Hawkins County, Tennessee, 1861–1865* (Rogersville, Tenn.: Hawkins County Genealogical and Historical Society, 1995), 3:37, 67–68. For the extramilitary violence that prevailed in eastern Tennessee throughout the war and into the Reconstruction era, see Fisher, *War at Every Door.* See also Michael Fellman, "Women and Guerrilla Warfare," in Clinton and Silber, *Divided Houses,* 147–65.

39. Entry for 2 April 1865, Fain Diaries. A week later, she again "closed the work of this day around the family altar with my dear children." Entry for 9 April 1865, Fain Diaries.

40. Entries for 24 July 1861, 10 April 1865, Fain Diaries. For similar efforts elsewhere, see Faust, *Mothers of Invention,* 185–86.

41. Entries for 11, 17 April 1865, Fain Diaries.

42. Entries for 14, 15, 19 April, 17 May 1865, Fain Diaries.

43. Donald Mathews, *Religion in the Old South* (Chicago: University of Chicago Press, 1977); Jean E. Friedman, *The Enclosed Garden: Women and Community in the Evangelical South, 1830–1900* (Chapel Hill: University of North Carolina Press, 1985).

44. Rable, *Civil Wars,* 202–21; Richard E. Beringer et al., *Why the South Lost the Civil War* (Athens: University of Georgia Press, 1986), 351–67.

45. On 27 April 1865, she wrote, "Yesterday I could not write as my spirit was overwhelmed within me. I felt so rebellious." Entry for 27 April 1865, Fain Diaries; Faust, *Mothers of Invention,* 191–93; *Civil Wars,* 217–19.

46. Entry for 31 December 1865, Fain Diaries. The end of an old year and the beginning of a new was frequently a time of serious reflection on the past. Rable, *Civil Wars*, 205.

For a discussion of the responses of white religious Southerners to Confederate defeat, see Daniel W. Stowell, *Rebuilding Zion: The Religious Reconstruction of the South, 1863–1877* (New York: Oxford University Press, 1998), 33–48; Eugene D. Genovese, *A Consuming Fire: The Fall of the Confederacy in the Mind of the White Christian South* (Athens: University of Georgia Press, 1998), 101–21; Charles Reagan Wilson, *Baptized in Blood: The Religion of the Lost Cause, 1865–1920* (Athens: University of Georgia Press, 1980), 58–78; Rable, *Civil Wars*, 221–39.

NINE

POWER, SEX, AND GENDER ROLES

The Transformation of an Alabama Planter
Family during the Civil War

Henry Walker

The contention that the American Civil War was a watershed in Southern history has long been the subject of debate. For nearly half a century, scholars have been concerned with the political and economic fate of the planter class.[1] More recently, historians have focused increasing attention on the social implications of the war and have tried to discover what impact it had on gender and familial relations.[2]

Scholars who see discontinuity in gender relations have amassed an impressive arsenal of scholarship. The first important contemporary contribution to this school of thought is Anne Firor Scott's *The Southern Lady: From Pedestal to Politics, 1830–1930*. Scott finds that although women's roles were changing before the war, the conflict offered and women embraced even greater opportunities for change. Much subsequent scholarship has tried to determine how the war affected gender roles by altering, in one form or another, the institution of marriage. Catherine Clinton contends that due to a lack of male companionship, a generation of Southern women was "forced into economic self-sufficiency." Carol Bleser and Frederick Heath's examination of a prosperous Alabama planter couple caused these historians to generalize that the war "produced profound alterations in the internal dynamics of many Southern marriages." In his study of nineteenth-century laws, Peter W. Bardaglio comes to the same general conclusion. He believes that women gained greater autonomy during the war and that postwar legislation reflected this reality. Focusing her attention more on the psychological changes the war wrought in interpersonal relations, Drew Gilpin Faust argues that Southern women perceived their men's failure to protect hearth and home as a grave weakness. This perception led women to become disillusioned with men and to begin asserting their own self-interest.[3]

Historians who argue for continuity in the Southern household have also produced much thoughtful work. The same year Scott's work appeared, H. E. Sterkx published an examination of Civil War women in Alabama which asserts that the independence women gained during the war was lost when peace returned. Suzanne Lebsock's painstaking research of women in Petersburg, Virginia, reveals that instead of offering women new opportunities, Confederate defeat actually confirmed their subordination. LeeAnn Whites's equally well researched study of Augusta, Georgia, finds both change and continuity. She states that postwar women did have greater power in the public sphere but used that power to restore traditional values. In a recent examination of women in Caldwell County, North Carolina, David McGee finds little change at all and argues that the war left women "relatively unscathed." In an even more recent work, Carol Bleser shows how the marriage between Varina Howell and Jefferson Davis attests to the survival of the patriarchal system.[4]

Many historians who have taken a somewhat broader view of the South buttress these case, local, and state studies. In *Confederate Women,* Bell Irvin Wiley contends that although the war diminished the patriarchy of the Old South, no gender revolution occurred. Jean Friedman, in her *The Enclosed Garden,* asserts that after the war women remained in traditional kinship networks that had been formed in the antebellum era. In his *Civil Wars,* George Rable overall agrees and shows postwar Southern women clinging to the region's traditional values.[5]

The following essay addresses many of these historiographical controversies by examining the Claytons of Alabama. A wealthy planter family for generations before the Civil War, the Clayton's story supports those who claim that the antebellum planter class survived the war and dominated the postwar South.[6] However, a thorough examination of the Claytons' correspondence and memoirs reveals that the family changed at its very core. The war may have left the family's position in society intact, but the transformation of sexual relationships and gender roles had a permanent impact on the power structure within the family. For the Claytons, the war was indeed a revolution: one within their own household.

The Claytons were a large landowning family in eighteenth-century North Carolina. By the early nineteenth century, the family had migrated into western Georgia. In 1839, they settled in Chambers County, Alabama, in the southeastern section of the state, where they owned a large cotton plantation and forty-two slaves.[7]

The patriarch of the family, Nelson, was an impressive man. In the 1820s and 1830s, he was a judge and also a member of the Georgia House of Representatives and Senate. When he moved to Alabama, he became a respected community leader and a proponent of scientific agriculture. He contributed articles to progressive farm journals and spoke at agricultural fairs.[8]

Nelson had assumed the role of family patriarch when his father died in 1820. Nelson took his responsibility seriously and conscientiously tried to help his family. In his papers, one finds many letters from distant relatives for whom Nelson administered wills, bought land, and conducted other business transactions. These family members were grateful to have Nelson look after their financial affairs and eagerly took his advice on money matters. However, with his immediate family, he did not fare as well. His younger brother, Delamar, had developed a dependence on alcohol early in life and, after suffering from severe depression for an extended period, committed suicide in 1837.[9] Although Nelson had done the best he could for Delamar, his early death by his own hand caused Nelson to question his abilities.

Nelson therefore began to overcompensate and became increasingly authoritarian with his immediate family members, especially his sons Henry and Joseph. Since Nelson's only goal for his three daughters—Jane, Sarah, and Susan—was a proper marriage, he believed they could manage without a great deal of supervision from him.[10] His sons were another matter entirely.

In 1845, both Henry and Joseph began attending Emory and Henry College in Virginia. Joseph was not academically gifted, so he returned home to learn to manage the plantation under Nelson's watchful eyes. Henry, on the other hand, flourished in college and relished the temporary freedom from his father.[11]

Henry wanted to become a scientist, but he knew his father would not allow him to pursue that goal. In an autobiographical oratory entitled "The Choice of a Profession," Henry bemoaned his father's forcing him to forgo his own choice of a career for the field of law. Henry believed that Nelson's and all fathers' interference in their sons' lives resulted from a type of self-interest that could cause a man to become "a complete *brute*." Henry argued that sons should follow their "natural inclinations," but lacking the courage to confront their fathers, they instead threw away their dreams and thereby wasted their real talents. Henry then warned that ultimately "the old men . . . must expect to receive their portion of the blame" for this intrusiveness into their sons' lives.[12]

Henry's strong words of protest were never uttered to Nelson. Rather, Henry "chose" the legal profession. In October 1848, he moved to the bustling town of Eufaula, Alabama, within a day's travel of Nelson's plantation, and began studying for the bar. He received his license to practice in 1849.[13]

After Henry started his law practice, he began courting and then married Victoria Hunter. The Hunter family had moved from South Carolina in 1835 to claim Indian land in eastern Alabama. The area was wild, and Indian attacks were still fairly common. Victoria received a traditional early education and attended Christ College, a female Episcopal school in Georgia. After her mother's death, she returned home to help her father, John Hunter, with the management of his large plantation. By the time she was twenty, she had received both the cultivation that often comes from a liberal education and the grit of her early years on the Alabama frontier.[14]

Victoria's upbringing allowed her to be tough and determined. Reflecting on her youth in her memoirs, Victoria felt that her experience on her father's plantation was an asset in finding a husband and states that "no practical man worth the favorable consideration of a young lady, desires a useless woman." Although Victoria believed that she was not merely decorative, she nonetheless saw her usefulness as important only if it related to the larger goal of attracting a man.[15]

Victoria's mindset helps explain why the Claytons' marriage was from the beginning a partnership but an unequal one. This inequality became clear in the management of their plantation. Victoria looked after the food, clothes, housing, and religious training of the slaves. And when Henry was away on business, she supervised the plantation. Yet she never possessed any real autonomy, since Henry insisted that she only implement his explicit instructions.[16]

Not only was Victoria subordinate to her husband; due to Nelson's dominance in Henry's life, she often had to defer to her father-in-law as well. A good example of this was Nelson's attempts to control Victoria's children. In the fall of 1854, her first child—who was four years old and named for Nelson—visited his paternal grandparents. When Henry and Victoria traveled to Nelson's plantation to retrieve their son, Nelson demanded that Henry extend the boy's stay. Victoria initially protested but finally had to acquiesce to the men's decision to leave young Nelson in his grandfather's care. On 23 September the child contracted a "congestive chill." Fearing that his condition might worsen, the elder Nelson sent one of his slaves to summon Henry and Victoria. They arrived on 25 September to find that their son had died the previous day.[17]

About the time of their son's death, Henry and Victoria became increasingly interested in the promotion of Southern rights. Since the late 1840s, Henry had belonged to the Eufaula Regency, a bipartisan Southern rights organization whose members have been called "the most consistent secessionists in the state during the fifties." Victoria shared her husband's political agenda. As she explains in her autobiography, "We of the South felt that we had become slave-holders under our common government with its most sacred sanction." With the Republican Party trying to prevent the expansion of slavery into the western territories, this "sacred" right in human property stood in danger. Consequently, Henry and Victoria decided to take bold steps.[18]

In September 1856, the couple led an expedition of over one hundred Southern emigrants to "Bleeding Kansas" in an effort to increase the number of proslavery voters in the territory and hence bring it into the Union as a slave state. On this trip, Victoria had to sleep on the ground, eat from tin trays, bathe when she could, and do without her usual comforts. These conditions were difficult for everyone, but probably worse for her, since she was three months pregnant. Once in the territory, Victoria saw the open warfare between Free-Soil and proslavery forces. She armed herself with a pistol and protected the women and children of the expedition while her husband joined a proslavery militia that threatened the Free-Soil town of Lawrence. Although Henry's army disbanded without engaging in combat, Henry and Victoria were proud of having settled more proslavery men and women in Kansas.[19]

The Claytons' ideological commitment to Southern rights led them to strongly advocate secession. From 1857 through early 1861, Henry served in the Alabama legislature, where he constantly stressed the need for Southern independence. In 1860, as a delegate to the Democratic state convention, he helped William Lowndes Yancey push through his program, which ultimately led to the disruption of the national Democratic Party and to disunion.[20]

When Alabama seceded on 11 January 1861, the Claytons were prospering. Henry had a promising political future. Victoria enjoyed a life of social prominence and was busy raising her five children. By 1860, they owned twenty-six slaves and had $37,000 in real estate and personal property.[21]

After Alabama seceded, Henry volunteered his services to the state. Alabama's governor, A. B. Moore, made him a colonel and gave him command of all Alabama troops stationed in Pensacola, Florida. (Henry was promoted to brigadier general in 1863 and then to major general in 1864.)[22] In the exciting days of early 1861, the Claytons expected war, but they could not have been prepared for the changes that it would bring.

The first change that the war wrought in Henry and Victoria's relationship concerned their sex life. Their separation not only interrupted their sexual relationship but also changed its terms. Henry was, except on rare occasions, unable to leave camp and return home. He expected Victoria to visit him whenever he asked. Victoria did not acquiesce to his demands and instead visited when *she decided* that her schedule permitted. Almost immediately, the power roles shifted. Henry was no longer the dominant sexual partner, choosing when the two would have sex. The decision now rested with Victoria.

For example, in February 1861, a little over a month after Henry arrived in Pensacola, he begged his wife to visit him in camp. She agreed. After a few weeks together, Henry requested that she stay longer, since no enemy attack looked probable. She again agreed and by her own choice stayed with him another two months. Not long after she had returned home, Henry asked her to prepare for another trip to Pensacola, but she refused. In June and July, he constantly wrote her about arranging visits to camp. In August, Victoria traveled to Pensacola but only to help Henry return home to recover from camp fever. Three months later, when he was stationed in Mobile, Victoria made a brief trip to see him, but clearly she now controlled the terms of their conjugal visits.[23]

That is not to suggest that Victoria did not want to see her husband. During the war, she overcame Victorian reticence and began expressing her own sexual needs to Henry. Speaking metaphorically in a letter with strong erotic undertones, she told him of a dream she had had in which the two were "holding sweet communion." It was her own desire to be with Henry that made her refusal to see him so emphatic. She would have liked to have given in to her sexual desires, but she believed that her place was on the plantation, where she tended her five children, produced clothing and other items for the war effort, and exerted greater influence over plantation management. Traveling would interfere with these duties, and so would the travails of being pregnant and then caring for an infant. She knew this all too well after becoming pregnant in early 1862 during one of Henry's rare visits at home between commands.[24]

Henry was powerless to counter Victoria's decision to remain home, but he did not agree with her reasoning. He did not share her opinion that she should solely manage the plantation. He therefore continued to give her detailed orders about how to raise the crops, and when and at what price to sell them. From Henry's perspective, Victoria was little more than a conduit through which his instructions flowed.[25]

Until early 1863, Henry asked Nelson to help manage the plantation. Nelson made several extended visits and kept Henry informed about his crops, animals, and slaves. In June, Henry wrote Victoria that Nelson "seemed not to be pleased with the way things were going," because he found "too much waste and extravagance." Henry and Nelson decided to hire an overseer to manage the plantation on a full-time basis. By July, a Mr. Powell was carrying out these duties. Henry communicated with him directly as well as via Victoria. By the fall, Henry had become disappointed with Powell and fired him. Rather than hiring another overseer, Henry continued relying on Nelson, believing Victoria incapable of such a responsibility. This perception soon changed.[26]

Henry's world, as he had known it, ended in the violence of the Battle of Murfreesboro, Tennessee. On 2 January 1863, his brother Joseph, who was in charge of an infantry company, was severely wounded. The next day, the Confederate army evacuated Murfreesboro and abandoned those who were badly wounded as prisoners of war. On 19 January while in camp at Shelbyville, Tennessee, Henry received word of his brother's death. Although it was expected, the news deeply unsettled Henry. Henry had always looked to his older brother as a confidant with whom he could share his hopes and fears. As he wrote his parents, "He was my only brother & more than a Brother." The loss left a vacuum in Henry's life.[27]

Indeed, Joseph's death caused great anguish to the family and led to an eruption of long-simmering tensions. Henry's mother, Sarah, was so distraught that she completely disregarded propriety and lashed out at Nelson. She confided to Henry about his father's physical and emotional abuse of her. In a rather extraordinary letter, Henry told his mother that she was "very mistaken in supposing I knew but little of your trials and troubles." He goes on to write that "brother and I have frequently spoken on the subject and our hearts have bled over it." Yet they feared that approaching Nelson about the matter would only make her situation worse. Then, as is common in matters of domestic abuse, Henry momentarily blamed the victim. After asking her not to become angry with him, he wrote, "I don't think you do right sometimes." Despite this comment to Sarah, Henry knew that Nelson was the culprit. He soon after asked him to change the way he treated Sarah.[28]

Coming on the heels of the trauma of Joseph's death, these delicate exchanges about family troubles among Nelson, Sarah, and Henry caused Henry to reevaluate his relationship to his family. Henry had always known of Nelson's abuse, but now his mother had confirmed this knowledge for him. Especially important was Sarah's honesty about Nelson's behavior, for it gave Henry permission to face the abuse. This in turn allowed him to confront his father. This confrontation between father and son altered their relationship. In many ways, Henry took a paternal role by scolding his father. Similarly, by becoming Sarah's defender, he assumed the responsibility normally held by a husband, not a son. As his father diminished as an authority figure, Henry assumed more leadership within the family.[29]

The dynamics became even more interesting as Henry's perceptions of Sarah changed. Sarah never tried to comfort Henry over the loss of his brother; she only expected Henry to comfort her. Moreover, Henry wrote Victoria that if he were killed, he feared neither his mother nor father would help her with the children. Henry had to face the terrible truth that, while off at war risking his life, he could not depend on his parents to care for his family. This revelation most certainly caused him to believe that his mother had failed in her maternal role.[30]

It was at this vital juncture, in early 1863, when power relationships in the family shifted radically. Henry stopped looking to his father for guidance. Rather, he saw Nelson as a pathetic individual who needed help. Henry could have just ignored his father's problems. After all, Nelson had never been a warm, loving father; he had interfered in Henry's life and had abused his mother. Yet Henry charitably tried to convince Victoria to be kind to Nelson and wrote her that in some ways Nelson had been "the best father to his children that ever lived."

Henry specifically asked Victoria to take Nelson to church and show him attention when he visited.[31]

Henry had become his mother's protector even as he realized her severe maternal deficiencies. And because he could no longer confide in Joseph, the only person to whom he could turn was Victoria. She was also the only one in the family who demonstrated any self-discipline and control. In Henry's state, these characteristics were paramount. He needed someone on whom he could count.

Victoria must have felt some satisfaction. She had long found her mother-in-law disagreeable and had long been subject to her father-in-law's criticism and interference. Furthermore, she still felt resentment toward Nelson for the death of her first son. At long last, Nelson and Sarah were not in positions to command deference. Victoria was the person to whom her husband looked for guidance, and together they began to assume joint leadership roles within the family.

Henry began to express his weaknesses and fears to Victoria. He had mentioned his fear of being killed in battle only one time before Joseph died. Following Joseph's death, he wrote on the topic often. Not long after the retreat from Murfreesboro, Henry wrote that he was afraid he would not live to help raise his children. Within two weeks, he again confessed his anxieties. This time he bluntly stated, "I may not live through the war, so take care of yourself."[32]

As the war continued, Henry's fears only increased. Immediately following the Atlanta campaign, his letters became chilling. On 2 September 1864, he informed Victoria about the army's retreat from Atlanta. Feeling an impending sense of doom, he wrote that "a trust in God is about all that is left us." He told her of having bullets coming so close to him during the Battle of Jonesboro that they killed three of his horses. He admitted that he was "having a pretty hard time" and wrote, "If I never see you again teach our little children that their father died like a man." Oddly, he then assured her that he was "still hopeful," but soon after stated, "I leave you and the children to God and the country."[33]

Henry was so troubled, in fact, that he could not hide his condition from one of his comrades, who wrote his wife that "Clayton is pretty nearly whipped." About two weeks later, Henry told Victoria, "I have rested physically and improved very much, but my mind still feels tired and I need very much to get away for a short time."[34]

Henry's growing emotional reliance on Victoria altered his overall perception of her. One direct result of this dependence was that Victoria ultimately gained control over the plantation. Henry still corresponded with her about plantation matters, but the character of his letters had changed. With very few exceptions, he no longer gave her specific orders or expected her to be a messenger to pass his directions on to others. Instead, he began to view her as an equal partner in managing the plantation and even sought her opinion. When he did give advice, he picked his words carefully. He commonly used phrases such as "I advise" or "I am glad you concluded" or asked, "What do you think of my suggestion?" In one letter, he actually asked her to look over his former letters and inform him which of his several suggestions she had chosen to implement. In the spring of 1864, after sending her a table of standard weights, he beseeched her, "Tell me freely . . . dear, what I can do to aid you." In Victoria's autobiography, she remembers that she informed Henry of the plantation's progress so that he could "make suggestions about various things *to help me* manage successfully"[35] (emphasis added).

During the first two years of the war, when Henry asked Victoria to visit him in camp, he did not give much thought to her concerns or schedule. This began to change by the spring of 1863. In May, he asked her to visit but then deferentially added, "Don't you think you can do so without home interests suffering much?" Less than a week later he wrote, "I am anxious to hear your opinion as to when you can most conveniently come to see me." Victoria did visit Henry during Christmas of 1863 to help him heal from a wound he had received at the Battle of Chickamauga. To her chagrin, she became pregnant during this trip. Consequently, she did not visit him again in camp during the war.[36]

When Henry and Victoria discussed the specific treatment of their slaves, they did so as partners. A good example of this partnership is their decision concerning the fate of their slave Amy. In August 1864, she told Victoria that she wanted to marry Frank, a slave she had met on a neighbor's plantation. The Claytons had always had a policy of not permitting "abroad" or interplantation marriages, but Victoria wrote Henry that she wanted to permit Frank and Amy to marry. Two years earlier Henry would surely have ignored Victoria's wish. Now, he wanted to reach a compromise: he told her, "I hope to be able to yield to your wishes whatever they may be." He wanted to "find a plausible pretext for breaking a rule" that he had always stringently enforced. He then suggested that Victoria should either sell Amy to Frank's owner or buy Frank. The final decision was Victoria's to make. While no record exists concerning the sale, it is obvious that Henry and Victoria worked together to find a solution to a thorny problem. Henry was conceding to his wife's wishes in a new, important way.[37]

As Victoria gained greater autonomy, Nelson played a much less significant role in Henry's business. The only time that Henry and Victoria discussed Nelson's having any sustained input on their plantation was in early September 1864, less than a month after Victoria had given birth to her daughter Mary. Henry feared that Victoria would "overtax" herself so soon after a difficult delivery. Although Victoria would not allow Nelson to take over the plantation even on a temporary basis, she agreed to let him "advise" her.[38]

Once given the freedom to run the plantation her own way, Victoria was extraordinarily efficient. With the aid of her slaves and the local women she hired, she produced a bounty of shirts, pants, and socks for the army. As the Union blockade took a greater toll on the South, Victoria became even more self-sufficient. She used ground sweet potatoes as a coffee substitute and also used fruit from her orchard to make wine and brandy. Years later, Victoria recalled, "My duties . . . were numerous and often laborious" and referred to her plantation as her "post of duty." Henry's letters show that he too recognized Victoria's contribution to the war effort. In April 1864, he wrote, "I am trying to do my duty, and you are doing yours."[39]

Indeed she was. Victoria was a committed Southern partisan who was dedicated to both her family and the Confederate cause. She had a family to raise, a plantation to manage, and a war to win.

Some things were not to be. In April 1865, the Confederacy collapsed. Henry returned home to discover currents of change and continuity. His slaves had been freed, but most of them still lived on or near the plantation and continued to work for him and Victoria. In 1866, Henry won election to the position of circuit court judge. However, when Radical Republicans passed a series of Reconstruction Acts in 1867 that disfranchised and removed from office former Confederate leaders, Henry lost his seat. With the Amnesty Act of 1872, he regained his civil rights, and in 1874 he was again elected to the circuit court. He served in that capacity for twelve years and retired voluntarily.[40]

Over the course of the war, Henry and Victoria's marriage had been rebuilt on the deepest trust. Consequently, Victoria retained the autonomy she had gained. Henry never questioned the wisdom of this development. Indeed, because his judicial duties required him to be away from home so much, it would have been nearly impossible for him to have continued his career without Victoria's continuing to run the plantation.

Victoria managed the postwar plantation with great skill. She made contracts with the freedmen and continued to market the cotton crop. Her ability to do business in this new, more complex environment certainly shows her entrepreneurial talent. Her children, who numbered eleven by 1874, grew up seeing their mother as a strong and capable woman.[41]

As parents, Henry and Victoria never tried to emulate Nelson. They wanted to leave their offspring free to make their own choices. The Clayton children became both independent and emotionally close to their parents. The strong bond within the immediate family is evident in postwar correspondence. Henry Jr., while serving in the U.S. House of Representatives, wrote his mother, "I realize more and more as the years go by how much I owe you for all that I am and all that I hope to be." Henry and Victoria also respected their children's career choices. Their son Bertram had entered college to study medicine but became dissatisfied with that field and decided on the military. Although his parents were initially concerned that Bertram was being impetuous, they did not berate him for failing at medicine. Henry used his influence to get Bertram an appointment to West Point, from which he graduated in 1886.[42]

Unlike previous generations of Claytons, Henry and Victoria encouraged their daughters to be independent as well. Henry wrote his daughter Mary that she should keep a careful account of her finances. He believed that if she learned to do this at her youthful age of nineteen, it would help her develop the "good habit" of managing her money. He also told Mary and his other daughter, Helen, that he was pleased that he could provide them with an education because it was "the heritage of a useful life." Victoria summed up her and Henry's wishes for their daughters when she wrote to Mary that "we all . . . hope to see you a very useful, good woman some day."[43]

The partnership forged by Henry and Victoria during the war had consequences that extended beyond their family. When Henry was elected president of the University of Alabama in 1886, he undertook the daunting task of continuing to rebuild the university, which Union troops had all but destroyed in April 1865. On the surface, Victoria's main duty was to entertain guests and students, a duty she carried out well. Yet Victoria did more than just entertain. She gave the university an atmosphere where students felt comfortable. As Henry traveled throughout the state recruiting students, he could honestly assure concerned parents that he and his wife personally looked after their boys and treated them like family. Upon visiting the university, parents saw firsthand that this was so.[44]

The Claytons' tenure at the university lasted only three years. In 1889, Henry suddenly fell ill and died. Victoria suffered from terrible grief but eventually carried on. By the mid-1890s, she had begun writing her autobiography, *White and Black under the Old Regime*, which was published in 1899. Influenced by Henry Grady's New South movement and by her own beliefs about the social structure of the Old South, it is not surprising that her work enthusiastically endorses the New South creed.[45]

The public loved the book. It sold well on both sides of the Atlantic, and reviewers in the North and the South praised Victoria's account of Southern culture. Today, the book is not only dated but is also offensive in its racial stereotyping. However, through this work, Victoria not only offers insight into the mindset of nineteenth-century white Southerners but also helps to show how the war changed the role of women both in the family and within society.

As dramatic as the Claytons' story is, can the historian assume that it is representative? Certainly, the Claytons suffered much that was common to other Southern families. Victoria, Nelson, and Sarah worried about the welfare of Henry and Joseph; Henry worried about Victoria and the children; Henry and Victoria's sex life was disrupted; Victoria faced many new challenges on the plantation; Henry feared death and suffered from physical and emotional wounds; and the entire family grieved over Joseph's death. What makes the Clayton drama unique is that family members reacted to the strains of war according to their individual personalities, their previous relationships with each other, and the weaknesses that already existed in the family's foundation. This was true of all families. Obviously, each family reacted to the deprivations and horrors of the Civil War in its own way. Despite different responses to similar events, however, Southern families ultimately experienced a common result: a change in gender relations and a corresponding change in the power dynamics within the family. The Claytons are peculiar only in the specific manner in which they were affected by the war, not in the alterations of previously held assumptions about gender.

As more case studies are done, perhaps scholars will discover patterns showing that gender and familial relations changed differently according to objective factors such as class, family size, or subregions within the South. Of course, the work must first be done. Historians should utilize their many skills in determining the fate of planters, yeoman farmers, and others who lived in the Old South and experienced the changes brought about by the war. Judging from the Claytons and from an appreciation of the enormous suffering felt by Southerners, one thing seems certain: by changing the family, the war changed the South.

Notes

1. See, for example, C.Vann Woodward, *Origins of the New South, 1877–1913* (Baton Rouge: Louisiana State University Press, 1951), and Laurence Shore, *Southern Capitalists: The Ideological Leadership of an Elite, 1832–1885* (Chapel Hill: University of North Carolina Press, 1986).

2. Catherine Clinton, *The Plantation Mistress: Woman's World in the Old South* (New York: Pantheon Books, 1982); Elizabeth Fox-Genovese, *Within the Plantation Household: Black and White Women of the Old South* (Chapel Hill: University of North Carolina Press, 1988);Victoria Bynum, *Unruly Women: The Politics of Social and Sexual Control in the Old South* (Chapel Hill: University of North Carolina Press, 1992); Stephanie McCurry, *Masters of Small Worlds: Yeoman Households, Gender Relations, and the Political Culture of the Antebellum South Carolina Low Country* (New York: Oxford University Press, 1995); Elizabeth R. Varon, *We Mean to Be Counted: White Women and Politics in Antebellum Virginia* (Chapel Hill: University of North Carolina, 1998); Carol Bleser and Frederick Heath, "The Clays of Alabama: The Impact of the Civil War on a Southern Marriage," in *In Joy and in Sorrow: Women, Family, and Marriage in the Victorian South, 1830–1900*, ed. Carol Bleser (New York: Oxford University Press, 1991), 253.

3. Anne Firor Scott, *The Southern Woman: From Pedestal to Politics, 1830–1930* (Chicago: University of Chicago Press, 1970); Catherine Clinton, *The Other Civil War: American Women in the Nineteenth Century* (New York: Hill and Wang, 1985), 87; Catherine Clinton, *Tara Revisited: Women, War, and the Plantation Legend* (New York: Abbeville Press, 1995), 166; Bleser and Heath, "The Clays of Alabama," 91, 152; Peter W. Bardaglio, *Reconstructing the Household: Families, Sex, and the Law in the Nineteenth-Century South* (Chapel Hill: University of North Carolina Press, 1995). See also Drew Gilpin Faust's following works: "Altars of Sacrifice: Confederate Women and the Narratives of War," *Journal of American History* 76 (March 1990): 1200–1228; *Mothers of Invention: Women of the Slaveholding South in the American Civil War* (Chapel Hill: University of North Carolina Press, 1996); and "'Trying to Do a Man's Business': Slavery,Violence, and Gender in the American Civil War," *Gender and History* 4 (Summer 1992): 197–214.

4. H. E. Sterkx, *Partners in Rebellion: Alabama Women in the Civil War* (Rutherford, N.J.: Fairleigh Dickinson University Press, 1970); Suzanne Lebsock, *The Free Women of Petersburg: Status and Culture in a Southern Town, 1784–1860* (New York: W. W. Norton, 1984); LeeAnn Whites, *The Civil War as a Crisis in Gender: Augusta, Georgia, 1860–1890* (Athens: University of Georgia Press, 1995); David H. McGee, "'Home and Friends': Kinship, Community,

and Elite Women in Caldwell County, North Carolina during the Civil War," *North Carolina Historical Review* 74 (October 1997), 363–88: Carol K. Bleser, "The Marriage of Varina Howell and Jefferson Davis:'I gave the best and all I had to a girded tree,'" *Journal of Southern History* 65 (February 1999): 5, 9, 11–13, 36–40.

5. Bell Irvin Wiley, *Confederate Women* (Westport, Conn.: Greenwood Press, 1975); Jean E. Friedman, *The Enclosed Garden: Women and Community in the Evangelical South, 1830–1900* (Chapel Hill: University of North Carolina Press, 1985); George Rable, *Civil Wars: Women and the Crisis of Southern Nationalism* (Urbana: University of Illinois Press, 1989).

6. Jane R. Pope, "The Clayton Family," unpublished manuscript, Henry Clayton Papers, William Stanley Hoole Special Collections Library, University of Alabama (hereafter as cited UA); Henry Walker, "Secessionist, Soldier, Redeemer: Henry Clayton of Alabama" (Ph.D. diss., University of Alabama, 1995), 35.

7. Pope, "The Clayton Family"; Margaret Russell, *James Clayton of North Carolina and His Descendants in the Old South-west* (Columbus, Ga.: Quill Publications, 1993), 1–5, 13–14, 35–36, 41–46.

8. For records concerning Nelson's judicial and legislative offices as well as the management of his plantation, see Nelson Clayton Papers, UA; 1840 U.S. Census, Slave Schedule, Chambers County, Ala., Nelson Clayton; Russell, *James Clayton of North Carolina*, 123.

9. Thomas Clayton to Nelson Clayton, 1819; Elizabeth Delamar to Nelson Clayton, 1 November 1822, 24 September 1824, 6 July 1825; Churchill Delamar to Nelson Clayton, 22 March 1824; and John Carruthers to Nelson Clayton, 24 February 1829, Nelson Clayton Papers; Russell, *James Clayton of North Carolina*, 85, 90–99.

10. Pope, "The Clayton Family."

11. Ibid.

12. "The Choice of a Profession," Henry Clayton diary, Henry Clayton Papers.

13. Unpublished biographical sketch of Henry Clayton, and Henry Clayton's diary, 22 December 1848, Henry Clayton Papers.

14. Lewy Dorman, "A History of Barbour County, Alabama" (unpublished manuscript, UA), 111–12, 145, 302–3; Victoria Clayton, *White and Black under the Old Regime,* with an introduction by Frederick Cook Morehouse (Milwaukee: Young Churchman Co., 1899), 20, 34–35, 38–42, 44; Thomas M. Owen, "John L. Hunter," *History of Alabama and Dictionary of Alabama Biography* (Chicago: S. J. Clark Publishing Co., 1921): 3:872.

15. Clayton, *White and Black under the Old Regime*, 42–43.

16. Henry Clayton to Victoria Clayton, 31 January 1858, 28 January 1860, Henry Clayton Papers.

17. Nelson Clayton daybook, 1841–58, Nelson Clayton Papers; Russell, *James Clayton of North Carolina*, 151–52.

18. Lewy Dorman, *Party Politics in Alabama from 1850 through 1860*, with a new introduction by Leah Rawls Atkins (Montgomery: Alabama Department of Archives and History, 1935; reprint, Tuscaloosa: University of Alabama Press, 1995), 36; J. Mills Thornton III, *Politics and Power in a Slave Society: Alabama, 1800–1860* (Baton Rouge: Louisiana State University Press, 1977), 250–54; Clayton, *White and Black under the Old Regime*, 64.

19. Henry Clayton, "Letter from Kansas," *Montgomery Weekly Advertiser and State Gazette*, 15 October 1856; "A Century Ago in the *Enquirer*," *Columbus Enquirer*, 7 September 1856, Margaret Russell Private Collection, Eufaula, Ala.; Clayton, *White and Black under the Old Regime*, 63–67, 74–75.

20. Owen, *History of Alabama*, 3:347; *Proceedings of the Democratic State Convention, 1860* (Montgomery: Montgomery Advertiser Book and Job Steam Press Print, 1860).

21. 1860 U.S. Census, Population and Slave Schedules, Barbour County, Ala., Henry Clayton.

22. Holman Drew Jordan, "The Military Career of Henry De Lamar Clayton" (master's thesis, University of Alabama, 1954), 8; Confederate Service Records, 1861–65, Alabama Department of Archives and History, Montgomery, Ala.; Henry Clayton to Charles C. Jones, 5 July 1861, Charles Colcock Jones Jr. Papers, William R. Perkins Library, Duke University, Durham, N.C.

23. Henry Clayton to Victoria Clayton, 2, 25 February, 10, 18, 25 June, 19, 27 July, 6 October 1861, Henry Clayton Papers; Clayton, *White and Black under the Old Regime*, 102.

24. Victoria Clayton to Henry Clayton, 19 July 1861, Henry Clayton Papers; Russell, *James Clayton of North Carolina*, 151–52.

25. Henry Clayton to Victoria Clayton, 31 May, 25 June, 2 October 1861, [?], 6, 10, 26 August 1862, Henry Clayton Papers.

26. Henry Clayton to Victoria Clayton, 25 June, 6 October 1861, 19 August, 14 September, 21 October 1862, Henry Clayton Papers.

27. Henry Clayton to Nelson and Sarah Clayton, 24 February 1863, Henry Clayton Papers.

28. Unidentified letter to Henry Clayton, 19 January 1863; Henry Clayton to Victoria Clayton, 22 February 1863; Henry Clayton to Nelson and Sarah Clayton, 24 February 1863; Henry Clayton to Victoria Clayton, 8 March 1863; Henry Clayton to Sarah Clayton, 17 March 1863; Nelson Clayton to Sarah Clayton, 23 March 1863, Henry Clayton Papers.

29. Henry Clayton to Sarah Clayton, 17 March 1863, Henry Clayton Papers.

30. Henry Clayton to Victoria Clayton, 22 June 1861, and Henry Clayton to Victoria Clayton, 22 February 1863, Henry Clayton Papers; Russell, *James Clayton of North Carolina*, 370–71.

31. Henry Clayton to Victoria Clayton, 2 May 1864, Henry Clayton Papers.

32. Henry Clayton to Victoria Clayton, 22 February, 8 March 1863, Henry Clayton Papers.

33. Henry Clayton to Nelson and Sarah Clayton, 17 February 1863, and Henry Clayton to Victoria Clayton, 13 August 1863, 1, 2 May 1864, Henry Clayton Papers; Jordan, "The Military Career of Henry De Lamar Clayton," 23.

34. Ray Mathis, *In the Land of the Living: Wartime Letters by Confederates from the Chattahoochee Valley of Alabama and Georgia* (Troy, Ala.: Troy State University Press, 1981), 111; Henry Clayton to Victoria Clayton, 2, 13 September 1864, Henry Clayton Papers.

35. Henry Clayton to Victoria Clayton, 2 June, 11 December 1863, 2, 3, 8, 12, 16, 24 April, 28 August, [?] 24, 28 September 1864, Henry Clayton Papers; Clayton, *White and Black under the Old Regime*, 116.

36. Henry Clayton to Victoria Clayton, 23, 27 May 1863, Henry Clayton Papers; Russell, *James Clayton of North Carolina*, 151–52.

37. Henry Clayton to Victoria Clayton, 5 August 1864, Henry Clayton Papers.

38. Henry Clayton to Victoria Clayton, 6 June 1863, 18 August, 2, 3, 22 September, 15 October 1864, Henry Clayton Papers.

39. Clayton, *White and Black under the Old Regime*, 100, 103, 107, 114–22; Henry Clayton to Victoria Clayton, 3, 8, 12, 16, 24 April 1864, Henry Clayton Papers.

40. "Alabama News," *Montgomery Daily Advertiser*, 19 May 1866; "Official Vote," *Eufaula News,* 3 December 1874; "The New President," *Tuscaloosa Gazette*, 1 July 1886.

41. See the Claytons' postwar farm records, Henry Clayton Papers; Clayton, *White and Black under the Old Regime*, 169; Russell, *James Clayton of North Carolina*, 151–52, 171.

42. Henry Clayton Jr. to Henry Clayton, 26 December 1883; Henry Clayton Jr. to Victoria Clayton, 10 February 1898; Henry Clayton to Bertram Clayton, 20 April 1880; and Bertram Clayton to Henry Clayton, 10, 21 May 1880, Henry Clayton Papers; unpublished biographical sketch of Henry Clayton Jr., Henry Clayton Jr. Papers, UA.

43. Henry Clayton to Mary and Helen Clayton, 24 January 1884, and Victoria Clayton to Mary Clayton, 4 January 1882, Henry Clayton Papers.

44. "University of Alabama," 9 March 1887, and "The Sophomores Accorded a Brilliant Reception by Mrs. Clayton," 15 May 1889, and "The Hop," 26 June 1889, *Tuscaloosa Times*; James B. Sellers, *History of the University of Alabama, 1818–1902* (Tuscaloosa: University of Alabama Press, 1953), 456.

45. Frederick Morehouse to Victoria Clayton, 30 October 1899, Henry Clayton Papers; Clayton, *White and Black under the Old Regime*, 10, 14–15, 21, 24, 26, 50–57, 131.

✳

TEN

TAKING UP THE CROSS

Conversion among Black and White Jews in the Civil War South

Lauren F. Winner

When James Mill returned home to North Carolina after the Civil War, he was by no means so naive as to expect that he could resume the rhythms of antebellum life without a period of adjustment. His worries were manifold: Although Mill had only owned (or possibly hired) one slave, a young woman who had split her time between the fields and domestic chores, he knew that labor would be a problem. He was worried, too, that his newly free black neighbors would "act ancy [*sic*] and assume airs." Finally, he was concerned that his native state might be rent asunder by internal strife. As he confided to his brother, North Carolina was home to many who had "resisted this war all along"; Mill did not want his Unionist neighbors to suppose they could "punish us and act like the outcome proved them right." All his fears proved justified—he did have trouble getting his few acres of land planted in time, and his crop that year was meager; he complained bitterly through at least 1873 that the freedmen he met acted haughty; and shortly after his return home, a family of Republicans who had remained loyal to the Union moved from their native bloody Madison County to Mill's home county, setting up house close enough to Mill to make them neighbors. But what proved to be Mill's biggest conundrum during Reconstruction was not one he had anticipated at all. His wife, who was a Jew when he left for the front in 1862, was a professing Christian of some "sectarian" variety by the time Mill returned. She was turning his children into "little Jesuses, saying the Our Father before they sleep," and redecorating his humble house, hanging a rustic, homemade cross on the wall and placing a Bible prominently on the table for permanent display and frequent use.[1]

Mill's experience was not unique among Jews in the South. While Jews throughout Southern history have occasionally abandoned the faith of their fathers for the evangelical Protestantism of their neighbors, the Civil War era saw more Jewish conversions to Christianity than any period prior to the war. The conversion of Jews to Christianity was not merely a religious choice with religious implications. Upon examination, it becomes clear that these wartime conversions had quite chaotic consequences, spilling over into many realms of individual Southerners' lives. As such, they shed light on many arenas— and orthodoxies—of Southern history: gender, family relations, the evangelization of slaves and the nexus between race and religion, the social meanings of conversion, the theological incentives to convert, and citizenship.

Recent scholarship has attempted to argue that Jews were accepted fully into the society of the Old South. One recent enterprising scholar has claimed that Jews in antebellum South Carolina, because they dueled, sported hoop skirts, and owned slaves, were full participants in Southern society. That Jews could not engage in that essential feature of the South's social landscape—evangelicalism—is, in this scholar's estimation, inconsequential at best.[2] But the voices of Jews themselves betray another experience. The letters of Rachel and Ellen Mordecai, for example, contain poignant expressions of a gulch they perceived between themselves and their Episcopalian neighbors. Recalling his Richmond childhood, Moses Jacob Ezekiel noted that "it would have been just as easy to have mixed oil and water as to have had our household mix socially with the people around us." Even Mill, several years before the war, wrote to his brother to complain bitterly about the treatment his wife had received from other women because she did not have access to the site of women's social activities—the church. On top of that, to be snubbed "openly, at the store and market . . . all on account of being a Jewess," was, Mill thought, more than "one person ought to have to suffer." Many a Jew recognized the two-pronged meaning of the word "communion," and they were quick to point out that they were excluded, in the words of one woman, from entering into "full communion with neighbors and friends at socials and parties" because they refused communion with the Christian God. Because of Jews' "reluctance to drink wine at one table," the communion table, Protestant neighbors and acquaintances sometimes proved unwilling to include them at their dining room tables.[3]

The Civil War, many Southern Jews felt, would change all this. Not unlike African Americans, who have believed throughout U.S. history that military service would guarantee them the rights of full citizenship, Southern Jews expected that if they embraced the Confederate cause wholeheartedly, they would in turn be embraced by the Confederacy and accorded a new role in the society of the new nation. The new nation did not come to fruition, and neither did Southern Jews' expectations of their support of the Confederacy. To the contrary, they found that during wartime, their support was not welcomed but, rather, received warily. Protestant Confederates blamed Southern Jews when any aspect of the war effort went wrong, accusing them of espionage, racketeering, and conspiracy.

Protestant sources richly document the hostility and suspicion Jews in the Confederacy faced. Captain R. E. Park recounted that his colonel attempted to block the promotion of Mobile's Captain Adolph Proskauer because the colonel was suspicious of Jews' loyalty to the Confederacy. A Jewish colonel assigned to a Texas regiment experienced such ridicule and antagonism that within forty-eight hours of joining up with his new regiment, he left. Many Southerners lambasted even those Jews whose devotion to the Confederacy might appear unquestionable. Eugenia Levy Phillips was so unswerving in her devotion to the Confederate cause that the Union suspected her of being a spy. Twice during the war she was arrested and imprisoned. Nonetheless, some in the Confederacy doubted her loyalty, suggesting that her "pretense" of devotion to the CSA had been "boldly calculated" in order to paper over her true Unionist sentiment. A proto–conspiracy theory developed around Phillips, with hostile Confederates suggesting that she was, in fact, a spy for Union forces and that she, her husband Philip Phillips (whose loyalties were with the Union), and certain high-ranking officials of the Union government had cooked up her ostensible Confederate convictions to make her espionage more convincing. Judah P. Benjamin, the Jewish member of Jefferson Davis's cabinet, likewise endured an onslaught of hostility throughout the war, as Rebels from Virginia to Mississippi blamed him for all the problems of the Confederacy.[4] A North Carolinian opined

that "all the distresses of the people were owing to a Nero-like despotism originating in the brain of Benjamin, the Jew." A man from
Tennessee labeled the secretary of war the "Judas Iscariot Benjamin"
of the Confederacy. Tennessee congressman Henry S. Foote made a
speech in the Confederate House of Representatives in January 1863
in which he declared that Jews had overrun the Confederacy and were
at that point in control of nine-tenths of all business interests in the
country. Benjamin, Foote went on, was the secret protector of all
these Jews and was covertly transferring ownership of property from
loyal Confederates to "foreign Jews." By the end of the war, Foote
predicted, Southerners "would probably find nearly all the property of
the Confederacy in the hands of Jewish Shylocks."[5]

Benjamin was only one of the many Confederate Jews whom
Confederate Christians plugged into age-old stereotypes of the Jew
qua extortionist, thief, shylock, of Jews driven by, in the words of historian John Higham, "cunning" and "avarice.[6] Confederate Christians,
as Gary L. Bunker and John Appel have shown, portrayed Jews as vul-
tures hoping to gain from wartime economic shortages.[7] Jewish merchants in Georgia were accused repeatedly of "unpatriotic conduct."
Fear and suspicion of Jewish merchants was only exacerbated by the
extreme shortages that became increasingly frequent as the war progressed. In one Georgia town, wives whose husbands were away fighting held up a Jewish merchant's store at gunpoint, and, accusing the
owner of speculating and making a fortune while their husbands died
in defense of their country, stole everything they could carry from the
store. Congressman Hilton of Florida frequently declared that Jews
controlled all of the Confederacy's trade and offered a number of il-
lustrations to prove the Jews' greedy and grasping nature, including the
tale of a blockade runner who landed on the Florida coast, only to
have his goods confiscated by the authorities. Florida Jews, however,
had somehow learned the whereabouts of the blockade runner, and
"at least one hundred" Jews "flocked there, led even to this remote
point by the scent of gain, and they had to be driven back actually at
the point of the bayonet."[8] Richmond Gentiles believed that Jews had
unique access to all manner of hard-to-come-by desirables: they called
one store, owned by a German Jew, "Noah's Ark" because it "seemed
capable of producing anything from a needle to firearms."[9] Even
commentators from abroad shared this suspicion of Confederate Jews.
One Englishman described how Jews stood by the Confederacy only
in hopes of turning a profit: "The Israelites, as usual, far surpassed the
Gentiles in shrewdness to the auspicious moment, and laid in stocks

(procured on credit) which, in almost every instance, were retailed at rates five hundred to one thousand per cent above ordinary prices; cash always being exacted. Many of these gentry proved unscrupulous knaves during the war; having husbanded their goods for one or two years, and converted them into coin, if they did not decamp from the Confederacy altogether, they found a thousand and one excuses for not bearing arms." Another English pundit observed that Charleston was the center of blockaded goods, adding that there appeared to be "more Jews in Charleston than . . . in Jerusalem."[10]

Such criticism of Jewish failure to support the war effort did not waver after the war had ended. In 1866, the editor of the *Augusta Sentinel*, while writing about North Carolina's refusal to abandon the religious test for office-holding, sought to defend Jews against "charges which we have frequently heard made by our street-corner gossiper and windy patriots, that the Israelites of the South failed to perform their duty during the recent war." Jews had welcomed the Confederacy with hopes that they would be received differently in the new nation, but that welcome proved every bit as elusive as the new nation itself.[11]

If male merchants were accused of extortion and profiteering, the women on the home front found no warmer reception. Jewish women plunged into voluntary societies with vigor, devoting themselves to caring for the Confederate sick and collecting food and clothing for soldiers. Many a women's charitable organization was sponsored by and met in the local church, and while some Jewish women had considerable familiarity with Christian houses of worship, others found themselves in churches for the first time in their lives. Jewish women in the North often supported the Union war effort through specifically Jewish organizations, such as the Ladies Hebrew Association for the Relief of Sick and Wounded Soldiers, established in 1863 in Philadelphia, and Pittsburgh's Hebrew Ladies' Soldiers' Aid Society. Southern Jewish women's groups, for reasons I have discussed elsewhere, by and large failed to coalesce, at least until after the war, when Southern Jewish women organized to support the Lost Cause. Southern Jews commemorated their war dead with rather more enthusiasm than did their Northern co-religionists—the Hebrew Ladies' Memorial Association of Richmond, organized in 1866 to care for Jewish Confederate graves in the Hollywood Cemetery on Shockoe Hill, was the most ambitious and elaborate Jewish memorial association.[12]

But some Gentile women were suspicious of Jewish women's contributions to the war effort. One group of Jewish women in North Carolina was devoted to collecting provisions for troops for their community. A neighboring Christian woman questioned whether or not clothing instead given to these women ever made it into the hands of North Carolina soldiers, suggesting instead that the supplies were distributed to Jewish soldiers of any regiment, North or South. Even Phoebe Yates Pember came under suspicion. Pember (sister of suspected spy Eugenia Levy Phillips) worked as a nurse at Richmond's Chimborazo Hospital from 1862 to 1865 and later published her memoir, *A Southern Woman's Story: Life in Confederate Richmond*. She was, by all accounts, unswervingly devoted to the Confederate cause and to the care of the sick and wounded that came through Chimborazo. Nonetheless, the occasional gossip-monger accused "Phebe [*sic*] the Jew" of seeking out Jewish patients and giving them special care and attention at the expense of other soldiers.

Antebellum Southern Jews, of course, did not live in ghettos. They were quite accustomed to interacting with their Christian neighbors in every walk of life. But the Civil War brought both Jewish women and men into more intimate contact with Christians, and it fostered explicitly religious encounters that would not have occurred during peacetime. This is especially true for men, who found themselves present at fireside prayer meetings and miniature revivals and who often turned to the only available chaplains—Christians—for solace, guidance, and support. Jewish women, too, found that the war brought increased exposure to Christianity and evangelization. As mentioned above, their charitable works often required Jewish women to spend an appreciable amount of time in churches, surrounded by material reminders of the Christian faith. And regardless of whether or not their charitable work was actually located in churches, Jewish women were subjected to the tellings and retellings of their evangelical friends' experiences of rebirth; with hours spent in one another's company and the work no more interesting than sewing rags for wounded soldiers, conversation almost invariably turned to spiritual matters. Finally, not a few Jewish women, whose commitment to Judaism may have been no more than a sense of history and heritage, were attracted to the peace and comfort their neighbors seemed to find in Christianity, which sometimes, in the hectic and bloody days of war, seemed the only source of peace available.

If the white Jewish merchants, soldiers, and pillars of the home front met hostility from Christian Confederates who believed the Jews' loyalty to the cause to be suspect, black Southern Protestants greeted black Jews with curiosity, and sometimes antagonism. Due to the dearth of information historians possess about black Jews in the Southern—or black Jews in the North or West, for that matter—the discussion of black Jews' experience of the Civil War that follows is necessarily tentative. Any assessment of Southern black Jewry during the Civil War era must be tempered by qualifiers: perhaps, probably, almost certainly the case.

Little is known about the position of black Jews in the Old South; in fact, it would not be an exaggeration to say that little is known of the *existence* of black Jews in the Old South. What is clear, however, is that though the numbers must have been incremental, some slaves who were owned by Jewish families considered themselves Jewish.[13] That these slaves ever formally converted to Judaism in a ceremony that would have met the exacting rabbinic criteria for *gerut*, conversion, is unlikely.[14] That they nonetheless may have received some instruction in matters Jewish from their masters or, more frequently, mistresses is not improbable. Finally, black Jews, although they identified themselves as Jewish, had slippery notions of the bounds between Judaism and Christianity and may well have engaged in some Christian practices—participating in Christian worship services or singing Christian songs. While Jews of European descent might have looked askance at such activities, many black Jews apparently saw no contradiction between proclaiming a Jewish identity and belting out spirituals. (Of course, before we leap to conclusions about what Ashkenazic Jews in the South would have made of such practices, it is worth noting that at least one ostensibly observant Jew in antebellum Wilmington took his family to the local Episcopal church every Sunday, seeing no conflict between church attendance and his self-professed Jewish identity, but responding with shock and fury when his wife converted to Christianity.)[15]

The best source for information about those Southern black Jews who converted to Christianity are the records of the churches where they ultimately came to be baptized. These records indicate that black Jews often participated in Christian communal practices even as Jews: they tell us, for example, that "brother George, though long a practitioner of the Israelite faith, on account of being [owned] by a Jew, has for many years been known by members of this body in fellowship, worship, and praise" and that "Sarah has had familiarity with the teachings of the Lord, though she was a Jew, just as the Lord knew the Truth even as he was a Jew."[16] In explaining why George, though identified as a Jew, was a suitable candidate for baptism, the elders of his new church explained that they had known him a long time and that George had made a habit of worshiping with them. Is the implication of their statement that he only identified as a Jew because he was owned by a Jew?

If white Jews felt some pressure to convert to Christianity in order to cement their loyalty to the Confederate cause, black Jews may have been under pressure in the African American community to reject any Jewish identity because it was perceived as being part and parcel of their slave status: part of being a slave was being forced to adopt a Jewish identity, and it follows that part of being free was being able to reject that identity and choose Christianity. If white Christians viewed Judaism as marking a Southerner's loyalty to the Confederacy as suspect, black Christians may have understood continued loyalty to Judaism as indicating continued loyalty to one's owner.

The story of an ex-slave named, appropriately, Paul is illustrative. Identified by no moniker other than "Paul the Jew," Paul had almost certainly been owned since at least the 1850s by one of the slaveholding Jewish families in South Carolina. Apparently, he identified himself as a Jew, and even considered Saturday, not Sunday, the Sabbath. During the war, he wound up in Virginia, where he mixed with a group of free blacks who ultimately convinced him to be baptized, on the grounds that "perpetuating his loyalty to the Jews was no more than perpetuating his loyalty to his owner." For Paul the Jew, freedom came to mean not only "Christian freedom" but also freedom from his owner to choose to be Christian. However, convincing Paul that the Sabbath fell on Sunday was an uphill battle, since the dictates of Constantine had little meaning for him.[17]

It is worth noting, however, that not all African Americans shared the assumption that rejecting a religious tradition inherited from one's former owner was part of their newfound freedom. At least one black Jew, whose wife Susannah later became a Christian, later identified so strongly with the Israelites' experience of being led out of Egyptian slavery that he maintained throughout his life that he was Jewish.[18]

Southern Jews who converted to Christianity understood their conversions in a variety of ways. Although these Jews-turned-Christians perceived their Judaism as a bar to social acceptance among their neighbors, few were so crass as to couch their conversions in the language of mere social climbing. The rare convert, of course, was forthright that her motivations for converting were social: as Elizabeth Parker put it to a correspondent, "This war has made me learn quite a few lessons. . . . [T]hat support of my home is not enough to garner the acceptance of all of my acquaintances. Supporting my home means also supporting their God."[19] If Jewish conversions to Christianity were motivated at least in part by the desire for acceptance into Southern society, the historian wants to know whether converts were successful in their quest for Southern identity. To put it bluntly, did conversion work? Did their Protestant neighbors view Jewish converts to Christianity as wholly Christian and no longer Jewish, like themselves, or did Protestants from birth continue to view Jewish Christians with suspicion? Working within the framework of European and American Jewish history, one might be tempted to suggest that Jews remained Jews in the eyes of hostile Christian neighbors, despite baptism and heartfelt professions of faith. In medieval Europe, for example, Christians remained suspicious of Jewish converts, insisting, in the words of one historian, that Jewish converts "retained some elements of Jewishness." Medieval Jewish men who converted to Christianity found it a special challenge to leave behind their Jewish identity, given that they were marked bodily as Jews through circumcision.[20] Research in progress suggests that in the colonial era, Christian settlers from Rhode Island to the Caribbean viewed Judaism as an immutable category that, presumably, could not be changed by merely accepting Jesus into one's heart.[21] But an eye attuned to the nuances of our particular context—the American South after the Great Awakening—might find clues leading to a different answer. Whether the gentleman who referred to Judah P. Benjamin as "Iscariot" would have been softened had Benjamin become a devout Methodist, one cannot say. But many women and men who all but badgered the Jewish members of their military regiments or sewing circles into considering Christ were indeed satisfied by their conversions. As a friend wrote to James Mill's wife, Eveline, in 1866, "In Christ, we have found a new identity, greater than anything we have known before. Greater than our earthly family, our now lost nation, greater than whatever you or I were before we came into this newness and life. As Paul wrote, "In God, there is no Jew or Greek."[22]

ELIZABETH PARKER'S OBSERVATIONS ABOUT THE SOCIAL REquirement of conversion notwithstanding, most Jewish women and men who converted to Christianity did more than formally convert; the majority participated in the ritualized, if not routinized, etiquette of conversion in the evangelical sense, experiencing a dramatic and datable rebirth. Whether brought to worship at the foot of the cross by the urgings of female evangelical acquaintances or by fellow soldiers on the front, most Jews who became Christian were at least as motivated by the soteriology of Christ as they were by the potential social benefits of conversion.

For newly evangelical Jews, the moment of conversion was not the end of the story but merely the beginning of a new life in Christ. So, too, it is only the beginning of our story. As the sketch of the Mill family suggests, the rub for Southern Jewish families came when the newfound religious commitments of one family member were not shared by other family members. Husbands converted on the front returned home to wives still firmly committed to Judaism. Wives brought to faith by the dogged efforts of friends in sewing circles and makeshift hospitals found their husbands less willing to speak the language of Canaan. Black families temporarily separated during the war learned upon reunion that the religious affiliations of mother or father, but rarely both, had changed. Daughters and sons who had committed themselves to Christianity during the war found themselves reunited with parents aghast at their decision. Family strife engendered by religious conversion was not new to Southerners and was by no means unique to Jewish converts to Christianity. As Christine Leigh Heyrman and others have richly documented, evangelical conversions throughout Southern history have sparked conflict between siblings, parents and children, and husbands and wives.[23] More readings of the records of flesh-and-blood conversions from unbeliever to believer, Methodist to Baptist, Catholic to Presbyterian is needed before we can say with any confidence whether the nature of the conflicts around Jewish conversions was more serious than that engendered by the many other conversions that shaped the South's religious landscape.

Before exploring the family dynamics of those families where the husband but not the wife, or the mother but not the son, converted to Christianity, it is worth noting that this conflict did not arise for the majority of Southern Jews, most of whom went through the war without even considering converting. If the existing historiography on Jews and the Civil War has overlooked the experience of what the rabbis would call *mumarim* (apostates), it has glorified those heroic and moving tales of Jews (almost exclusively Jewish men) struggling to maintain some semblance of a Jewish identity while on the front. There is Isaac J. Levy's well-known letter to his sister movingly describing the Passover meal he and his brother Zeke cobbled together; the impassioned but unsuccessful pleas of Rabbi Maxmilian J. Michelbacher to General Lee requesting that Jewish soldiers be granted a furlough to observe Rosh Hashanah and Yom Kippur; and the heartfelt prayers that synagogues across the Confederacy offered for the government and the army, prayers that Jefferson Davis appreciated, if God did not. For a handful of Confederate Jews, wartime experiences seem to have strengthened their faith: there are reasonably banal accounts of Jewish soldiers moved to prayer by the horrors of war, stories of Jewish soldiers inspired by their comrades' sincere Christian faith to explore not Christianity but Judaism, and the remnant of Jews still determined to demonstrate that Jews qua Jews could contribute to the Confederate effort. As mentioned above, we know of at least one African American Jew whose commitment to Judaism was strengthened by his understanding that the God of Israel had finally made good on his promise to free the slaves and deliver them from Egypt. These instances of unwavering Jewish devotion have been emphasized in the historiography, to the exclusion of Jewish experiences to the contrary,[24] not just because a minority of Jews converted to Christianity but also because much of the historiography of American Jewry—and Southern Jewry in particular—has been written not by historians but by rabbis, seminarians, and laypeople, whose explicit interest is often to chart the consolidation of American and Southern Jewry through time. That the stories recounted in this essay detract from a narrative of increasing Jewish unification and solidarity cannot be denied.[25]

IN CONSIDERING THE EXPERIENCES OF JEWISH FAMILIES REuniting and reconciling after the Civil War, it becomes clear that as with the rest of American religious history, gender is a key component of the story. The process of reconciling with their families was far different for women who converted than for men who converted. If a woman converted to Christianity during the war, there seemed to be little hope that her husband could be compelled to participate in her adopted religion, although several annoyed husbands confessed that they eventually capitulated and began attending church just to "shut up" their wives' "nagging."[26] Wives of men who had become Christian, however, were offered little choice about participating in Christian rites. Even if their husbands could not coerce them to be baptized, receive the Lord's Supper, or profess acceptance of Christ, they could at least insist that their wives accompany them to church. But Jewish women created strategies to resist their husbands' new Protestant piety.

One husband in Mississippi was disappointed to learn that his wife had no interest in becoming baptized, taking communion, reading the

New Testament, or "quitting her Friday night rituals," and he refused to take dinner with his wife on Friday nights, saying that until she ceased lighting the Sabbath candles, she would have to do without his company in the dining room. This disgruntled husband's efforts failed to achieve his desired goal: his wife seemed not to miss his presence at dinner at all, and for several weeks she went on with her "Friday night rituals," eating alone in peace and equanimity while her husband sulked in some other part of the house. Finally, she did pick up the New Testament—but not because she was inspired by the religious sensibilities her husband hoped she would cultivate. Rather, she flipped her husband's "new book" open to Acts and pointed to passages that indicated that Jewish Christians were still required to keep Mosaic law. Her husband rather shockingly responded by asking his wife when she had come to acquire such a deft knowledge of Torah and suggested that if she wanted a religion where she could "engage the Bible," she might do well to join him in his pilgrimage to the Baptist faith, where the "Holy Spirit speaks equally to husbands as to wives." There was, he added, no such "equalizing Holy Spirit to be found" in Judaism. (On this point, he seemed a bit addled: in a later battle, he pointed to Genesis 1:2 and various passages in Psalms as evidence for the Spirit's workings in the Old Testament.) After nearly eight months of debate, the couple adopted what the husband, perhaps in an effort to save face, presented as a compromise, though it was no compromise at all. What was described as a via media was really the husband's capitulation. Every Friday night for the rest of his wife's life, he ate dinner at her table, bathed in the warm light of the candles that had so perturbed him.[27]

Other Jewish women were similarly feisty and found creative ways to resist their husbands' attempts to draw them into Christianity. One Virginia woman was shocked to learn not only that her husband had been born again at the Battle of Gettysburg but also that he expected her to follow suit. When she refused to be baptized, her husband made it clear that she was not to refuse to attend church. Dutifully, Rosa accompanied her husband to Sunday morning services. But she refused to adopt the habit that most of the ladies in church had embraced in the flush of the Lost Cause. While they had decorated their church fans with the likenesses of Robert E. Lee and Stonewall Jackson, Rosa fanned away with a picture of Judah P. Benjamin.[28]

Newly Christian husbands were irate at their wives' refusal to capitulate to their religious wishes. One husband, who possessed a greater sense of humor and self-irony than most of his co-religionists, astutely noted that "religion is meant to cause problems in the other direction. . . . Among my friends, it has been their wives who have gotten religion and turned their houses upside down trying to get everyone . . . into church. Quite the opposite spirit seems to have taken . . . this house. Perchance the ride will be less rocky with a husband and a father at the helm."[29] But to the chagrin of most husbands and fathers, the ride proved no smoother for the male steering the religious ship. The constant complaints of religiously unsatisfied men are double-edged: they were worried, as good Christians, about the salvation of their wives' and children's souls, but they were also worried about their inability to control their households as they would have liked. "I think I am being made to look like a woman," one man wrote regarding the situation in his South Carolina home. "My wife is coming to church now regularly . . . but everyone can plainly see that she makes a mockery of the liturgy by saying the prayers for the bread and wine and refusing to partake." It was not merely the host that this man was worried his wife was mocking, but him as well.[30]

The fierce resistance of many Jewish spouses and parents to their relatives' embrace of Christianity begs the question of what Judaism meant to the Jews in question. While a detailed consideration of this question is outside the scope of this essay, it is worth noting that many of the relatives in question were not, at first blush, attached to Judaism themselves in any meaningful way: these were parents who made little or no effort to educate their children about Judaism, spouses who failed to observe even the most major Jewish festivals or rites, and so forth. In one case of a conversion of the antebellum period, alluded to above, Aaron Lazarus responded with vitriol to his Jewish wife's profession of Christianity. Recall that Lazarus, however, was in the habit of taking his family to church every Sunday. For Lazarus, church attendance was merely a social activity that betokened no religious or spiritual feeling or commitment, and he was shocked when his wife formally abandoned Judaism for Christianity. Clearly for these Southern Jews, Judaism may not have had a meaning that historians of the South, viewing them with lenses steeped in the study of evangelicalism, would construe as religious. Nor can the persistent attempts to maintain Judaism in the family be chalked up merely to men's attempts to control their families, since, as we have seen, many Jewish women were no more pleased with the conversions of their mates than were Jewish men. Nonetheless, Judaism had a deep claim on their souls, such that the conversions of their spouses or children incited fury, fear, and immense frustration.

The familiar reading of nineteenth-century religion tells us that women were considered to be innately more religious than men, and they were thus held responsible for men's religious lives. The experiences of Jewish women whose husbands converted to Christianity suggests that this model does not necessarily hold true for Jewish women; while Rosa and fellow travelers may have refused to abandon Judaism, they made no particular efforts to convince their husbands to return to the fold. They may have believed that continued devotion to Judaism was the right thing to do in their own lives, but they evinced no special concern for their husbands' religious well-being. In fact, in those cases, Christian husbands—not the Jewish wives—played the role of the nineteenth-century woman charged with the burden of her loved ones' salvation.

An examination of Jewish women who converted but whose husbands did not raises further questions about the dominant interpretation that ostensibly spiritually superior women assumed the burden of bringing their "erring men," in the words of historian Barbara Welter, to Christ. There were, to be sure, Jewish women who converted to Christianity without the sanction—and sometimes without the knowledge—of their husbands or fathers. Evidence exists that at least two black women who had identified themselves as Jewish before or during the Civil War had converted to Christianity by the end of Reconstruction. These two women, identified in the sources only as Sister Sarah James and Sister Susannah, became devout Christians and active members of their church. Their husbands did not join them in adopting the cross. Recognizing Jews as "the Chosen People of God" and understanding conversion to be "the work of God," not the job of humans, Sister Sarah James and Sister Susannah were content to let their husbands, and even their children, persist in their Jewish identity.[31]

That Sister Sarah and Sister Susannah exhibited little interest in converting their husbands to Christianity at first seems puzzling. But when we consider something that the standard account of nineteenth-century women's religiosity and subsequent desire to convert their families overlooks—theology—the story begins to make much more sense. Susannah and Sarah were Baptists—theologically, they were in the Calvinist vein, committed to the idea that people could do nothing to earn their salvation. Either a person was saved or she wasn't. That they demonstrated little interest in converting their husbands appears curious by the standards of a historiography that plugs all women into a gendered Arminianism whereby women are concerned with the souls and eternal disposition of their menfolk. This historiographical tradition, however ignores theology.

Unfortunately, we do not have the theological musings of Sarah and Susannah, but we can surmise that they, and many other reformed Protestant women with them, evinced little interest in converting their husbands because they eschewed Arminian theology. The thesis that nineteenth-century women were desperate to convert their families ignores reformed theology, with its disinclination to openly convert anyone, its tendency to allow the Holy Spirit to do such work. While even reformed theology may have imbibed huge doses of Arminianism after Charles Finney, the experience of Sister Sarah and Sister Susannah suggests that we may need to reexamine a cherished article of faith within our study of women and religion.

Doubtless Jewish conversions were a question of faith for many Southern Jews, who, could we resurrect them, would explain that they were called by Jesus to embrace Christianity. But religion encroaches upon, and reveals much about, many other areas of people's lives. In this brief investigation into Jewish conversions to Christianity, we have touched on issues that have far wider implications: how husbands and wives related to one another, the extent to which theology tempers evangelistic zeal, the social meanings of religion, the impact of war on faith, the requirements for a place at the Confederate altar. All these questions and more are raised by Jewish Southerners' conversions to Christianity during the Civil War era.

Notes

I am grateful to David L. Chappell and Beth Barton Schweiger, who both offered their usual trenchant criticisms and faithful insights on a draft of this article.

1. James Mill, North Carolina, to "My Dear Brother," Petersburg, Va., 8 September 1866. James Mill diary, 17, in possession of Mrs. I. H. Mill, Philadelphia, Pa. Typed manuscript in author's possession. This and all subsequent pages numbers refer to the typed manuscript. Mrs. Mill also has in her possession miscellaneous bits of additional family correspondence, hereafter cited as Mill Family Papers, and some papers relating to the Helm family of Georgia, hereafter cited as Helm Family Papers.

2. James William Hagy, *This Happy Land: The Jews of Colonial and Antebellum Charleston* (Tuscaloosa: University of Alabama Press, 1993).

3. See the correspondence of Ellen Mordecai and Rachel Mordecai Lazarus in the Mordecai Family Papers at the Southern Historical Collection, Wilson Library, University of North Carolina at Chapel Hill. For a treatment of the Lazarus-Mordecai family, see Myron Berman, *The Last of the Jews?*

(Lanham, Md.: University Press of America, 1998), and Emily Simms Bingham, *Mordecai: Three Generations of a Southern Jewish Family, 1780–1865* (Ph.D. diss., University of North Carolina at Chapel Hill, 1998); Stanley F. Chyet, "Moses Jacob Ezekiel: A Childhood in Richmond," *American Jewish Historical Quarterly* 62 (March 1973): 289; James Mill to "My Dear Brother," 13 September 1858, Mill Family Papers; Elizabeth Parker, Virginia, 18 May 1863, to Eveline Mill, North Carolina, Mill Family Papers.

4. Bertram W. Korn, "Judah P. Benjamin as Jew," *Publications of the American Jewish Historical Society* 38 (September 1948): 171.

5. Ella Lonn, *Foreigners in the Confederacy* (Gloucester, Mass.: Peter Smith, 1965), 335; Bertram W. Korn, *American Jewry and the Civil War* (Philadelphia: Jewish Publication Society of America, 1961), 175–88.

6. John Higham, "Social Discrimination against Jews in America, 1830–1930," *Publications of the American Jewish Historical Society* 47 (September 1957): 3–7.

7. Gary L. Bunker and John Appel, "'Shoddy,' Anti-Semitism, and the Civil War," *American Jewish History* 82: 43–72.

8. J. B. Jones, *A Rebel War Clerk's Diary at the Confederate States Capital* (New York: 1935), 165–66: Korn, *American Jewry,* 175–88; R. E. Park, *Sketch of the Twelfth Alabama Infantry, 10* (Richmond, 1890); Max J. Kohler, "Judah P. Benjamin: Statesman and Jurist," *Publications of the American Jewish Historical Society* 12 (1904): 79. See also *Memphis Daily Bulletin,* 28 April 1863, and Leonard Dinnerstein, "A Neglected Aspect of U.S. Jewish History," *American Jewish Historical Quarterly* 41 (September 1971): 55–59.

9. Lonn, *Foreigners in the Confederacy,* 336.

10. Korn, *American Jewry,* 180; Lonn, *Foreigners in the Confederacy,* 337.

11. Korn, *American Jewry,* 181.

12. For a discussion of one antebellum Jewish women's benevolent society, see Mark I. Greenberg, "Savannah's Jewish Women and the Shaping of Ethnic and Gender Identity, 1830–1900," *Georgia Historical Quarterly* 82 (Winter 1998): 762–63.

13. On Jewish slaveowning see Bertram W. Korn, "Jew and Negro Slavery in the OLd South, 1789–1865," *Publications of the American Jewish Historical Society* 50 (March 1961): 153–54. On black Jews, see Clive Webb, *A History of Black-Jewish Relations* (Ph.D. diss., Cambridge University, 1997), 18.

14. Many Jewish congregations would not permit black members. In Charleston, for example, Beth Elohim accepted converts as members of the congregation if they "are not people of colour." But there is evidence of a "free man of color," who was converted to Judaism by his owner, attending services in Charleston in 1857. Korn, "Jews and Negro Slavery," 175.

15. See the correspondence of Aaron Lazarus in the Mordecai Family Papers at the Southern Historical Collection, Wilson Library, University of North Carolina at Chapel Hill. For a treatment of the Lazarus-Mordecai family, see Bingham, *Mordecai.*

16. Baptismal Record Book, n.p., Canaan Tent Bible Church, Orange County, N.C.

17. Anon., *Christian Conversions of the Negro Variety* (New York: n.d.), 5.

18. Ibid., 3.

19. Elizabeth Parker, Virginia, 18 May 1863, to Eveline Mill, North Carolina, Mill Family Papers.

20. Jonathan M. Elukin, "From Jew to Christian?: Conversion and Immutability in Medieval Europe," in James Muldoon, ed. *Varieties of Religious Conversion in the Middle Ages* (Gainesville: University Press of Florida, 1997), 171. Miri Rubin, "Conversion without End," unpublished paper.

21. Holly Snyder, paper presented at "Coastal Cultures in North America, 1500–1860," University of Warwick, Coventry, England, 7 December 1997.

22. Sarah Jenkings, Raleigh, N.C., 1 January 1866, to Eveline Mill, North Carolina, Mill Family Papers.

23. Christine Leigh Heyrman, *Southern Cross: The Beginnings of the Bible Belt* (New York: Knopf, 1997).

24. As Ira Rosenwaike has noted in the context of early America, there is a "practice among historians of recording the lives of settlers in American communities who were of Jewish background, regardless of their degree of participation, or total lack of it, in Jewish religious life. Indeed, examination of a drift away from religious practice is important to understanding" history, too. Ira Rosenwaike, "The Mussina Family: Early American Jews?," *American Jewish History* 75 (June 1986): 397.

25. Writers, however, are not singlehandedly responsible for the fact that the story of Jewish converts has remained unexplored. Archives, too, are partially to blame. As these footnotes attest, much of my information comes from several family papers that remain in private hands. In fact, this article could not have been written were it not for the generosity of two women who shared their family papers with me. According to these women, an attempt was made a number of years ago to place some of these papers in several Jewish archives, but in each case the archive was uninterested, because the papers dealt so explicitly with Jewish conversions.

26. James Mill diary, 27.

27. Marcus Helm to Peter Righter, 15 April, 12 October, 2 November 1866, 18 February 1867, Helen Family Papers.

28. Teresa Walter, (Lousia County?), Va., 8 August 1866, to Rebecca Cohn, Philadelphia, Pa., papers of Rebecca Cohn, in possession of Ms. I. M. Hedley, copy in author's possession.

29. Jeremiah Walter, (Lousia County?), Va., 13 September 1866, to Hermann Cohn, Philadelphia, Pa., papers of Rebecca Cohn, in possession of Ms. I. M. Hedley, copy in author's possession.

30. M. Peters to Philip Mosie, 5 January 1867, papers of Leon Moise, in possession of Ms. I. M. Hedley, copy in author's possession.

31. Anon., *Christian Conversions of the Negro Variety*, 5.

ELEVEN

✴

IN THE FAR CORNER OF
THE CONFEDERACY

A Question of Conscience for
German-Speaking Texans

Anne J. Bailey

In the neighborhood of San Antonio, one-third of the population is German," observed Colonel Arthur Fremantle, an Englishman who passed through Texas in the spring of 1863. "The houses are well built of stone," he added, and Menger's Hotel, owned by a German, was a "large and imposing edifice." To the casual observer, the number of foreign-born in the picturesque city nestled in the Texas hill country was striking. Another traveler, Frederick Law Olmsted, had also noted the varied ethnic groups in the heart of the city: "The sauntering Mexicans prevail on the pavements, but the bearded Germans and the sallow Yankees furnish their proportion." In no other Confederate state, barring Louisiana, were residents of foreign birth so conspicuous.[1]

At the time of the secession crisis, the number of European-born families in America was unusually large. Almost one-third of the North's male population was foreign, and one out of every four Union soldiers was a first- or second-generation immigrant. Germans and Irish made up the two largest ethnic groups in both the North and the South. While the numbers were not as large in the South, less than 14 percent of the foreign population of the United States lived in a slave state; there were some 84,763 Irish, followed closely by 73,579 Germans, in the eleven Confederate states at the beginning of the war. Almost half of the Germans, about 33,000, had settled in Texas.[2]

The story of Texas Germans is complex, for it would be the only Confederate state where a large number of aliens openly opposed the government in Richmond. In 1860, four of the state's largest cities, Galveston, Houston, San Antonio, and New Braunfels, were located in predominantly German counties. But the German-speaking settlers were not united over the issues of secession and war. The path of least resistance, and the one that many chose, was to follow the state into the Confederacy. Many foreigners saw compliance simply as a matter of self-preservation. A significant percentage of Germans who joined the Confederate army did so for reasons unrelated to those that prompted tens of thousands of men to swear their allegiance to the new nation. The family of Ernst Coreth, an Austrian nobleman and a Catholic, was one of those. Count Coreth sent three of his four sons to fight in a war in which he felt little personal stake; he would pay a great price for that decision.[3]

The Coreth family was one of hundreds that emigrated to Texas in the 1840s. In Europe, the leaders of the loose German Confederations did not allow people much social, political, or religious freedom, and in 1842, some noblemen organized a society with the idea of purchasing land in Texas for colonization. This initial immigration was the work of the *Verein zum Schutze deutscher Einwanderer in Texas* (Society for the Protection of German Immigrants in Texas). Prince Carl of Solms-Braunfels made arrangement for colonists to move to the American Southwest in 1844, and the following year he founded New Braunfels in Comal County, the first of the German towns. German immigration increased, and early in 1846 some 2,300 more arrived in Galveston. It is not known whether Coreth was one of the noblemen who took part in the planning nor why he left Austria, but he brought his growing family to New Braunfels in that year.[4]

Although German immigrants settled throughout South Texas, there was a heavy concentration in a triangle outlined by the western counties of Travis, Medina, and Mason. Germans in this region were divided into two groups: the "grays," conservative settlers, who arrived before the revolutions of 1848, and the "greens," liberal intellectuals, who came after. Coreth proved atypical. When the revolutions erupted in Europe, he was already comfortably settled in Texas. In an unusual move, he uprooted his family and returned to the land of his birth. He remained in Europe for two years, from the spring of 1848 until 1850. Upon his return to Texas, he was classified as a "forty-eighter," although it is doubtful that he had taken part in any fighting in his homeland. Neither was he an intellectual, like many late arrivals; Ernst Coreth was a cultivated but not profoundly educated nobleman.[5]

The political beliefs of the Germans who came before the revolutions of 1848 and those who emigrated after them had some bearing on their attitudes toward the Confederacy. The Germans who arrived in the mid-1840s were mainly provincial and conservative. They were not opposed to the philosophy of states' rights, nor were they anxious to antagonize the slaveholding elite who ruled Texas. The ones who came after the revolutions in Europe were often republican, nationalist, and liberal. In Texas, the first group settled a large number in Comal County, while the second moved farther west to the frontier counties. The split among Texas Germans during the war also followed clear geographical lines and tended to be directly related to their proximity to the hostile Indian territory to the west. The threat of Indian raids, more than any ideological beliefs, tested the loyalties of many Germans during the Civil War.[6]

New Braunfels, near where the Coreths lived, was in the heart of the western German settlements. It had a large population and a stable economy and was distant from the frontier. This stability produced greater assimilation and acceptance of the prevailing culture. Frederick Law Olmsted reported that the New Braunfels population was made up of around 3,000 Germans and only twenty Anglo-Americans. To this he added that there were only 100 slaves, most of whom were in the outlying regions of Comal County. The 1860 census indicated 193 slaves, or 4.8 percent of the population. Significantly, only one New Braunfels resident owned slaves. Still, local politics reflected an acceptance of the existing political order. Although few people voted in New Braunfels, those who did vote had gone solidly Democratic in the national election of 1860 and had rejected the "Black Republicans." This was not true of all the German regions, however, for a number of counties with a plurality of voters born in the German-speaking European states did not support the Democratic candidates.[7]

Like the majority of Comal County residents, the Coreth family accepted the state's decision to go to war. Twenty-four-year-old Carl Coreth wrote his brother Rudolf, a year younger: "There are people here who say they would not leave, they had not started the thing, etc. I feel duty bound to go though, and what pleases me greatly is that Hedwig [Kapp] agrees with me." Nonetheless, Carl's apparent enthusiasm did not translate into immediate action, for Carl did not enlist at the outset of hostilities. In fact, he did not leave until the passage of

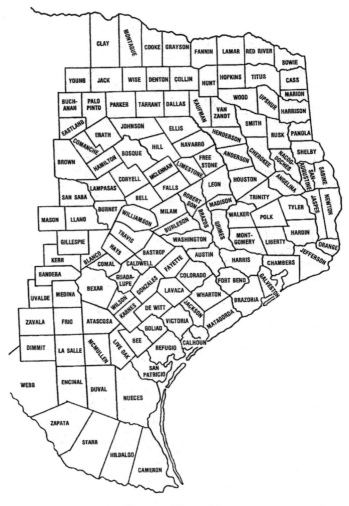

Figure 1   Texas, 1861

the conscription law in the spring of 1862. This delay might have had something to do with Hedwig Kapp, for Carl and Hedwig had obtained a marriage license in July 1861. For a variety of reasons, though, including illness, they did not marry until April 1862. Still, Carl's letter to his younger brother reveals a man who considered it one's duty to fight. Undoubtedly this strong belief in military obligation came from his father's expectations. Ernst Coreth had served in the military for over a decade, until he was discharged from the service of the Imperial-Royal Duke of Sachse-Coburg in 1832. Moreover, Ernst's father, a soldier in the Austrian army, had fought in the Napoleonic wars.[8]

The decision to support the Confederacy may have been rooted in the family's military traditions, but it was also a practical move. Certainly foreigners had cause for concern after the Confederate government passed the Banishment Act on 8 August 1861. This law required all males over fourteen years of age who were considered hostile to the Confederate government to leave within forty days. For those who stayed, the question of military service became an obvious dilemma. In modern times, a foreign national is not required to serve in the military, but the situation was not that clear during the Civil War. It was generally accepted that a foreigner should serve in the defense of his home, even if he did not join a regular military unit. In Texas, Governor Francis Lubbock recommended that anyone who refused to enlist should be forced to leave the state.[9]

Faced with the prospect of losing everything, the Coreths chose to obey Texas's Confederate leaders. This was not a difficult decision, for the residents of Comal County in general backed secession; they sent two companies of cavalry and one of infantry to the Confederate army. Throughout the war, the local paper remained committed to secession and states' rights. Because the county remained basically conservative, there were few problems with the handful of Germans who opposed the state's action. Criticism of Germans was widespread because most Texans generally believed that foreigners remained loyal to the Union. When the Confederates evacuated Galveston in December 1861, a Texas infantryman wrote that "every body run when the guns went except a few Yankees and Dutch who remain to welcome the Lincolnites when they come."[10]

Those Germans who wanted to avoid difficulties at home elected to back the Confederacy. The first Coreth to enlist in the army was twenty-three-year-old Rudolf. Even though he could barely speak English and had met few Texans outside his small closed community,

Rudolf, along with his good friend Adolf Münzenberger (who had emigrated from Lübeck, near the Baltic Sea), joined the Confederate army in October 1861. The two men enjoyed a certain prestige in being the only foreigners in their unit, a cavalry company organized for coastal defense. "We are treated as well here as we could possibly wish. The company consists almost entirely of Americans; we are the only Germans here." Yet this also had drawbacks, for Rudolf clearly recognized that he was an outsider. "The other people, officers and enlisted men, are all acquainted with each other," he told his family. "They are almost all planters from Brazoria County, who, it seems to me, only went to war to lead quite a comfortable life."[11]

While Rudolf was not one of the planter class, he certainly recognized where his family fell in the social hierarchy. Although his father had dropped his title when he moved to Texas, many Comal County citizens still called the elder Coreth "Count." Soon after enlisting, Rudolf wrote home that he had seen another company of foreigners, one composed almost entirely of German soldiers. "They behaved quite crudely all along the way," he complained, and, "in a word, [acted] like a real bunch of German yokels." And when another German-speaking recruit joined his own company in February 1862, Rudolf echoed the disdain many Austrian Catholics still maintained toward Silesian Protestants from the Old World. "I think he is a Silesian, a boor," Rudolf wrote of the new recruit. "We would have been just as happy to be the only Germans in the company. But the others know the man and seem to like him quite well, and then we don't pay him much attention so that we won't be held responsible for his actions, and so I don't think he will detract from our status here much."[12]

Status was important in the Confederate army. This was particularly true for the foreigners, who could often overcome their place of birth by bravery in battle. Unfortunately, even if a man earned the respect of his comrades, this did not necessarily translate to respect for his family among the American-born in his hometown. Ethnic discrimination, which grew as discontent with the war spread, formed an outlet for various frustrations of the native-born. In Texas, these attitudes coalesced into open distrust of the Germans living in the isolated settlements of the hill country.

There was no open hostility toward foreigners until the spring of 1862, when the passage of the conscription law incited widespread resentment in many of the scattered German settlements. In March, Brigadier General Paul O. Hébert, who commanded the District of

Texas and Louisiana, declared martial law in the state and required that all males over sixteen take an oath of allegiance to Texas and the Confederacy. To make this requirement clear, Hébert ordered the declaration printed in both English and German. Those who failed to appear before the provost marshal were fined five dollars, and the *Neu Braunfelser Zeitung*, a German paper in New Braunfels, printed the warning that anyone refusing to comply would "be vigorously dealt with." Those who refused to sign the oath could obtain a permit to leave the country. Colonel Fremantle observed that the Germans "objected much to the conscription, and some even resisted by force of arms."[13]

The Germans in the hill country countered by organizing a Union Loyal League. The professed reason was to provide frontier settlers with protection from the Indians, but the state government doubted that purpose, believing that members conferred more about opposing the laws. In response, state officials ordered two companies of Confederate cavalry to Fredericksburg, a German town in Gillespie County that was a hotbed of Unionist sentiment. Rudolf Coreth belonged to the regiment selected for this duty, but only companies composed entirely of American-born soldiers were designated for the assignment.[14]

Although tension increased, Rudolf Coreth and Adolf Münzenberger did not feel any repercussions from the civilian problems until the reorganization of the regiments in the spring. As the disagreements between Confederate officials and the German population mounted, it was impossible for the Coreths at home, or Rudolf in the army, to escape the rising wave of resentment. Moreover, if the Coreth family chose to remain loyal to the state, Carl, now twenty-five, and Johann, nearly eighteen, would have to enlist. Quite naturally, Rudolf preferred being in a company with his brothers. His frustration with the Confederate bureaucracy swelled when he could not secure a transfer to the company they joined. He wrote his brother that he and Münzenberger had "positively made up our minds to sign up for the duration of the war only if we are allowed to go with you all. If they do not want to give us any opportunity to do that, they can defend their cause without us."[15]

Rudolf was becoming increasingly skeptical about Confederate service. When he could not secure permission to join his brothers, he complained to his family that his regiment was "completely disorganized" and that both he and Münzenberger were unhappy. "The next time I write," he added, "I hope I shall have adjusted to the circumstances." His concern about the changing attitude toward foreigners in the army made him worry about his siblings. While he had initially enjoyed a special status within his own company because he was German, he was now slighted for that same reason. Rudolf did not want to see Carl and Johann in the same situation. He hinted that he would rather see his brothers join the resistance. "I hope," he concluded, "that Carl and Johann have not gone yet when you get these lines."[16]

The pressure on Texas Germans to conform finally reached a crisis in mid-1862. Throughout the late spring and early summer, Confederate soldiers patrolled the hills around Fredericksburg looking for men eluding the draft. Germans evaded capture by heading for Mexico, where a large community-in-exile formed at Matamoras. When one party of around sixty men started the long trek south in August, a Rebel detachment followed. Confederate troops caught up with them at the Nueces River on 10 August and in the battle that ensued, approximately thirty Germans were killed and twenty wounded. The Texans, however, had determined to take no prisoners and soon murdered the Germans they had captured. Not all the Rebels condoned the massacre, however, and R. H. Williams, an Englishman in the regiment involved, was particularly critical, and later wrote an account of the "shameful day." But the bloodbath only indicated the rising hostility toward German unionists.[17]

Texas authorities remained firm in their distrust of hill country Germans. Even after the affair on the Nueces, disgruntled Germans still held secret meetings and found a variety of ways to elude the draft. Thomas Smith noted: "There is now a daily guard around Fredericksburg. The 'bushwhackers' or traitors are plentiful in this country but keep themselves hid, and they have selected a good country for the business. When *one* chances to fall into the hands of the C.S. soldiers he is dealt pretty roughly with and generally makes his last speech with a rope around his neck. Hanging is getting to be as common as hunting." As a result, small parties continued to flee to Mexico.[18]

Although Smith condemned those whose loyalty was in question, he was put off by the brutal treatment they received. "The *creeks* in this vicinity are said to be full of dead men!!" he wrote. "I witnessed yesterday a sight which I never wish again to see in a civilized & enlightened country. In a water hole in Spring Creek (about 2 miles from camp) there are 4 *human bodies* lying on top of the water, thrown in and left to rot, and that too after they were hanged by neck and dead." The eighteen-year-old soldier was appalled. "If they are traitors no doubt they deserved their reward," Smith added, "but they should have at least gave them a burial."[19]

Loyal Germans worried that the continual trouble could upset the

delicate balance that kept their settlements safe. Yet when Rudolf
Coreth heard of the massacre, he shrugged it off as propaganda. He
would not believe the rumors, particularly since the soldiers involved
came from his own regiment, the Thirty-second Texas Cavalry. He
told his father: "I cannot give that report any credence though, because the man said, after the fight was over, the soldiers dragged the
wounded away from the camping ground and had them shot dead one
by one, and that," he insisted, "seems very improbable to me, really."
Still, Germans knew it was important to maintain a distinction between the settlements in open rebellion and the towns that professed
loyalty to the Confederacy. Suspicion and distrust was widespread. The
Coreths, hoping to avoid any disruption of their daily lives, walked a
fine line.[20]

One way to remain out of harm's way was to refrain from anything
political. As Germans began to take sides, Ernst Coreth did not want
to draw attention to the fact that he had three sons serving in the
Confederate army. As a result, he insulated his family from the outside
and tried to maintain a normal lifestyle isolated on their farm. "We
live a rather lonely and peaceful life together; we all work, Mother
above all," Ernst told his son. "She has a very beautiful garden." The
peas were abundant, the greens were coming along, and she had about
one hundred tobacco plants. Besides the garden, the family planted
sweet potatoes, cotton, melons, rye, barley, and corn. They had five
young calves and all the milk, cheese, and eggs they needed. The in-
dustrious family also made shoes. Ernst told Rudolf they had recently
finished sixteen pairs, but their profit fluctuated, as a pair of shoes
could be sold in town for $10.00 one day and $15.00 the next. But one
never knew, mused Ernst, for he had recently read in an old book that
during the French Revolution a pair of boots cost the equivalent of
$6,000 in Confederate money.[21]

While stability was important, anonymity became critical. There
was safety in obscurity. Unfortunately, while the Coreths wanted to
preserve the status quo by supporting the Confederacy, others factors
were at work undermining their loyalty. The first crisis came in the
summer of 1863, when the family learned that Johann was ill. John (as
Johann preferred to be called) and Rudolf were on scout with their
regiment in the barren region between the Nueces River and the Rio
Grande when dysentery struck the younger brother. Although Rudolf
received permission to take his ailing brother home, Johann did not
survive the journey, and his older brother buried him in an unmarked
grave on King's Ranch. As Rudolf neared the family home, he sent a

message ahead warning that he brought bad news. "In a few minutes I will be with you myself," he told his father. "Unfortunately I am bringing along a very sad report; what it consists of you can already imagine when you hear that I am coming alone. I am sending these lines ahead so that at least I won't frighten you by my arrival." To add to the family's sorrow, the first child born to Carl and Hedwig died after only nine days.[22]

The family tragedies fueled a growing cynicism. Rudolf Coreth became increasingly critical of both American-born Texans and the Confederate army. In July 1863 he told his family that his company had been ordered to Goliad, an American settlement near the coast. The town, he decided, was "quite a pretty place. There are many rather large stone houses here, which look quite decent because they aren't coming apart the way they are in most American towns." Of the army, he told his family: "I should like to advise Carl to try everything he can to have his leave extended, or else to get employed in a shop in San Antonio, because life in the company is sure not to please him."[23]

Discontent within the army was not limited to foreigners, for by mid-1863 the war was also unpopular with many Americans. Boredom, of course, was the main culprit. The government had moved the Thirty-second Cavalry from the Rio Grande to a point near Corpus Christi, where the troopers were charged with protecting the coastline from Padre Island to Louisiana. From Victoria, Rudolf told his family: "Here in the vicinity there is a very bad mood prevalent. The men acknowledge quite openly that they are Unionists, Germans as well as Americans, and all Unionists as well as Secessionists wish very much that the war might soon come to an end, and I hope that most emphatically too. . . . I hope the business is over with soon, so that we can get together again."[24]

In Comal County, the Coreths tried to carry on with life as usual, although it became increasingly difficult to do so. In September, Ernst told his son that it was "too early to harvest corn and too dry to plow" but they had "a nice supply of fodder for the winter" as the "horse stall and the vinegar storeroom are full." They also had a good harvest of straw, which they could use for roofing. But even the war could not prevent local disputes, as the elder Coreth was being sued by a neighbor for diverting a stream into his fields to irrigate the parched soil.[25]

Although Texans tired of war, it remained essential for residents of the German communities to demonstrate loyalty in order to avoid trouble. Ernst, however, refused to participate in the sham meetings held throughout the region. "In San Antonio a War Meeting Barbecue in the grandest style has been announced for this coming Saturday," he wrote his son in September 1863. "So naturally there is also a War Meeting in Podunk ['*Krehwinkel*,' meaning New Braunfels]. It is enough to make one explode when one has heard each and every one of the shop-keepers individually and sees their shameful souls lie fully exposed before one, and hears them sing 'War, Brother, War' in chorus." With two sons in the army, Coreth knew he had demonstrated his loyalty to the Confederacy and criticized those who only gave lip service to the Southern cause. Yet he recognized that as the tension increased between Germans and state authorities, many Texans of foreign birth felt compelled to exhibit their allegiance in a visible way.[26]

An undercurrent of discontent also spread throughout the military units after the fall of Vicksburg in July 1863 isolated the states in the Trans-Mississippi. "Confidence in this war has now sunken very much, even among the Americans," Rudolf wrote on Christmas Eve. The soldiers, he added, "would rather have mules than Negroes and Confederate money." By February 1864 he claimed there was "absolute demoralization."[27]

The frustrations that often accompany inactivity ended abruptly in the spring of 1864, when the soldiers headed for Louisiana to stop Major General Nathaniel P. Banks's Federal army from marching up the Red River toward Shreveport and the fertile cotton fields of East Texas. Rudolf, having never been in battle, was convinced he would die. He felt obligated to tell his father about his financial condition, which, he confessed, "consists exclusively of debts." Nonetheless, he felt sure his father would want to "straighten them out" in case he did not survive. He hoped his estate—namely, his horse, which he calculated worth $40 to $50 in silver—would be enough to cover the bills. Rudolf naively counted on his horse surviving, even if he did not.[28]

Both Coreth brothers, Rudolf and Carl, weathered the Red River campaign, but their letters between April and July 1864 were infrequent. The regiment remained in Louisiana even after Banks was repelled and the threat of invasion ended. From the spring of 1864 until the first months of 1865, the unit was stationed in central Louisiana. Both Coreth brothers eagerly awaited news from home, for Carl's wife Hedwig was pregnant again.[29]

In Texas, the family ignored the war as much as possible. "The ladies," noted Ernst in May, "Mother above all, it goes without saying—are busy binding." The peas had to be mowed, hauled, and threshed; they harvested around nine bushels. "Mother was foreman again," he added. "Corn and peas were money crops and could be sold in San Antonio for a good profit." He did tell his son that he had heard that "ten men, the murderers of the poor Germans, have been arrested [at Fredericksburg], but those are just rumors, and there is nothing in the newspapers about it yet."[30]

By the end of 1864 Carl and Rudolf were fed up with both the war and their American comrades. When, two days before Christmas, the company held an election for lieutenant, Rudolf threw his name in the ring. "[William] Hoym and I were urged by many to run," he told his family, "and there was nobody who wanted to run against us. Then Lt. Bitter and his clique put up an American who has been in our company several weeks and made him my opponent. They kept after the men, and at the casting of votes he beat me by one vote. Almost all those who had asked me to run voted against me." Rudolf was furious. One soldier confided to Rudolf that he had not voted for him because he "thought it would make the company look very fine if we elected an American." Rudolf was so upset that he vowed "to get out of the company and maybe even out of the army." Two weeks later his anger had not abated, and he told his parents, "I am now rather indifferent to everything."[31]

Unfortunately for the Coreths, the war did not end soon enough. Both Carl and Rudolf had become totally disillusioned after the company election, and another Christmas spent far from home in what they now called "the American war" made them both despondent. Carl was particularly bitter because he wanted to be with Hedwig when their child was born. But during the holidays he was in no condition to travel: he had been suffering from intermittent diarrhea and a persistent fever. "I can say that soon it will be all the same to me how the war comes out," he complained to his parents, "if only it would end soon. There is nothing but betrayal, robbery, and lies wherever one looks anyway." In a shaky hand, he closed: "My head hurts too much for me to be able to write you a long letter. . . . So for today, farewell again. With a thousand warm regards as ever, your loyal son Carl." Two days later Carl was dead of "congestion of the brain." He never knew about the birth of his son a month earlier, a boy Hedwig called Karl in honor of his absent father.[32]

For the Coreths, the sacrifice had been too great. Although Rudolf remained in the army five more months, his resentment increased. The family back in Texas fell under increasing scrutiny. When Ernst wrote his son about conditions in Texas, the elder Coreth warned: "Burn this letter when you have read it. It could perhaps get into the wrong hands." The Coreths's loyalty to the Confederacy had dissolved.

Rudolf had buried two brothers. "It is horrifying that such great sacrifices have been made in the firm belief that something would be attained," Rudolf concluded in May, "and that it is now clear everything was in vain."[33]

The family never recovered from their sacrifice to the Confederate war. Hedwig and her son Karl returned to Germany. She never remarried, although Rudolf admired her greatly and clearly hoped she would consider him. Even Rudolf eventually left Texas; he died in Vienna in 1901. In an odd twist of fate, his family did not realize that a periodic fee was required to retain claim to a burial plot, and at some point his body was moved. All three Coreth brothers lie in unmarked graves.[34]

The Coreth family had entered the American war with few convictions about slavery, states' rights, or secession. If they took up arms for a cause, it was in the defense of liberty and the political and economic freedom denied them in the land of their birth. The pressure to conform was particularly strong in the Texas hill country, and the Coreths, unwilling to sacrifice everything they had worked for since emigrating to America, chose to adapt. The Coreths were not rich, but they were solidly upper middle class and hoped to protect all they had gained. Building on the elder Coreth's military background, the family initially saw the war as an act of Northern aggression and the Union army as a threat. Their conscience dictated that they take up arms. Yet they never converted to the secessionist point of view, nor was there a burning zeal for Confederate independence. They, like many Germans in the Texas hill country, concealed their real sentiments to avoid persecution. To remain in the Confederacy, however, the family had to send three sons to fight. The Coreths would lose no matter which choice they made: by dissenting, they would have forfeited everything they owned; by declaring allegiance to the Confederacy, the family sacrificed two brothers for a cause in which they did not believe.

Notes

1. Diary entry dated 25 April 1863 Arthur James Lyon Fremantle, *Three Months in the Southern States, April–June 1863* (1863; reprint, Lincoln: University of Nebraska Press, 1991), 53, 55; Frederick Law Olmsted, *A Journey through Texas; or, a Saddle-Trip on the Southwestern Frontier* (New York: Dix, Edwards & Co., 1857), 150. In 1860, San Antonio counted 4,000 Mexicans, 3,500 Americans, and 3,000 Germans. Germans also comprised a large percentage of the inhabitants on the surrounding farms. Ella Lonn, *Foreigners in the Confederacy* (1940; reprint, Gloucester, Mass.: Peter Smith, 1965), 22.

2. Some 200,000 Germans and 150,000 Irish wore the Union blue. James I. Robertson Jr., *Soldiers Blue and Gray* (Columbia: University of South Carolina Press, 1998), 27–28; Jason H. Silverman, "Germans" and "Irish," *Encyclopedia of the Confederacy*, ed. Richard N. Current (New York: Simon & Schuster, 1993), 2:675–76, 822–23. Silverman estimates that there were roughly 53,000 Germans in Texas, Louisiana, and Virginia, and only around 20,000 in the remaining eight Confederate states.

3. Galveston is located in Galveston County, Houston is in Harris County, San Antonio is in Bexar county, and New Braunfels is in Comal County. The letters that this essay are based on were written by Ernst Coreth and his family in German. Ernst Coreth used essentially standard New High German, interspersed on occasion with other foreign terms and sometimes with his own Austrian dialect. Rudolf Coreth, who wrote the majority of the surviving letters, came to America when he was eight. His writing reveals that he was weak in mechanics; he would often spell words phonetically. Also, both Rudolf and his mother used far more Upper German coloration than other family members. The collections includes a handful of letters from Carl Coreth, but none from the youngest brother, Johann Coreth. Minetta Altgelt Goyne, ed., *Lone Star and Double Eagle: Civil War Letters of a German-Texas Family* (Fort Worth: Texas Christian University Press, 1982), ii–iv. Also see Glen E. Lich, *The German Texans* (San Antonio: Institute of Texan Cultures, 1981).

4. The Society was also known as *Adelsverein* or *Verein*. New Braunfels was founded on the Comal River in April 1845. In 1850 Germans numbered 11,534, or 5.4 percent of the state's population. By 1860 they numbered over 30,000, or 5 percent of the total population and 7 percent of the free population. Terry G. Jordan, "Population Origins in Texas, 1850," *Geographical Review* 59 (January 1969): 85; Robert B. Shook, "German Unionism in Texas during the Civil War and Reconstruction" (Ph.D. diss., North Texas State College, 1957), 8. For detailed maps of the settlements, see Terry G. Jordan, *German Seed in Texas Soil: Immigrant Farmers in Nineteenth-Century Texas* (1966; reprint, Austin: University of Texas Press, 1994). For more on New Braunfels, see Oscar Haas, *History of New Braunfels and Comal County, Texas: 1844–1946* (Austin: Steck Co., 1968).

5. At the time of the revolutions of 1848, Coreth was forty-five years old. German settlements extended throughout South Texas, from Galveston and Houston to the edge of the frontier. In 1862 the legislature of the state of Texas created a new county, Kendall, from parts of Kerr and Blanco. Sisterdale, where the Coreths owned land, was located in Kendall County. The Coreths also owned town lots in New Braunfels, the region's urban center. Goyne, *Lone Star and Double Eagle*, 7–14. Also see A. E. Zucker, ed., *The Forty-Eighters: Political Refugees of the German Revolution of 1848* (New York: Columbia University Press, 1950).

6. James Marten, *Texas Divided: Loyalty and Dissent in the Lone Star State* (Lexington: University Press of Kentucky, 1980), 27. See also Rudolph L.

Biesele, *The History of German Settlements in Texas, 1831–1861* (Austin: Von Boeckmann-Jones, 1930). Historian Terry Jordan cautions that it is not accurate to make too much out of the split between the Germans who came before the revolutions of 1848 and those who came after. He warns that most Germans were "not politically oriented" and that it is incorrect to assume all Germans fell into neat categories. Jordan, *German Seed,* 182–85.

7. Olmsted, *A Journey through Texas,* 181. In the presidential election, New Braunfels voters gave John C. Breckinridge 137 votes, John Bell 15, and Abraham Lincoln none. Only 86 of 325 men or 26 percent would later vote against secession in Comal County. Shook, "German Unionism," 16, 20. A comparison of Comal and surroundings counties can be found in Judith Dykes-Hoffman, "'Treue der Union': German Texas Women on the Civil War Homefront" (Ph.D. diss., Southwest Texas State University, 1996), 22, 28, 78. Joseph Landa, the one German who owned five slaves (a family of four women and a young male who drove their wagon), had to flee to Matamoras during the war. Harry Landa, *As I Remember* (San Antonio: Carleton Printing Co., 1945), 19–27. Also see Walter Buenger, *Secession and the Union in Texas* (Austin: University of Texas Press, 1984).

8. Ernst Coreth had attended the Theresianum, an elite military academy in Vienna, and had later served in the army. Carl Coreth to Rudolf Coreth, 6 May 1861, Goyne, *Lone Star and Double Eagle,* 5, 6, 17, 54.

9. It is not known how many Germans served in Texas units. An examination of the muster rolls give an estimate of the number by counting the German names, but that can be misleading because Germans often Americanized their names. Even Carl, Rudolf, and Johann Coreth took the names Charles, Rudolph, and John Coreth. Also see Shook, "German Unionism," 42.

10. In actuality, many of foreign birth were committed to the Confederate cause. For a look at Comal County in particular, see Gregg Woodall, "German Confederates from Comal County: Some German Immigrants Made the Difficult Decision to Embrace the Confederacy," *Columbiad: A Quarterly Review of the War Between the States* 2 (Winter 1999): 46–56. Still, the Texas German communities remained suspect. E. P. Petty to "Dear Wife," 5 December 1861, *Journey to Pleasant Hill: The Civil War Letters of Captain Elijah P. Petty, Walker's Texas Division CSA,* ed. Norman D. Brown (San Antonio: Institute of Texan Cultures, 1982), 12. Petty referred to the Germans as "Dutch," *deutsch* (German). See also Dykes-Hoffman, "Treue der Union," 74–75.

11. Although Rudolf joined in New Braunfels, not all men of military age enlisted. On 20 April 1861, T. J. Thomas reported that the town's residents tended to evade enrolling officers, and he believed nothing short of a draft would stir them. Lonn, *Foreigners in the Confederacy,* 312. The quote is found in Rudolf to family, 13 November 1861, Goyne, *Lone Star and Double Eagle,* 23.

12. Rudolf Coreth to family, 3 November 1861 and 9 [8] February 1862, Goyne, *Lone Star and Double Eagle,* 19, 41.

13. When it became clear that many Germans intended to avoid military

service, Texas vigilance committees took matters into their own hands. A San Antonio newspaper reported in July that the bones of Germans "are bleaching on the soil of every county from Red River to the Rio Grande and in the counties of Wise and Denton their bodies are suspended by scores from the 'Black Jacks.'" *San Antonio Herald,* 19 July 1862. See also *Dallas Herald,* 14 June 1861; diary entry dated 25 April 1863 Fremantle, *Three Months in the Southern States,* 56.

14. Robert W. Shook, "The Battle of the Nueces, August 10, 1862," *Southwestern Historical Quarterly* 66 (July 1962): 32; Claude Elliott, "Union Sentiment in Texas, 1861–1865," *Southwestern Historical Quarterly* 50 (April 1947): 455.

15. All three older Coreths were of military age. Carl Coreth was born on 16 January 1837, Rudolf Coreth was born on 7 May 1838, and Johann was born on 19 February 1845. The only other male, Joseph, was just eight years old. For the quote, see Rudolf Coreth to Carl Coreth, n.d. [probably 4 April 1862], Goyne, *Lone Star and Double Eagle,* 50.

16. Rudolf to family, 11 May 1862, ibid., 57.

17. Reports of the number of Germans killed and wounded (and later murdered) vary. The Confederates had two killed and eighteen wounded. After the battle the Confederates were interred in a common grave, but the Germans were left unburied. The remains were not recovered until August 1865, when they were reburied in Comfort, Texas, under a monument that was inscribed *Treue der Union.* Shook, "The Battle of the Nueces," 39–41. See also R. H. Williams, *With the Border Ruffians: Memories of the Far West, 1852–1868* (New York: E. P. Dutton and Company, 1907), 250; John W. Sansom, *Battle of the Nueces in Kinney County, Texas, Aug. 10th, 1862* (San Antonio, 1905); Rena Mazyck Andrews, "German Pioneers in Texas: Civil War Period" (Ph.D. diss., University of Chicago, 1929), 40; and Lonn, *Foreigners in the Confederacy,* 423–36. For another point of view on the Confederate commander involved, see Richard Selcer and William Paul Burrier, "What *Really* Happened on the Nueces River" James Duff: A Good Soldier or the Butcher of Fredericksburg?," *North and South: The Magazine of Civil War Conflict* (January 1998): 56–61. It should be noted that R. H. Williams, who wrote an account of this incident, was English and often critical of his American comrades.

18. Entry dated 27 August 1862 Thomas C. Smith, *Here's Yer Mule: The Diary of Thomas C. Smith, 3rd Sergeant, Company 'G,' Wood's Regiment, 32nd Texas Cavalry, C.S.A.: March 30, 1862–December 31, 1862* (Waco: Little Texan Press, 1958), 19.

19. Diary entry dated 27 August 1862 Smith *Here's Yer Mule,* 19, 20.

20. All three Coreth Brothers eventually ended up in the same regiment, a unit officially designated the Thirty-second Texas Cavalry, Company F, organized by Theodore Podewils, and immigrant Prussian with European military experience, included a significant number of Germans. Carl and Johann enlisted on 31 March 1862. Ironically, Rudolf and Münzenberger, who had to

obtain a release from their old company, are not even listed on the muster rolls of their original unit. These two men officially joined the Thirty-second Texas Cavalry on 27 April. Carl L. Duaine, *The Dead Men Wore Boots: An Account of the 32nd Texas Volunteer Cavalry, CSA 1862–1865* (Austin: San Felipe Press, 1966), 23. For the quote see Rudolf Coreth to family, 26 August 1862, Goyne, *Lone Star and Double Eagle,* 66.

21. Ernst Coreth to Rudolf Coreth, 15 May 1863, Goyne, *Lone Star and Double Eagle,* 86.

22. Carl had returned home to be with his wife Hedwig for the birth of their first child. Rudolf Coreth to father, n. d. [June 1863], Goyne, *Lone Star and Double Eagle,* Duaine, *The Dead Men Wore Boots,* 98.

23. Rudolf to family, 27 July 1863, Goyne, *Lone Star and Double Eagle,* 97.

24. Duaine, *The Dead Men Wore Boots,* 42–43; Rudolf Coreth to family, n.d. [August 1863], Goyne, *Lone Star and Double Eagle,* 101.

25. Coreth's neighbor was undoubtedly also German, so the dispute was purely over water rights. Ernst Coreth to Rudolf Coreth, n.d. [3, 20 September 1863], Goyne, *Lone Star and Double Eagle,* 103–4.

26. Ernst Coreth to Rudolf, n.d. [20 September 1863?], ibid., 105.

27. Rudolf Coreth to family, 24 December 1863 and 4 February 1864, ibid., 115, 119.

28. Rudolf Coreth to Ernst Coreth, 9 April 1864, ibid., 127.

29. Duaine, *The Dead Men Wore Boots,* 89.

30. The incident on the Nueces River was only one of many that involved the murder of Germans. One such slaughter is found in the reminiscences of Mathilda Wagner, who lived in Fredericksburg. Mathilda Doebbler Gruen Wagner recollections in *Texas Tears and Texas Sunshine: Voices of Frontier Women,* ed. Jo Ella Powell Exley (College Station: Texas A&M University Press, 1985), 111. For the quote, see Ernst Coreth to Rudolf Coreth, 29 May 1864, Goyne, *Lone Star and Double Eagle,* 134.

31. Rudolf Coreth to family, 23 December 1864 and 12 January 1865, Goyne, *Lone Star and Double Eagle,* 154–55, 157.

32. Carl Coreth died on 13 January 1865. He was buried in an unmarked grave at San Augustine. His son, Karl Coreth Jr., had been born on 3 December 1864. Carl Coreth to parents, 12 January 1865, ibid., 157.

33. Ernst Coreth to Rudolf Coreth, 19 May 1865, and Rudolf Coreth to family, 19 May 1865, ibid., 173–74.

34. Ibid., 174, 202.

✴

PATRIARCHY IN THE WORLD WHERE THERE IS NO PARTING?

Power Relations in the Confederate Heaven

Ted Ownby

A s they went off to join Confederate regiments, many young Southern men confronted two things for the first time: separation from their families and the possibility of dying quickly. How did separation alter their language about and understandings of family life, and how did those understandings of family life relate to their images of life after death? Would life after death continue the wartime separation of families, or would it be a great family reunion?

These questions seem especially important in light of what scholars have written about patriarchy and paternalism as organizing themes in Southern social life. Men off at war had to wonder whether they could keep their ideals about patriarchy and paternalism working during their sustained absences and, ultimately, in death. In the minds of Confederate men, was there patriarchy in heaven? Was there paternalism? In their letters about the afterlife, they were not simply reporting ideas they had heard; they were imagining or even building a heaven, and in those visions one can see which parts of their lives they hoped to continue, to enhance, and to forget.

Two perspectives on separation and death dominated the thinking of men in the Confederacy. One was a stoic mode that tried to confront battle as a duty without thinking about possible consequences.

The stoic perspective stressed a patriotism that subsumed the individual into a broad identity encompassing household, community, state, and country. From this perspective, men should be willing to die, if death was necessary, with no assurance that everything would be okay. The second was a romantic mode, which was broadly sentimental, imaginative, idealistic, dreamlike, maybe but only maybe too good to be true. It was also romantic in the sense that it included love and affection between men and women. In the romantic mode, soldiers fought with the hope that they would meet family members in what so many referred to as the world where there was no parting. Some Confederates fit into one category, some the other, and some showed signs of both. Although it is difficult to track such changes, considerable reading in the letters of Confederate soldiers and their families suggests that as the war continued and the death toll mounted, the stoic perspective gradually declined, and the romantic perspective grew increasingly popular.

For the stoic, the goal was to fight without thinking much about separation from family or the possibility of death. For stoics who wrote letters, separation from family members was simply a reminder of the reason to be fighting—to protect the household and serve the new nation. What they felt, we do not know. Part of being a stoic was not discussing feelings, and stoics by nature did not write long, expressive letters. For such men, letters home included straightforward messages full of war news, requests for information, and instructions about running their households.

Perhaps the clearest way to understand the stoic is by examining a young soldier who feared he was not stoic enough. Mississippian Columbus Sykes wrote a series of letters telling his wife how much he missed her and their children. But he repeatedly reminded himself not to dwell on his affections, because he feared that sentimentality and nostalgia for home would hinder his ability as a soldier. He wrote in 1864, "Tell the children that 'dear papa' thinks often of them, and wishes that he could form one of the fireside at home, but it wouldn't do to indulge this thought until this 'cruel war' is over, as I might become demoralized, and that, you know, would be dreadful."[1] Dreaming about home seemed to Sykes a weakness—an indulgence— because it made him long to be somewhere other than the battlefield. A month later he wrote that while preparing for battle, he often thought about his children, started to "imagine that I see them as in days that are gone," and prayed that God would protect them. Significantly, he stopped himself. "Such thoughts sometimes unfit me to be a soldier, and I cannot indulge them as I would. When the hated foe is driven from our soil, and balmy peace once more spreads wide her silvery pinions, we may luxuriate in the idea of home—comforts and pleasures."[2] When Sykes had romantic thoughts of home, he tried to put them out of his mind.

Other letters by would-be stoics who failed in their stoicism took the form of admissions of emotional weakness and dependence. Patriarchy demanded independence and control over the emotions, but prolonged absence from family members left many men concerned about their ability to command everything, including their own feelings. Georgia doctor George Peddy confessed to his wife, "Kittie, my dear, I would tell you how much I think of you & little Laura if I was not ashamed."[3] Ugie Allen tried but failed to be a stoic and admitted to his wife how much he depended on her. "Long, long have I strugled to conciel the agony of feeling I endure by being absent from you. In vain have I endeavored to assume an air of indifference to smother those outbursts of sorrow that continually rise. But I am not my own master and confess my weakness to you only now."[4] Overcoming shame and asserting mastery were central to the virtues of white Southern men.[5] These Confederates were making significant admissions by saying that affection for their wives had undercut those virtues. Stoicism was not easy to achieve.

The stoic did not dwell on a heaven, although he probably believed such a place or condition existed. Columbus Sykes, for example, never mentioned the afterlife in his letters. He wanted to get home to his children and wife, but he did not choose to imagine a heaven in which he might be with them forever. When heaven mattered for such men, it was less as a source of comfort or an ultimate destination and more a source of assistance. Family and country both seemed worth dying to protect. As a young father from Georgia wrote his wife, "If I die in the struggle, be assured I die for you & our little ones."[6] A wealthier Confederate from Texas wrote in the stoic mode that he was "determined to conquer or die. I know that I love life & the pleasures of it as well as anyone, but I feel, or pray to feel, willing if necessary to sacrifice it for the good of my country."[7] A Louisiana man combined the two, writing his wife, "I had rather fall in this cause than to live to see my country dismantled of its glory and independence. . . . If I should fall, Oh! teach my boy to love his country."[8]

Stoics tended to close their letters to family members by saying they were "Yours until death," or "Your husband until death." For some, such a form carried little theological meaning—it was a simple expression of lifelong loyalty. But it was the closest thing some made to a theological statement in their letters, and it suggested that human connections did not continue into an afterlife. A few weeks before he died, Florida Confederate Winston Stephens wrote his wife with stoic advice about his possible death. "Grieve as little as you can for your lost husband and take consolation that I died a soldier defending a just cause."[9]

The stoic perspective, to conclude, gave little consideration to an afterlife, and when stoics thought about family life, they imagined protecting their families or sacrificing for them rather than spending eternity with them. It may be important that stoics did not choose to consider hell as an option for the afterlife; in their letters they simply tried to avoid the subject.

Confederates who wrote the most about home and heaven were romantics who envisioned both as settings for secure and happy family relations. They were usually men writing to women or women writing to men. When men wrote to fathers, sons, brothers, and male friends, they usually avoided sentiment or imagination. But when men and women wrote each other, they increasingly envisioned futures with affectionate family relations, first in earthly reunions, then in eternal life.

Separation hit many men harder than they had expected, especially as the war continued for years. In their letters, many men showed a degree of feeling some of them found surprising and even embarrassing. As separations grew longer and men became more desperate, many letters became less stoic and more openly affectionate. One wealthy Mississippian exemplifies the soldier who tried to balance romantic and stoic perspectives and ended up on the romantic side. Early in the war, William Nugent wrote his wife Nellie that he hoped God would allow him to live long enough to have an heir "to take my name and represent me hereafter in the affairs of men." But even without that ultimate claim to the immortality of the family name, he made the clearly stoic point, "One cannot die too soon in the discharge of his duty."[10] Nugent's letters contained eloquent passages about his love for his wife and home. Like many absent husbands, he said his affection increased daily; he wrote about wanting to "assemble around our family hearth" and someday soon to "go somewhere, where I cannot be at all disturbed, and pet you and the baby to my heart's content."[11] Like the stoic Columbus Sykes, he worried that he should not dream so much about homes—heavenly or earthly—and that he should develop "a firm trust in the God of battles."[12] But the hearth was at the center of his vision for the future, in both earthly life and the next life. In a long letter in 1864, he contrasted his public self and his private, more affectionate self. "I believe I am brave & strong, but I have an excessively tender heart as far as you are concerned and lean upon your affection more than you will ever believe. In contact with men I am philosophic, to a certain extent stoical and self possessed; with you I am swayed by an impulsive affection, and the simple story of love can always steal its way into my innermost feelings, rule dominant over them, and evoke the softest emotions, emotions that struggle for utterance and can only express themselves in the unsought tear and warm embrace." He continued that he could "never speak of the tenderest feelings that lurk within me without giving vent to them by involuntary weeping."[13]

This newly discovered willingness to tell family members about "the softest emotions" is important and representative. Male letter-writers wrote that they were changing or wanted to change due to new realizations they made during wartime. Countless men wrote that they missed their parents or their wives and children more than they had ever expected. Many used bland clichés to make the point that their hearts had indeed grown fonder. An Arkansas man wrote, "You do not know dearest wife how much I prize you—how much I have learned to love you since this war began."[14] An Alabama farmer, John Cotton, wrote his wife, "I never new what pleasure home afforded to a man before."[15] Some men went beyond clichés to use language one might not expect of men in the Confederacy. Edgeworth Bird, a wealthy Georgian, wrote in a long series of affectionate letters to his wife Sallie, "Ah, old Birdie, in every letter I tell you of how necessary you are to me, how complete a void your absence makes in my heart." He continued with language that is perhaps surprising: "I never knew my complete dependence upon you till I lost your support."[16] Some men, almost with a sense of having had conversion experiences, told their wives they planned to change how they treated their families. One reported that he "heard a man say that if he ever got home again he would be a model husband. He had always thought he was doing well; but if he got home he would do evrything that his wife even hinted or suggested without ever being asked. And that his whole time should be spent in a way conducive to her pleasure."[17] William Dorsey Pender, whose musings on family life and the afterlife led him to tell Fanny Pender, "I have almost come to feel that you are a part of my religion," spelled out ways he wanted to improve once he got home. "I often think darling that when we get together again that I will not be cross and look mad and refuse to talk as I used to do."[18] The effusive William Nugent wanted to hurry home to prove to his wife Nellie how much he valued the "power and beauty, and grace, and equanimity" of "marital affection." "I have buffeted with the world long enough to know the value of peace and quiet, and if God spares me through the war, I shall cultivate them with a hearty zest."[19]

These expressions of newly found pleasure in family life and newly discovered dependence on their wives led, in the context of wartime and the immediacy of death, to considerable discussion of the after-life. Many men and women of the Confederacy shifted in their letters from discussions of separation to considerations of eternity. As the war progressed, more wrote with a sentimental conception of heaven—a conception at odds with the stoic's belief that one should fight out of duty without wondering about a future after death. In the sentimental or romantic conception, heaven was a happy place full of enjoyable human contacts and without human problems.

This, of course, was not a novel idea or an idea completely new to the South. In their history of ideas of heaven, Colleen McDaniel and Bernhard Lang list four features of the romantic vision of heaven first elaborated by Emanuel Swedenborg in the mid-1700s and popularized in England and the American Northeast in the early 1800s. First, heaven was close in time and personality to life on earth. The romantic heaven deemphasized the idea of purgatory—a condition of limbo for the soul—and emphasized the similarities between human potential and the heavenly condition. Second, heaven was "a continuation and fulfillment of material existence." Senses were fine things, and heaven would gratify them. Third, the romantic conception of heaven placed less emphasis on rest and more emphasis on activity, especially spiritual progress toward understanding the beauty of God. Finally, the modern heaven included the possibility of human love within a heavenly society.[20] American historians such as David Stannard, Mary Ryan, and Gary Laderman have analyzed the sentimentality of the romantic view, stressing the importance of nuclear families, loving mothers, innocent children, and fathers who loved and enjoyed family members without having to assert authority. Heaven, then, consisted of the affectionate family at its most idealized, without work, pain, disciplining patriarchs, or anything threatening or sinful.[21]

Such a perspective seems strange in light of the gender ideals and gender relations that prevailed in the antebellum South. How did male Confederates—who had such strong conceptions of male control, male leadership, male assertiveness, and male honor—think about heaven? Would there be patriarchy in the world where there was no parting?

A few Southern historians have analyzed antebellum ideas of heaven. Virginians in the 1700s, according to Mechal Sobel, believed in heaven as a family reunion. She interpreted such beliefs as signs of the cultural interaction of whites with their slaves, who believed in communing with the spirits in western Africa.[22] In the late antebellum period, as Stephanie McCurry has shown, many women expected families to be reconstituted in heaven, and preachers used the threat of family division as a common device in their sermons.[23]

Letters of Confederates often included reassurances of family reunions in heaven. Said one, "My Dear Parents, it may be that we will never meet on earth again but if we do not I hope that we will meet again in that world that is all pleasure, peace and joy."[24] Another: "Dear wife if I never see you again in this life I hope to meet you again & them sweet little children in Heaven the land of rest."[25] A third: "Give my love to all of our connection kiss the children and think of me. May the Lord bless and assemble us together in heaven if not on earth."[26] Another wrote in a letter of consolation, "Tell Aunt Margaret just to pursue her present course and she will meet him in that beautiful and happy place, never again to be separated by death."[27] A fifth dreamed with "raptures of bliss" about being with his wife again but had the consolation that death "will only prepare us for an ever lasting union in another and better world."[28] Although this was not a new sentiment in Southern history or a new conception of the afterlife, the immediacy of death made the issue a much more frequent topic of discussion than it had been in antebellum letter-writing. Also, numerous reports of dreams, dying words, and deathbed sightings of dead relatives suggested that heaven was to be a reunion of family members.

Many depictions of heaven went far beyond expressions of resignation or consolation and promised joy and excitement about the nature of eternal life. Dying was not a duty, as the stoic would say; instead, it would be a great pleasure. William Nugent spent long pages discussing how thoughts of death should inspire a more loving family life. He loved to imagine the time his whole family would be together in the "'Mansion not made with hands' beyond the surging billows of life's troubled sea. To that mansion may we all so live as happily to terminate our pilgrimage, when we shall have passed the Jordan of death."[29] Like many Confederate letter-writers, W. J. Mims paired a family reunion at the end of the war with the notion of family reconstitution in heaven. "Oh! for that long looked for, that much prayed for day, when we shall meet under the bright auspices of a happy & lasting peace when we shall unite our voices in praises to the Great Giver of all Good." It is not clear whether he was referring to a reunion in this life or the next one, but he saw those things as so closely related that it did not matter. "May God bless us & ours, grant us a speedy reunion & ultimately a place in his kingdom above."[30] Joshua Callaway also wrote love letters about heaven. Shortly after he followed his wife Dulcinea in the decision to join a church, he wrote home with what he called "a delightful thought, an absorbing theme." "And may you, my dearest love, and I go hand in hand through a long and peaceful life, stand together acquited at the bar of God and then on the wings of angels fly away [to] heaven to cast our crowns at the feet of Jesus and spend eternity in singing his praises, followed by our dear little children."[31]

If letters about heaven could be love letters, they could also include religious inspiration. Evangelical religion demands that all Christians go about trying to convert the unconverted. But the command took on a special urgency in an age with so much sudden death. Numerous letter-writers wrote to ask their spouses to hurry up and get converted so they would not have to face eternity alone, or so they would not have to spend their old age wondering if their spouse would greet them in heaven. Mississippian Warren Magee was delighted to read that his wife Martha had converted and joined a church. "Oh how my heart fluttered when I saw that. . . . Suppose I had died when I was sick I would Oh died Saying I leave an unconverted Wife behind, but Oh Such is not the case."[32] William Gale wrote in 1863 to assure his wife Kate that he had converted and taken communion for the first time. He knew she worried about his religious condition, but he promised "to lead a new life" that would allow them to be together "*in all things through all time*."[33]

William Dorsey Pender worried that his wife Fanny might go to heaven without him. "Oh! honey the idea that when we go to our final rest you will go to everlasting life and bliss and I to everlasting damnation agonizes me. Let us go together." His letters about heaven were love letters. Hoping to enjoy "everlasting bliss together," Pender found it excruciating that "two who love each other as I know we do, may be separated at any time for eternity." Pender was finally baptized and felt a degree of reassurance about the next life, but like any good evangelical, he still worried about his motives. In a combination of proclaiming love and fearing idolatry, he admitted, "I am forced to say, if I say the truth, that my fear of death arises more from the disinclination to leave you, than the proper motive, fear of damnation."[34]

The imagery Confederate letter-writers and diarists used to describe heaven was not unusual for Anglo-American Protestants in the nineteenth century. Heaven was the "happy world where sorrow & pain is not known,"[35] or the place "where ther is no parting for ever."[36] Elijah Odom, a devout teenager from Lee County, Mississippi, called heaven a place "free from pain, disease, sorrow, death, and all the troubles of the world," where he hoped to "bask forever in the sunshine of the Son of God."[37] It is tempting to see the construction of heaven as a place without the problems Americans faced in the years of the Civil War—dislocation and separation, fear, illness and death.

The views of heaven popular among Confederates seem remarkable only in their remoteness from the workings of everyday Southern home life and gender relations. The northeastern romantic idea of heaven took bourgeois ideals of domestic privacy, affection, motherly sentiment, and childish innocence, blocked out society's problems, and imagined the result as eternity. As Reid Mitchell writes in his study of Union soldiers, "The newly imagined heaven turned out to look very much like the idealized Victorian home. Americans could anticipate death as the means to be reunited with their loved ones; heaven was conceived of as a place where friends and family resume their social intercourse."[38] But the shift toward small families, privacy within the home, separation from the world of work, and motherly affection had not taken place in Southern households as they had in bourgeois households in the North. According to virtually everything historians have written about the antebellum South, men did not organize their households around the principle of affection. Farming men wanted large families of hard workers, and plantation patriarchs demanded discipline over large households for the operation to run smoothly.[39] While statements of romantic love were not uncommon in upper-class gender relations in the antebellum South, such expressions of affection generally seem to have been peripheral and perhaps even antithetical to the social ideals white men in the region held most firmly—control, honor, responsibility, independence.[40] Among Southerners, there seems no obvious reference point for the widespread popularity of the romantic, sentimental vision of a family heaven.

Two omissions stand out about the Confederate heaven. Slaves were absent. Letters often mentioned slaves—their presence in camp, salutations to them and calls for news about them, instructions about how to deal with certain slaves, news about slaves who left home and those who did not, and references to the "family white and black." Occasionally but not often, letters mentioned slaves who died. But with extremely few exceptions, Confederates' wartime letters did not include slaves in their visions of heaven. Perhaps since they did not imagine anyone working in heaven, they had no place for them. Perhaps the growing frustrations of wartime slaveholding made slaveholders doubt the continued status of slaves as members of the household. White Southerners might have imagined a segregated heaven, but they did not mention it in their letters. It seems more likely that they were developing such an idealized view of heaven that they ruled out anything or anyone who was problematic.

Also absent in discussions of the afterlife were fellow soldiers who were not relatives. Letters and diary entries often mentioned that a dying fellow soldier talked about going to heaven, and officers wrote letters of condolence to relatives describing the last words and planned destinations of the dead. Despite all their feelings of brotherhood and shared purpose and despite the wartime revivalism in which so many Confederate men converted together, soldiers did not mention that they hoped to see fellow soldiers in the next life.

For Confederates who wrote about it, heaven consisted of small mixed-gender units of family members. These imagined units were families, not the *households* that labor and gender scholars have shown constituted the day-to-day working reality of preindustrial life. Confederates did not expect to see slaves, friends, or fellow soldiers. Some mentioned grandparents and uncles and aunts, but the great majority of heavenly units imagined by Confederates consisted of husbands and wives, parents and children, and siblings.

There was no patriarchy in the Confederates' view of heaven, and there was no paternalism. Heaven, as they imagined it, was a place without power relations, except for the power of God. Patriarchy and paternalism were always works in progress, not conditions free men simply inherited and enjoyed, and not ideals Confederates envisioned for their eternal lives. Patriarchy required work to enforce and uphold. Paternalism demanded negotiation to determine the paternalist's responsibilities, and then required the paternalist to live up to those responsibilities. Heaven, as a place with no work or burdens, no conflict or struggle, was not a place for exercising power. Nor was it a place where honor mattered. The competitions over character, the protection of the family name, the struggle for control over all things within the household—none of them had a place in the Confederates' views of the next life.

What should we make of a view of the afterlife so profoundly different from the everyday lives and ideals common in the antebellum South? How can we explain this romantic view of heaven? It is surprising, in light of the differences in family structures in the antebellum North and South, that Confederates' heaven looked a great deal like the heaven imagined by Union soldiers and their families. Perhaps the war experience itself helped bring on and intensify white Southerners' notions of a heaven as a happy, affectionate family. Somewhat similar to the ways middle-class jobs separated men in the antebellum Northeast from their homes, the Civil War separated Southern men from their households and encouraged them to imagine and idealize wives and children rather than to deal with them. Also, the fears of Confederate men that war was demolishing their homes and scattering their families may have inspired new idealizations about the home life those men could now picture only in their memories. It seems likely that the Confederate men who wrote love letters about home and heaven were not merely envisioning the afterlife—they were reassuring themselves and their family members about the ultimate value of their relationships.

Removed from home and perhaps fearing for the existence of their homes, Confederate men chose to imagine personal relations that were almost assuredly happier and more loving than they had actually been. Some of the letters represented a form of courtship. Married men, many of them young men who had not written to family members before, used language to reassure their wives that they would remain faithful in spite of their absence. Distant spouses could address the complaints typical of young lovers—why haven't you written, why did your last letter seem so cold, why can't you get away to see me more often, how can I be sure you won't forget me—with flowery descriptions of sharing eternal life. This was their form of poetry, and discussions of heaven as home typically came at the end of letters full of more mundane matters. I would never leave you or forget you, the men said, in this life or in the next.

The romantic view of heaven also allowed Confederate men to deal with some of the contradictions and tensions inherent in their assertions of control. Patriarchy was full of tensions already, but practicing patriarchy in absentia posed new difficulties. In their letters home, men tried to retain power over major decisions by spelling out instructions about workers, crops, livestock, and goods to purchase. But as Anne Firor Scott and others have shown, Confederate women ably took on these roles during wartime.[41] A second challenge to patriarchy came from women whose support for the war declined as they felt betrayed by the loss of life and support.[42] To put it simply, it was hard for men to feel confident as patriarchs when they were absent from their households, troubled by women's assertiveness within those households, and failing to win the war.

It seems likely that envisioning an afterlife without conflict allowed Confederates to avoid confronting such issues by making them irrelevant. It is never easy both to rule and to love, but it was especially hard to do both in wartime. Confederate men may have envisioned heaven as an affectionate home as a way to avoid any tensions between the two. The notion of a heaven without such worries must have been appealing for men who were wondering who—if anybody—was in charge of the household, wondering if the war would ever win protection over those households, and wondering how to balance tensions between manly self-control and feelings of weakness and dependence.

Imagining a heaven without slaves was likely a way for Confederates to deal with the tensions in wartime slaveowning. The actions of slaves during the Civil War consistently challenged slaveowners' self-image as paternalists who secured social order through their kindly control over dependents. Perhaps men who were thinking about what mattered most to them were ready to dismiss slaves as too complicated, too untrustworthy, or too troublesome to have a place among their acquaintances in the next life. The Civil War was a dividing line in so many things in Southern history; whether we believe labor and political relations changed dramatically or only slightly, it is clear there was a revolution in the place of African Americans in the self-definition of white Southern men. By the end of the war, white men in the South no longer imagined blacks as extended members of their households. African Americans now lived outside the control of whites' households, and many white Southerners considered them threats to the household rather than extended parts of it. It is no wonder, then, that white men off at war envisioned a heaven without any of the questions and worries related to slavery.

Finally, one must speculate about possible consequences. If the romantic conception of heaven as an affectionate family did indeed become more prevalent among white Southerners during the Civil War, did such ideas affect their behavior after the war? It is clear that wartime thinking about affectionate family life did not encourage white Southern men to temper their interests in manly aggressiveness and physical violence. Armed terrorism in the postwar generation and the rise of lynchings in the succeeding generation dramatized men's willingness to use violence to assert their interests. While heaven may have become more affectionate and less patriarchal, life in the South did not.[43]

Perhaps the soaring idealism about loving family life and the violence of the postbellum period actually developed together. Men were proven to be unable to achieve either of their highest goals—being an affectionate husband and father and being a patriarchal protector. They failed in the first goal because of the sheer difficulty of being the kind, loving member of the idealized household; they failed in the second by the reality of military defeat. As Charles Reagan Wilson has argued, Confederates who lost a war they considered holy chose to view defeat as a time of testing their commitments to sacred ideals.[44] Perhaps the paired sacralization and romanticization of family life during wartime had the tragic consequence of urging ex-Confederates to fight on in the name of ideals of family life that had always been too good to be true. Rather than altering their behavior to conform to ideals they associated with the perfect home in this life and their ultimate home in heaven, they chose to fight, intimidate, and kill in the name of those ideals.

Notes

1. Columbus Sykes to "Dear Darling," 1 May 1864, n.p., "Pre– and Civil War Letters of Lt. Col. Columbus Sykes, 16th Regiment, Mississippi Infantry," comp. Jim Huffman, p. 53, Mississippi Department of Archives and History, Jackson.

2. Ibid., 1 June 1864, p. 59.

3. George W. Peddy to Kittie Peddy, Camp Harrison, Ga., 9 November 1861, *Saddle Bag and Spinning Wheel, Being the Civil War Letters of George W. Peddy, M.D., and His Wife Kate Featherston Peddy,* ed. George Peddy Cuttino (Macon, Ga.: Mercer University Press, 1981), 11.

4. Ugie Allen to Susie Allen, Camp near Manassas, Va., 4 February 1862, *Campaigning with "Old Stonewall": Confederate Captain Ujanirtus Allen's Letters to His Wife,* ed. Randall Allen and Keith S. Bohannon (Baton Rouge: Louisiana State University Press, 1998), 73.

5. On ideals common among Southern white men, especially wealthy ones, see Bertram Wyatt-Brown, *Southern Honor: Ethics and Behavior in the Old South* (New York: Oxford University Press, 1982); Steven M. Stowe, *Intimacy and Power in the Old South: Ritual in the Lives of the Planters* (Baltimore: Johns Hopkins University Press, 1987), Kenneth S. Greenberg, *Honor and Slavery: Lies, Duels, Noses, Masks, Dressing as a Woman, Gifts, Strangers, Death, Humanitarianism, Slave Rebellions, the Proslavery Argument, Baseball, Hunting, and Gambling in the Old South* (Princeton: Princeton University Press, 1996).

6. Joshua Callaway to Dulcinea Callaway, Corinth, Miss., 19 May 1862, *The Civil War Letters of Joshua K. Callaway,* ed. Judith Lee Hallock (Athens: University of Georgia Press, 1997), 17.

7. Thomas Jewett Goree to Mary Frances Goree Kittrell, Centreville, Va., 18 February 1862, *The Thomas Jewett Goree Letters,* vol. 1: *The Civil War Correspondence,* ed. Langston James Goree V (Bryan, Tex.: Family History Foundation, 1981), 135.

8. William Edwards Paxton to Rebecca Puxton, Corinth, Miss., 27 March 1862, Ken Durham, ed., " 'Dear Rebecca': The Civil War Letters of William Edwards Paxton, 1861–1863," *Louisiana History* 20, no. 2 (Spring 1979): 183.

9. Winston Stephens to Tivie Stephens, Lake City, Fla., 13 February 1864, *Rose Cottage Chronicles: Civil War Letters of the Bryant-Stephens Families of North Florida,* ed. Arch Fredric Blakey, Ann Smith Lainhart, and Winston Bryant Stephens Jr. (Gainesville: University Presses of Florida, 1998), 317.

10. William L. Nugent to Eleanor Smith Nugent, Vicksburg, Miss., 19 August 1861, *My Dear Nellie: The Civil War Letters of William L. Nugent to Eleanor Smith Nugent,* ed. William M. Cash and Lucy Sommerville Howorth (Jackson: University Press of Mississippi, 1977), 46.

11. Ibid., Camp Holly near Vicksburg, 22 June 1862, p. 91.

12. Ibid., Near Lost Mountain, Ga., 9 June 1864, p. 179.

13. Ibid., Pikeville, Miss., 22 January 1864, p. 156.

14. James Mitchell to Sarah Mitchell, Little Rock, Ark., 17 April 1863, Frances Mitchell Ross, ed., "Civil War Letters from James Mitchell to His Wife Sarah Elizabeth Latta Mitchell," *Arkansas Historical Quarterly* 37, no. 4 (Winter 1978): 312.

15. John W. Cotton to "My dar wife and children," Chattanooga, Tenn., 3 August 1862, in *Yours till Death: Civil War Letters of John W. Cotton,* ed. Lucille Griffith (University: University of Alabama Press, 1951), 14.

16. Edgeworth Bird to Sallie Bird, Camp Walker near Manassas, Va., 2 September 1861, *The Granite Farm Letters: The Civil War Correspondence of Edgeworth and Sallie Bird,* ed. John Rozier (Athens: University of Georgia Press, 1988), 21.

17. Ugie Allen to Susie Allen, Camp near Centreville, Va., 19 October 1861, Allen and Bohannon, *Campaigning with "Old Stonewall,"* 59.

18. William W. Hassler, ed., *The General to His Lady: The Civil War Letters of William Dorsey Pender to Fanny Pender* (Chapel Hill: University of North Carolina Press, 1965), 185, 226–27.

19. William L. Nugent to Eleanor Smith Nugent, Elyton, Ala. 20 April 1864, Cash and Howorth, *My Dear Nellie,* 169–70.

20. Colleen McDannell and Bernhard Lang, *Heaven, a History* (New Haven: Yale University Press, 1988), 183.

21. David E. Stannard, *The Puritan Way of Death: A Study in Religion, Culture, and Social Change* (New York: Oxford University Press, 1977); Mary P. Ryan, *Cradle of the Middle Class: The Family in Oneida County, New York,*

1790–1865 (NewYork: Cambridge University Press, 1981); Gary Laderman, *The Sacred Remains: American Attitudes toward Death, 1799–1883* (New Haven:Yale University Press, 1996).

22. Mechal Sobel, *The World They Made Together: Black and White Values in Eighteenth-Century Virginia* (Princeton: Princeton University Press, 1987), 223–24.

23. Stephanie McCurry, *Masters of Small Worlds:Yeoman Households, Gender Relations, and the Political Culture of the Antebellum South Carolina Low Country* (NewYork: Oxford University Press, 1995), 171–76. See also Jean E. Friedman, *The Enclosed Garden:Women and Community in the Evangelical South, 1830–1900* (Chapel Hill: University of North Carolina Press, 1985), 47–50; Laura F. Edwards, *Gendered Strife and Confusion:The Political Culture of Reconstruction* (Urbana: University of Illinois Press, 1997), 133–34. Jane Turner Censer's study of family relationships in North Carolina planter households discusses bereavement among affectionate families but not the notion of family reconstitution in the afterlife. Jane Turner Censer, *North Carolina Planters and Their Children, 1800–1860* (Baton Rouge: Louisiana State University Press, 1984), 28–31.

24. Samuel Blackwell Gulledge to "Mother and Father," Corinth, Mississippi, 12 July 1861, *Letters to Lauretta, 1849–1863, from Darlington, S.C., and a Confederate Soldier's Camp*, ed. W. Joseph Bray Jr. and Jerome J. Hale (Bowie, Md.: Heritage Books, 1993), 164.

25. Elijah M. Odom to Sarah H. Odom, 25 March 1862, Folder 1, Elijah Odom Papers, Mississippi Department of Archives and History, Jackson.

26. John McDonald to Susan McDonald, 10 October 1862, n.p. John McDonald, "Civil War Service Records, Article on Barksdale's Brigade, and Letters (dated July 5, 1862–December 2, 1864," Mississippi Department of Archives and History, Jackson.

27. Harry Miller to Richard Franklin Simpson, Dalton, Ga., 24 September 1863, *"Far, Far from Home":The Wartime Letters of Dick and Tally Simpson, Third South Carolina Volunteers*, ed. Guy R. Everson and Edward H. Simpson Jr. (NewYork: Oxford University Press, 1994), 286.

28. William Dudley Gale to Kate Gale, Atlanta, Ga., 29 October 1863, Gale and Polk Family Papers, Southern Historical Collection, Wilson Library, University of North Carolina at Chapel Hill, in *Southern Women and Their Families: Papers and Diaries* (University Publications of America), Series A, Reel 2.

29. William L. Nugent to Eleanor Smith Nugent, Pikeville, Miss., 22 January 1864, Cash and Howorth, *My Dear Nellie*, 156.

30. W. J. Mims to Kathleen Mims, Petersburg, Va., 22 September 1864, "Letters of Major W. J. Mims, C. S. A.," *Alabama Historical Quarterly* 3, no. 2 (Summer 1941): 224.

31. Joshua K. Callaway to Dulcinea Callaway, Missionary Ridge, Ga., 26 October 1863, Hallock *The Civil War Letters of Joshua K. Callaway*, 154.

32. Warren Magee to Martha Magee, Johnson Island, Ohio, 23 March

1864, in Bell Irvin Wiley, ed., "The Confederate Letters of Warren G. Magee," *Journal of Mississippi History* 5, no. 4 (October 1943): 213. Drew Gilpin Faust makes this point in *Mothers of Invention: Women of the Slaveholding South in the American Civil War* (New York: Vintage Books, 1996), 185–87.

33. William Dudley Gale to Kate Gale, Shelbyville, Tenn., 1 March 1863, Gale and Polk Family Papers, Southern Historical Collection, Wilson Library, University of North Carolina at Chapel Hill, in *Southern Women and Their Families in the Nineteenth Century: Papers and Diaries* (University Publishers of America), Series A, Reel 2.

34. These letters appear in Hassler, *The General to His Lady,* 57, 62, 64, 97.

35. J. Miles Pickens to Richard Franklin Simpson, Camp near Rapidan, Va., 1 October 1863, Everson and Simpson, *"Far Far from Home,"* 293.

36. Elijah M. Odom to Sarah H. Odom, Two Mile Bridge, Camp near Vicksburg, Miss., 15 July 1862, Elijah Odom Letters, Folder 1, Mississippi Department of Archives and History, Jackson.

37. Ibid., 3 July 1862.

38. Reid Mitchell, *The Vacant Chair: The Northern Soldier Leaves Home* (New York: Oxford University Press, 1993), 141. See also Phillip Shaw Paludan, *"A People's Contest": The Union and the Civil War, 1861–1865* (New York: Harper & Row, 1988), 364–70.

39. In *Masters of Small Worlds,* Stephanie McCurry argues that the notion of fatherly control was as important in yeoman households as in plantation households.

40. On affection and romance within a framework of honor and control, see, for example, Censer, *North Carolina Planters and Their Children*; Stowe, *Intimacy and Power in the Old South*; and Jan Lewis, *The Pursuit of Happiness: Family and Values in Jefferson's Virginia* (Cambridge: Cambridge University Press, 1983).

41. Anne Firor Scott, *The Southern Lady: From Pedestal to Politics, 1830–1930* (Chicago: University of Chicago Press, 1970).

42. See Faust, *Mothers of Invention.*

43. My thanks to Margaret Ripley Wolfe for suggesting that I clarify this point.

44. Charles Reagan Wilson, *Baptized in Blood: The Religion of the Lost Cause, 1865–1920* (Athens: University of Georgia Press, 1980).